JoySo

JoySong

A 365 days Inspirational Guide
to the Music In Your Soul

Ann Stewart-Porter

To order additional copies of this book, contact:
Xlibris
1-888-795-4274
www.Xlibris.com
Orders@Xlibris.com
537209

CONTENTS

Acknowledgements

You never write alone.

I joyfully acknowledge that the Holy Spirit gave me words and blessed me as I tried to be obedient.

To my husband, Daniel, who never once questioned my late nights or distracted moments.

To my incredible daughter, Suzanne, who has been my constant confidant and friend through all my writing.

Thanks!

To my friend, Diane Newton, who did the first draft, and to David Whitehead Jr. who finished the work with joy.

And to all my Facebook Friends who kept encouraging me to keep writing every single day. You are real and wonderful to me.

Thank you all.

Dedication

*I dedicate this book to the people who have never stopped believing
in me, who never asked me to change to please them, who prayed for
me a thousand times and waited for the finished work.
From the time I can remember, my Mama would wake up at
5:00 a.m. each morning to pray, read God's Word, and always
had a few devotionals she read through. Each year at Christmas,
one of us would get her a devotional. After you eat breakfast
with Mama, she has daily devotions you read at the table.
So...This devotional is dedicated to my Mama, Dr.
Clara Gaynelle Stewart, whose love of Jesus and faithful
testimony have bore much fruit for the kingdom.
Her life is a daily devotional.
Thank you Daniel Paul Porter.
There are none like you. You have been my own personal JoySong.
I could not love you more.
To Suzanne Sarters.
Being your mother has been a gift. Thank you for honoring me and God.
To my sister, Sarah Mathias,
who kept reminding me of my JoySong when I would forget.
You bless me. May we ever be friends.
Most of all, I praise my Jesus, Who put the JoySong in my soul and
His Spirit in my heart. You are above all Loves. You are the eternal Joy
of my every moment. I love You more than life itself.*

Introduction

Joy changes your life. It's a day after day choice, so I've written practical, everyday inspirations to help you get familiar with the feelings of joy. So much so, that you will want to foster that choice in your life.

Joy is a choice.

It's available in circumstances that have brought deep pain in your life. It's available when you grieve; when life is mundane and when you can't bear to go another step.

Let's walk together and choose joy every day.

Ann Stewart Porter

JANUARY 1

"If you don't like something, change it. If you can't change it,
change your attitude." – Maya Angelou

WE SIMPLY CAN'T change everything. We just can't no matter how hard we try. Certain people will always remain the same. Certain circumstances will continue intact and no amount of scheming will fix them. As a friend of mine said several dozen times after her husband's ski accident a thousand miles from home uprooted their life for nearly a year, *"It is what it is."* Her sense of humor remained intact and became a bulwark. She didn't always feel strong and capable but she didn't let her fear keep her from the work at hand. There really wasn't anything else to do about it. It had to be the *attitude* that changed.

If you spend too much time trying to change circumstances into something you want them to be, you might find it hard to learn the lesson right in front of you. If you can change it, then by all means feel free to do so. But if it isn't your call, that is, if it isn't your business or is something beyond your ability to change, then change your attitude toward it. You might find that is where the change truly needed to be anyway.

The mind of Christ is an attitude of constant obedience to *God's plan*, not yours. You will be trained by being placed in situations that require this attitude.

"Let this mind be in you which was also in
Christ Jesus." (Philippians 2:5)

JANUARY 2

"Hope is like the sun, which, as we journey toward it, casts the shadow of our burden behind us." – Sam Smiles

WE USE THE word *hope* in so many ways today, but to walk in *hope* is the infrastructure of divine position. *Hope* is tethered to faith and faith is tethered to love. All three work together in synergy, creating our life that braves the realities, and speaking into existence the substance of life. When we are immersed in *hope*, we are capitalizing on "letting go and letting in."

We change the focus.
We take what is and exchange it for what is to be.

A burden so sure, becomes a story God weaved into a remarkable, unlimited exception to every rule. We swipe away a yesterday with the beauty of the eternal speculation. Like a piece of coal hidden in the deepest, darkest cave, our burden becomes a glistening diamond others look to see. That's what *hope* can do.

Hope is an abiding manufacturing of the unseen. To believe in its power, is to touch the sun. Let it cast its shadow for indeed it is the shadow of the Almighty. He, Who gives the very sun its heat and time, can also change the burden of any heart into a glowing opportunity of grace.

"You will be secure because there is hope." (Job 11:18)

*"Be careful not to become so addicted to the wounding,
that you miss the healing."* – Ann Stewart Porter

THE HUGE BODY of a quarterback stood larger than usual. With broken ribs and a broken hand, bundled like a mummy; he was poised for play. When asked why he felt he had to play, he said he would rather play in pain than sit on the sidelines in pain. While I can't vouch for the intelligence of that decision, the message is worth the keep.

Whenever you are in pain, there is a tendency to step out of life.

There is a grief you want everyone to share. You feel like you won't be able to get past this hurt. But there is healing in resting, getting help and staying in the game. Even if you have to play in pain, stay in the game. Reach out to others at places you most hurt yourself. When you are most discouraged, try your best to pen a note to a person you know is discouraged. Or drop a muffin by to a friend who is hurting. Resist the temptation to lather yourself in pity and deserved coddling.

Yes, take your time to rest, to process, to bandage up, to take your medicine. Talk it through to acceptance. But remember that you cannot just make a life out of what was or is at any given moment. Be willing to try and play, even in your pain. It will help change your focus, give you good distractions and give you a different perspective. Never give up too soon.

*"Let us not grow weary of doing good, for in due season, if we
don't give up, we will reap."* (Galatians 6:9)

JANUARY 4

"Live well, it speaks so much of us."

I HAVE LEARNED THAT you can tell a lot about a person by the way they handle these three things: a rainy day, lost luggage, and tangled Christmas tree lights.

My mother will take on the craziest jewelry mess and tediously restore it to its glory, no matter the tangle or the hours. Me? I give it a shake or two and throw it away.

I met a gal in the park one day. She was telling me she wanted to move to Portland, Oregon because Colorado was..."too sunny!"

Once when we landed in Papua, New Guinea, the airport was straight out of an Indiana Jones movie set with whirring ceiling fans and all. We didn't realize one of our suitcases was missing until the next morning. We called the airport. The woman acted as though she had always known us. She told us yes, our luggage was fine, they knew who we were and it would be delivered shortly. (In America that probably would have taken days!)

Life is fun when there are so many of us looking at things so differently. We can be constantly bothered by this and frustrated at that, but wisdom enjoys the fact that we all have our place. We are all experiencing life in slivers of intellect, emotion and physical stitches. We all get different gifts handed out to us. We all learn the values of life hidden in those tangled up messes, those days of no sunshine and the losses of our lives.

"Rejoice always; pray without ceasing, give thanks in all circumstances, for this is the will of God in Christ Jesus concerning you." (1 Thessalonians 5:16-18)

JANUARY 5

"There are two basic groups of people: Those who toss coins in the fountain and those who fish them out."

WHICH ONE ARE you? Is tossing in the coin and dreaming big just part of who you are? Would you rather stick to doing the work and getting something done? I mean, why waste time dreaming, when there's work to be done.

Funny thing is...these two different kinds of people usually *get married!*

That can be quite advantageous if one of you thinks the other one has amazing dreams and wants to help you accomplish the very best in your life or one of you thinks the other is a great practical asset to your home.

Of course, many people just fight over why the dreamer dreams or why the worker bee has no vision, or argues over why the dreamer can't pull their weight or why the boring one lives for tedious mundane things.

It's about perspective!

The Dreamers need the Doers. The Doers need the Dreamers.

If you can find a way to lock in on the goodness of the other's gift you might just enjoy dancing together in the moonlight...and in the fountain. Share your life.

"Do nothing by strife or vain glory, but in lowliness of mind let each esteem the other better than himself." (Philippians 2:3)

"Miracles do not happen in contradiction to nature, but only in contradiction to that which is known in nature." – St. Augustine

MIRACLES SELDOM HAPPEN within a belief system that merely allows them to show up, unannounced and unexpected. However, practicing *"intentional creation"* will increase one's openness to miracles.

How do you practice miracle living? You speak it and produce the emotions associated with it. You can begin by remembering a moment of happiness or of profound emotion. Purposely relive the event. Use every sense possible. What does it look like? What does it smell like? What do you hear? Is there a taste in the air, a feeling? That is what you must do when expecting a miracle.

For instance, I need a wood floor. This will take a small miracle. I have two pieces of the wood lying on my floor. It is waiting for the rest to come.

It will come. I see it. I smell the smell of wood. I feel the grain. I see how beautiful it looks. I hear the sound I make walking on it.

I am working in cooperation with the miracle.

What is it you need that will take a miracle? Begin to imagine it as it would be.

Let's say you want a great marriage. What does that look like through each sense? Define it within the parameters of sense alone. Picture it. Say you want you and your spouse to be close again. Imagine it in every detail. Now, turn these *"video intentions"* over to God. Give

Him authority to do His will in all things, including timing. Don't be surprised if a miracle comes your way.

My wood floor is now three years old by the way, and I love it.

"You are the God Who performs miracles, You display Your power among the people." (Psalm 77:14)

JANUARY 7

*"Seek the wisdom that will not untie your knot.
Seek the path that demands your whole being." –* Rumi

MY GRANDSON NATHAN was watching Celtic Thunder and imitating the singers. We began to talk about what it would take to be a part of a group like that. We talked of singing in church choir and school, then singing in concerts and the training needed. But Nathan said he just wanted to go from right now and go sing *"there."*

Yes, Nathan, that is how most of us want to do things. We want comfort, easy, money, positioning and things that take work to be instant. We want others to untie our knots. We want things that don't require our whole being. But that which takes us to a place where we do or die is the place that gives us our strength. The mundane, irritating days of working out our salvation are the days in which our character is forged. That pain that broke us and changed us is the place we met the power of the resurrection.

If it can't consume you, is it worth having? Seek that which demands your whole being.

*"Whatsoever you do, do it heartily as to the Lord
and not unto men."* (Colossians 3:23)

JANUARY 8

"Scars carry pictures of our healing." Ann Stewart Porter

THERE IS THE one on the left side of my face from childhood chicken pox. There's one on my hand from the needle from blood work. There's one on my arm from a *"pic- line"* that saved my life. There's one on my foot from a fall.

Scars. We all get them.

But my deepest scars are the ones you cannot see. The death of my children, the damaged heart, the things said that cut deeply, the things l said l wish l could take back, the sin I knew better than to do, the regrets.

Scars are marks of pain, but also of healing.

Scars show that we have been there and they show how far we have come. L once went to a doctor who asked why l had so many scars on my hands. I told him because I had been healed so much. It reminded me of some scriptures that say *"to whom much is given, much is required."* Or the other one that says: *"Her sins, which are many, are forgiven; for she loved much: but to whom little is forgiven, the same loveth little."*

You see, to those of us given more pain, I believe we are given more healing. To us who have done the worst sins, we know most the value of our forgiveness. So, I do not begrudge my scars. They carry messages of healing and hope. So do yours.

"Her sins which were many, are forgiven; for she sinned much. To whom little is forgiven, the same loveth little." (Luke 7:47)

JANUARY 9

"It's always the little things."

WE MOVED INTO this cute little house in a nice neighborhood without noticing this little kudzu in the wall of our daughter's bedroom. When we did notice it, we snipped it, put weed killer on it and called it done. But it wasn't done. It continued to grow and it grew so fast it could fill a pot within a day. We asked advice of all we knew. Because there was a garden on the other side of the wall, it had managed to find a crack and wiggled its way in, forever to astonish us. We moved out with that kudzu still trailing the wall, and, as far as I know, it still does. I am thinking it would take a new foundation to stop it.

But oh, the lesson there!

Watch the cracks in your foundations. Watch what you choose to feed your mind and spirit. These make a difference in your thinking, and ultimately, in your doing. Not every crime will be so heinous, and some folks will debate that you can watch what you wish, but I would take you to the sites of the slain, the broken homes, the mental hospitals and the prisons and let you rethink that idea. Little secret sins, little secret hates, little cracks in our character are kudzu in our walls. It's the little things that often matter the most.

Live wisely. Evil is like kudzu. Give it a place and it will take all.

"He that hath no rule over his spirit is like a city that is broken down with no walls." (Proverbs 25:28)

JANUARY 10

"Joy is not able to grow in the air of disrespect and selfishness." – Ann Stewart Porter

THERE SHE IS, all dressed in her finest expectations, but HE has already fallen once, his shoes scuffed with insecurity. She rounds him out with her invisible pen and checklist.

…He went on about the business of wishing and hoping and grinding his teeth. He felt the crunch of the first egg shell and lifted his foot away. He learned to walk that peculiar way, because there was no other way to keep her tethered to him.

…He had thought love was freer, more selflessly inclined.

…He should have bought a ticket to a shrine. They would have appreciated him more.

…He didn't know how to make it different.

…Worst of all, he really loved her. He does try to please her. Most women he knows think he is fine.

…A man was not born to be cut down at every turn. He cannot breathe in critical air. He loses his ability to find himself…

…His backbone becomes his wishbone.

If you are the person he is living with and you are bent on keeping that critical spirit, you should know something right now. Eventually, he dies inside…or he leaves. He leaves whom he loved…But at least, he can breathe again.

"Therefore, however you want people to treat you, so treat them."
(Matthew 7:12)

"Joy can be a crying thing."

D ID YOU KNOW...THAT scientifically speaking, crying is not a sign of sadness or joy? It's just a sign of deep emotion. It's a reaction to feelings far below the surface. Some of us cry at the drop of a hat, but in truth, our vein of emotion is connected to our innermost self.

That is why crying is significant.

That is why when you experience something and you feel this swell inside you, you might want to pay close attention to why. Aside from obvious attachments, what is it that rakes you back to that burning? Is it a passion, a discovery, a mystery, a recycling, an undone, a discrepancy in the tales of your life?

Often, tears are road maps; navigations of the heart.

We tell ourselves to stop crying, but perhaps we would do better to stop pushing down our emotions. Crying is a message. Take time to read it.

"You keep track of all my sorrows, You collect my tears.
You have recorded each one." (Psalm 56:8)

JANUARY 12

"A lot goes on in the in-between." – Ann Stewart Porter

IN-BETWEEN. LOTS OF living goes on in-between.

In-between the years of 5 and 13, most of us are itching to be 16. In-between 16 and 21, most of us are living for the day we will be on our own. In-between changing jobs, somebody finds a career. In-between moving, an entire family puts down roots. In-between handshakes, a deal gets made. In-between coffee breaks, friendships are formed. In-between sheets, babies are conceived. In-between losing ourselves, we find what we wanted. In-between gaining a few pounds and losing a few more, we find out what we compromise. In-between dating and getting married, we might find the right one. In-between the years we are married and divorce, we find out the wrong ones. In-between circumstances, we find our strength and weaknesses. In-between our worst and our best, we become ourselves. In-between the years of soccer and piano lessons, we raise children; the fruit of our labors. In-between the living and the dying, we find out that time passes quickly, and somewhere between here and now, then and there, yesterday and tomorrow, we will find out the truth.

"So teach us to number our days, that we
may apply our hearts to wisdom."
(Psalm 90:12)

JANUARY 13

"Live in the Yes!"

I HAVE DECIDED MORE and more to live my life on the basis of this glorious truth: **I have been created in the image of God.** I have been given access to God's goodness, grace, mercy and anointing! All the promises of God are YES! Think about that. The promises of God are for His glory.

There are Yes's just waiting for us to find them. Edison had 2,000 failures before he invented the first light bulb. Reporters asked him how it felt to have so many failures. He explained he had none! He just knew 2,000 ways that did not work.

I have wondered about things that seemed like failures in my life. I have listened to lesser wisdom.

Everything that happens leaves a deposit inside of you and me. Everything is part of the preparation in our life to be full of glory and joy unspeakable.

Live in the Yes!

"For all the promises of God in Him are Yes and Amen,
unto the Glory of God by us." (2 Corinthians 2:20)

"There is joy in letting go."

ALTHOUGH THE NIGHT was sweet, she could not enjoy it. Lt reminded her of too many nights of waiting; waiting for the feet shuffling toward her, the smell, the sickness that overcame her; the father who would forever be remembered as her molester.

He was just a little boy. He didn't know better, but that never stopped the beatings, the accusations, the worthlessness he carried like a bag of rotten food inside of him. All he ever wanted was the man he called his father to say that he was proud of him. He would have taken another beating just to hear the words; but it was too late now; his father was dead.

How often we wait for the apology that never comes. A friend's betrayal. A siblings envy. A costly ordeal with a trusted partner. A marriage dissolved. Things taken from us. We want some sort of restitution, something we can sink our teeth into. Usually though, there are only memories bearing emotions and grief that regurgitate throughout our lives.

Call me crazy, but you have to let go. The past is the past; it is **not** the present unless you let it be. It does nothing for your spirit, much less for your soul. The choices they made are not yours.

Do not hold out for an apology before you allow yourself to be free. Let it go, and let the joy in.

"Who shall give account unto Him that is ready
to judge the quick and the dead."
(1 Peter 4:5)

JANUARY 15

"God never chooses comfort over conformation." – Ann Stewart Porter

OFTEN, GOD DOESN'T change your circumstance because He is busy...changing your heart. We are humans. We take in our piece of data and we make a conclusion. We drop off our chart and we have to have answers. We get stuck in the here-and-now, forgetting there is a there-and-forever. We often take on our role as victim, all the while squirming for the why of it.

There is a big lie that says God just wants you to be happy, snappy, healthy, wealthy and comfortable.

He never said that.

When it comes to the choice between making you comfortable or the choice to conform you to the image of the fullness of Christ, God will always choose to conform you. He wants you to learn how to trust, manifest goodness, reveal His glory, express His joy, and know how to live as a warrior and a peacemaker.

Conforming to His image is how you grow.

To grow, is to conform to His image.

He changes us from glory to glory, and that is what is happening in your life right now!

"...That I may know Him and the power of His resurrection, and the fellowship of His sufferings, being made conformable unto His death." (Philippians 3:10)

"Primum non nocere."
"When you hurt another, you hurt yourself first."

"FIRST, DO NO harm." As you may or may not know, your doctor had to memorize those words. They are part of the Hippocratic Oath. Medical professionals are required to take this oath as a promise to those who trust them to provide medical services. (It might not be a bad idea if we all raised our right hand and took that oath.)

We have become a nation, led by leadership, both godly and ungodly, to a throne of self-righteousness. It has led us to paths of unrighteousness, and we have hurt many in this *"screech of own righting."*

Before you go to wake up the stubborn child, first, do no harm. Before you speak to your angry mate or unfair ex, first, do no harm. Before you reach your friend, first, do no harm. Before you get to work, resolve to first, do no harm. Before you speak in church, first, do no harm. Before you enter your parent's home, first, do no harm. When you speak to an employee, first, do no harm.

Already, the very thought may be alerting your spirit to compassion and honor.

Oh that we may choose health over wealth, peace over war, and life over death just by employing the attitude of a heart that promises *"to do no harm."*

"Paul cried with a loud voice, saying, Do
thyself no harm for we are here."
(Acts 16:28)

JANUARY 17

"Joy is not a box thing. Joy is a deeper thing."

SEVENTY TWO PERCENT of the Obsessive Compulsive Behavior (OCD) patients who underwent Neurological Navigation have been freed from use of medications and from the condition itself. While parents have known for years it was more than just *"getting attention,"* it has been hard to imagine a real fix for it. Opinions were as varied as the compulsions. Because it is changing the terrain of OCD, it is also having some effects on Bi-polar issues.

Historically, these were thought to be reactions to anxiety overload. This assumption has often led to a *"diagnosis from a box,"* so to speak. Rather than looking deeper into each significant life, it was a quick *"take-two, don't call me in the morning."*

Unfortunately, this happens with just about everything. We put things in boxes that we don't quite have time to decipher, or more truthfully, don't want to take the time for.

When it comes to healing, it is the responsibility of the patient and the doctor to work together. Certainly, we are all guilty of not following through, including those in the medical profession.

Always look deeper. Healing is an awesome thing.

"Call unto Me and I will answer thee and show thee great and mighty things, which thou knowest not." (Jeremiah 33:3)

"Joy lets others in and in doing so, lets us out."

SHE WAS PETITE, not an ounce of fat, sleek, shining hair, an expressive touch and an alluring smile, maybe 25 years young. I began sizing her up, the way you do the most popular girl in school; the way a cat watches a bird.

What's her story, I wondered, as her husband seemed so clingy. I felt left out of her *"little sweet talk to me everybody"* world. But strangely, I liked her too. She was like the skinny me; the one tucked inside the fat me. She was like the part of me few people knew. We seemed to have an unusual connection that I couldn't explain.

I mentioned her to my hubs, who said she was very sweet, loved to tease him and was so friendly, comfortable, *"...like you always are,"* he added matter of factly. Maybe that was the connection thing I felt.

One morning, she stopped to ask me to pray. She said she had so loved my alto voice. Her eyes glistened as she told us how she needed us and the example of our marriage. Theirs had been so hard. They were fighting for survival.

Sometimes we judge people from the cracked clay of our own insecurities.

Sometimes, just letting someone in lets you out. Be brave enough to love past your judgments. We all need each other.

"The Lord said to Samuel, Do not consider his appearance or his height, for I have rejected him. The Lord does not look at the things man looks at. Man looks at the outward appearance, but the Lord looks on the heart." (1 Samuel 16:7)

JANUARY 19

"Speak your heart in joyful kindness."

I HAD SOMETHING TO tell my friend that she didn't want to hear. She wouldn't like it, so she wouldn't listen. I had breached the subject before and had been shut down, so I knew where the line in the sand was drawn. I knew it involved a part of her life that was being hurt but I could not fix it. It was really only selfishness keeping her tied to it. If it had been love, she would have let it go, but fear grabs everything like it's grabbing your throat.

So, I pondered how to say it, when to say it, if it was my business, how it would go, if the friendship would remain intact.

I chose to wait. Some things must wait for the appropriate timing.

It was several months; almost a year, before it surfaced. The timing worked out beautifully and I was able to put my two cents in, without taking away. It was such a sweet collaboration. She knew my heart. I knew hers. She has strengthened me plenty of times in the past and I hope I have returned the favor.

Sometimes, we get to jumping around with our own agenda, yelling for the world to change right this very moment.

Correct timing is a gift. Don't be afraid to wait.

"Speak the truth in love, so we will grow to become in
every aspect the mature Body of Christ."
(Ephesians 4:15)

JANUARY 20

"Take my bread away from me if you wish, but do not take from me your laughter…it opens for me all the doors of life." – Pablo Neruda

THE DAYS OF life and rust can be ruthless, dotted with the sarcasm of the sigh.

Experiencing my daughter's fifty-plus seizures a day was no picnic; holding each other and learning to ride the waves.

In a fascinating book by Jill Bolte, a neuroscientist who rebuilt her brain after a stroke tells us that emotional suffering is a 90 second episode. It takes only 90 seconds of experiencing the emotion caused by a negative event before the body finishes processing the hormones and returns to its baseline setting.

The body returns to normal and the emotion subsides…**unless you decide to relive it.** Then like a looped recording, the hormones are triggered again, and your body and emotions go through the same trauma.

Applying this lesson was very difficult for me at first, especially when it came to my daughter's seizures. However, I have found if you allow your 90 seconds and ride it hard, you can keep your positivity, and keep yourself from reliving events. You will begin to have days where laughter will rise up within you. On the *"weary can't-handle-this"* days, feel free to rest, find the reprieve of your heart, and recharge with the positive.

"She is clothed with strength and dignity, and she laughs without fear of the future." (Proverbs 31:25)

JANUARY 21

"Keep your eyes on the God beyond the multitude."

WHAT DO WE do with our joy when it rains and pours, and we feel powerless and like there's just too much coming at us? It's so easy to start talking about the issues. It's easy to be kidnapped by emotions. It's easy to put all our energy into the challenge or into the people in our way.

God says an anxious heart causes depression. So, He requires that we not worry about when or how or who He judges. When we feel powerless, it's an opportunity to get our eyes fixed.

Let God be God.

He makes all things beautiful in His time.

"Oh our God, will You not judge them? For we are powerless before this great multitude who are coming against us; nor do we know what to do, but our eyes are on you." (2 Chronicles 12:20)

"Fill your paper with the breathing of your heart." – William Wadsworth

TO STAY IN the joy, I highly recommend journaling. It's good for relieving everyday stress. It's good for *"writing out"* negatives and filtering positives. It's helpful for building strong bones of thanksgiving. It's a way of knowing yourself better; of seeing what you forget. It's good for the soul. It's profitable for keeping the emotions of an event intact. It's a place where you can divulge and indulge. It keeps a record of days you often forget in the journey.

Journaling can be a friend to mourners. Those things that can be shared in the deep, dark night on paper can be ways of maneuvering through sorrow. Words we write become stories to consider.

I keep a *"Thanksgiving Journal"* because it keeps me. It is only five lines long. It is simple. I can do it in five minutes and it keeps me centered. I keep a Prayer Journal as well, also simple, always changing, but a great reminder of those I pray for and answers l might forget.

I also keep a *"Life Journal."* I write three pages a day for one day, and then none the next. It's like an old friend waiting for me. This way, I can say it without hurting anyone and let go of feelings I need to release. It also allows me see how I am growing.

I am getting ready to try a *"Life Art Journal"* where you draw what you feel instead of write. That should be fun. Everybody should enjoy the benefits of feeling and filling your paper, with the breath of your heart.

*"The Lord answered me and said, "Write the vision and make it plain, that one may run that readeth it." (*Habakkuk 2:2)

JANUARY 23

"Healing requires more than just the desire not to die."

THE JOY OF healing is the desire to live. There is a far deeper commitment needed, to rise up out of the deep and live profitably. You are going to rustle through memories like you were dealing cards. Then you find out, you have to take them out and virtually rewrite them. If you plan on living a truly honest life, you will be required to face life openly, confronting the whys and the patterns.

Joy does not come by hiding and reckless accounting. It is never easy to heal.

You must learn to communicate with all of yourself. You have likely not been able to do that for a long time.

It will hurt to do it now.

Sometimes, it hurts to forgive, especially when it comes to forgiving yourself. The whole of a Being is in the spiritual, mental, physical and emotional healing. You can't fix one and call it good. Healing is a joint effort. Wholeness is completeness, not perfection. As you heal, you will understand how all of your parts intertwine. You come to know the synergy of your wholeness. It is a beautiful thing.

"Heal me O Lord, and I shall be healed; Save me,
and I shall be saved, for Thou art my praise." (Jeremiah 17:14)

"Find your own voice and sing your heart song."

WHEN I WAS in the 7th grade, a new girl came to our school. Her name was Patricia. She was a gorgeous *"almost woman."* She and I were very different. She had chestnut hair, was very feminine, and was an only child. She was wealthy, sophisticated, AND she wrote with her left hand! Who ever heard of such a thing?

We became fast friends.

I was the oldest of six children; a middle class preacher's kid. I was a tomboy and yet I was all girl; boring, and worst of all I was right handed! As you can imagine, our homes were so very different. She had 20 Barbie dolls with tons of Barbie clothes. Me? I had one Tammy doll and homemade outfits.

So I tried to become Patricia. I dyed my hair dark.

It turned green.

I tried to be sophisticated. I stopped wearing my glasses. I tried like mad to write left handed; to no avail. I even wrote *"Bunny"* as my name on school papers, but they figured out it was me.

IDENTITY CRISIS!

Stop. Smile. Relax.

I soon grew into the glorious me I have come to love and cherish. I have beautiful right hand handwriting, eyes that will weep with you, and nary a Barbie doll. I play piano, sing, write and love people. I don't know where Patricia is today, but that's okay. I found my voice, my handwriting, and my me.

"For we are His workmanship, created in Christ Jesus unto good works." (Ephesians 2:10)

JANUARY 25

"Put away what you don't need."

IF THERE'S ANYTHING contrary to joy, it's anger. I tend to see it as something you choose to wear, so to speak. We aren't just born angry. We might cry because we need a drink or a diaper change, but anger is a learned behavior. A tantrum or two is one thing, but when it has graduated to wrath or malice, there is a degree of contempt which marks us.

Wrath is an extreme, over-the-top anger. Malice is anger with intent to hurt. Blasphemy is anger with intent to hurt God. Filthy communication is anger with intent to speak hurtfully. Profanity is an extension of anger. It publicly reveals and communicates what is wrong in our own heart. Where there is a continual flow of cursing, there will be lives marked by the curse.

Where there is continual anger there will be bitterness. Be mindful that you can often create a person's life by what you speak into them; much like a parent who constantly tells their child they are stupid. Speak joy and gladness into the lives of others. Live in joy, not anger.

"You must also put away all the following: anger, wrath, malice, slander, and filthy language from your mouth." (Colossians 3:8)

"Faith is the heart's response to the character of God." – Adrian Rogers

DYLAN WAS THREE. We were folding clothes. He had put on a scarf and announced he was Superman. I said, "Jump Superman, Jump!" He was three, so his own experience in such things was quite limited. He trusted me without question.

I was worthy of his trust. I had loved him before he was born. I had fed him, clothed him, and changed his worst diapers. He did not question me when I told him to fly. So, he flew...all the way to the carpet where he burned his nose. Then, he looked up at me and in a quizzical voice and said "Grandma, I can't fly!"

I felt pretty rotten. Dylan had faith in my character. So, he could easily see himself flying.

That is the kind of faith I want to have; the kind that doesn't hesitate to trust, because I know how much God loves me. I know He has fed me, clothed me and changed some of my stinkiest messes. He is worthy of my trust. He has proven all He needs to prove. In response to that goodness, my heart chooses faith. What about you?

"Faith is confidence in what we hope for and assurance
about what we do not see." (Hebrews 11:1)

"There is joy in failing and taking an opportunity to grow."

I FAILED AGAIN. NO, I mean…a colossal failure. Okay, it isn't THAT big, but failure is like that first big acne blemish. There is just no convincing me it's small.

I set myself up to win. I thought I had it conquered. (Fine, I'll go ahead and confess before God and everybody.) I wanted to see if I could go into a massive store and come out with the three small things on my list: coconut, milk and bread.

I picked a big new king of a store. Confidently I walked in and headed for my product. But then I saw the 39-cent beans! And orange juice marked from six dollars to $1.50! By the time I left that store, the buggy was almost full.

I got home. Dan called to see if I needed anything from the store. "Yes, we need…coconut…and bread!"

See? Big failure. Stupid failure. Talk about stealing my joy!

Shame. Guilt. Self-pity. Feeling out of control. Wanting to be free of this thing l have yet to conquer. Does any of this sound familiar? Because l know what my failures can do to me, l know it's important for me to *"catch and release"* (as the fishy guys say). Catch the lesson. Release the rest. It's done. I might do it again. But l will also choose to try again.

Failure isn't final. Failure isn't a self-diagnosis. Failure is my colossal opportunity to grow. There. That's the right spirit. We will try again. I will be more ready next time. So will you.

"May the God of all hope fill you with joy and peace as
you trust in Him, so that you may overflow with hope by
the power of the Holy Spirit." (Romans 15:13)

JANUARY 28

"Listen for the joy stories."

WHEN YOU LOOK at a person, any person, remember that everyone has a story. Everyone has gone through something that changed them. Being in my line of work, I not only hear stories, I hear deep stories. I hear stories that no one else hears. I hear stories that have been buried for a very long time.

I know that people are made up of stories. Stories that change who we are and what we do. It changes our emotional, spiritual, mental and physical patterns. We now know that when a child is abused, the stress from that actually causes the brain to change. We now know that emotional trauma can keep a person's behavior and choices at the age of the trauma. If they were ten years old, much of their life will be thought of from that age perspective. Stories reflect lives.

This accounts for a great many things in our world. I have an old friend. When we go out to eat, he always asks the waitress how she got there. There's always a story. There is much we have learned from human stories. Feel free to tell yours and always know that someone is waiting to share theirs too. It helps us all grow.

"Do not neglect to do what is good and to share, for God is pleased with such sacrifices." (Hebrews 13:16)

"There is healing in joy."

WHAT STRENGTHENS US? It might surprise you that the findings of secular research say those "who have a strong attachment to their church have less heart disease, emphysema, cirrhosis, high blood pressure and even less abnormal pap smears."

Go figure.

Women in happy marriages had enhanced immune function. Men have less depression and live longer.

People with pets are healthier. People who have a social support group are stronger and are more able to fight disease. Social isolation actually raises the risk for disease. Men were twice as likely to have angina if they were not in a loving good relationship.

The research continues to point to strong connections, relationships, happy marriages and faith as leading contributors to good health. Be good to yourself. Let people into your life. Find a good church. We strengthen each other. In doing so, we make a difference...even in our health.

"Above all, love each other deeply because love covers a multitude of sins."
(1 Peter 4:8)

"A thankful heart is a joyful heart."

I HAVE A CAR, a home of my own, a hobby requiring some cash-flow and a tiny bit of money in a bank. Know what that makes me? It makes me one of the top 5% richest people in the world. This just boggles my mind. I can look at richer people right across the street who might tell you they aren't rich at all, who have way more than us.

We, who have so much, forget that we are benefactors of such goodness. If you are anything like me, you have already talked about what you don't have in some form today. While a good deal of the world doesn't have inside toilets, you will likely have two of them to clean today. While your car needs work, most of the world will never have a car. While you say funds are low, you don't mean you have no bank accounts, electricity or water in your home.

We are so wealthy. We often pray for more while living in most. We are richer than over half the world and we will still want more at the day's end. I think there's a lesson in the knowing of these things. A friend of mine who runs an orphanage said the orphans were running away…because there was no food. That will break your heart. Let us give more, be thankful more and stop spending on worthless things. We are a giving people. May this spur us on to good works.

"Give thanks to the Lord for He is good, His love endures forever." (Psalm 136:1)

JANUARY 31

"Nothing in life happens to you. It happens FOR you." – Joel Osteen

J UST THE OTHER day, I told someone they were having a really hard time because they were in the middle of the story. Middles are hard places. The yesterday doesn't make sense. The future looks scary. The now just seems frustrating. It takes a great deal of courage and strength to get through the middle. But if you have ever had surgery, you know the middle of surgery is just part of the healing process. How's that? You can't heal without the surgery. It has to be part of the journey. It's for your own healing.

Life doesn't happen to you. It happens *for* you. It's not always comfortable. It's not always understandable. God does NOT make life without purpose. He conforms us to His will through life. How do you teach your children to do things that are best for them – through the experiences of their everyday life. You don't get them and wait until they go to school to learn how to eat with utensils or go potty or be nice or clean up their toys. You do it from day one, right there in their life.

It is to your advantage to thank God for whatever He is doing in your life. You don't have to understand it, to trust that it is the best for you, that God knows what s happening. Trust He is doing His goodness *for* you...not to you.

"He Who began a good work in you will perfect it until the day of Christ Jesus." (Philippians 1:6)

FEBRUARY 1

"Let your flesh rest in hope."

WHEN YOU CHOOSE where to rest, you choose how it affects every area of your life.

We were traveling cross country and landed in New Mexico. It was way into dark thirty when we had enough. We pulled into a park in the pitch dark and laid our seats back to catch some sleep. Later we were in that hard drive kind of sleep, when a train horn scared every one of us out of our sleep. It was bigger than loud. It was early morning and dawn was outlining the tracks. We had parked right beside them!

Another time, we were at Camp in the rainy season in the Ozarks. A dear friend had felt we needed to get away and rest. Sure enough, it rained hard, and in our tent we found ourselves soaking in several inches of water. You could actually wring out our thin little mattresses. So between the snakes, bugs, a sprained ankle and the water, resting was out of the question.

Too many people choose to make their bed right next to the noise; the drama, the overwhelming, and wonder why they get no rest.

Choose to rest in hope. Choose to let your tongue know gladness and your heart to know joy. You must watch where you choose to rest, to abide; to live your life.

"Therefore did my heart rejoice, and my tongue was glad;
moreover also my flesh shall rest in hope." (Acts 2:26)

FEBRUARY 2

"There is joy in accepting you as you are."

A MAN IN CHINA was only five feet and one inch tall. After his girlfriend left him because he was too short, he went through a year of surgery to lengthen his legs. A woman in America thinks she lost her husband because she was fat. She underwent a year of lap band surgeries. A woman in Indonesia had her teeth shaped like spikes so her husband would not leave her and she would be beautiful by her village's standard.

Another had her face tattooed to make her *"marriageable."* Oh, the lengths we will go to, just to be loved and accepted. Ironically, some people even try to be unique while also attempting to fit in.

Have you seen all the tattoos lately? Individuals marring themselves to look like monsters, all in the name of finding themselves. Others try to look as perfect as a Barbie Doll; some of them tragically succeeding because of so much plastic surgery.

These kind of personal changes are only skin deep, and do not bring happiness or joy. What these people are really looking for is a purpose; an eternal purpose and they are attempting to fill a hole in their life that only God can fill.

An eternal purpose in life is much more unique than any tattoo. Today, find the joy in accepting you as you are, precious and loved by God.

"I praise You, for I am fearfully and wonderfully made.
Wonderful are Your works, my soul knows it very well." (Psalm 139:14)

FEBRUARY 3

"Don't let life change your name."

NAOMI WAS A happy woman. Her name meant *"Lovely."* But she faced the death of her son, the loss of her husband, and one thing after another it seemed. She actually changed her name to Mara, which means *"bitter."*

Years ago, your name signified what you were or what you did. In our family, we still believe a name is very important. My name Ruth means *"beautiful friend."* Ann means *"Grace."* I have always been able to make friends and perhaps being named such helped that process. I continue to grow into grace.

Naomi endured so much pain, she couldn't do it anymore. Life changed her name. It wasn't until her daughter-in-law, Ruth, came in to her life and truly became her friend, that she became Naomi again. God used Ruth (beautiful friend) to restore Naomi's spirit. We can do that for each other. We can change another's life by the very act of being. Don't let life change your name. Don't let bitterness change your heart. Don't let God's purpose go.

Grief and disappointment may wrestle you to the ground. You still have the choice to rise again. Let others bless you. Let others love you, lift you up and challenge you.

"We know all things work together for good, to those who love God, for those who are called according to His purpose." (Romans 8:28)

FEBRUARY 4

"There is joy in honor and respect."

WE WERE WATCHING an intense movie scene with the grandkids. The man was two inches from the woman's face yelling like a madman. Natalie asked if that was his wife. Grandpa affirmed, then he asked *"Isn't that the way your parents fight? That's how I treat Grandma all the time."* All three spoke fast and loud: *"NO! Our parents never fight like that...and you do not treat Grandma that way at all!"* He laughed and said that was true. (He can be pretty loud and we tease him about that at the soccer games.)

Natalie got quiet as she said that he should not talk to his wife that way. She's right. If you have to intimidate your wife to get a point across, you have lost your honor. She will have no respect for you. You will be left with a big voice and a lonely heart. We had a great impromptu exchange on treating each other with respect and honor. If you wish for your children to respect you, you must be an example of respect.

"Husbands, love your wife as you love yourself; and wives, respect your husbands." (Ephesians 5:33)

FEBRUARY 5

"There is joy in speaking truth."

S HE CAME TO me with a need for mediation. We were on the opposite sides of the issue. She knew exactly what I would say. She knew the questions I would ask. When it came down to it, she affirmed that she came to me because I would tell her the truth. I agreed. I replied that she would not trust me if I did not tell her the truth. She agreed.

There is something powerful about being trusted with the truth. It speaks life into us, even when we don't like it.

There is an excess of dishonesty in our world. It can be an overwhelming thing to address at times. Everyone seems bent on spewing out something less than truth. While the unvarnished truth is not always appreciated, it is still trusted for its value is worth more than any lie. As we love one another more, I believe we will find truth is the rule, not the exception. Truth makes way for a seat at any table.

Be a truth speaker of the House, a representative of truth. Keep telling the truth and others will have no trouble trusting that you will. Integrity speaks for itself.

"Teach me Your way, O Lord: that I may walk in Your truth; Unite my Heart to fear Your Name." (Psalm 86:11)

FEBRUARY 6

"Respond with joy where the Holy Spirit excites you." Rumi

WHAT EXCITES YOUR spirit? What's the passion you carry with you everywhere you go? What gives you great joy in the doing of it? I carry a way to write everywhere I go, literally. I have tried not to write. That thing inside me goes crazy without the words.

I adore teaching. It is my second spiritual gift. Added to my first spiritual gift, which is exhortation, there is a twin positioning of purpose I cannot turn off or walk away from, no matter what. I find the joy of doing these things is inexpressible. I find people respond well to these gifts in me.

Counseling and grief coaching is the perfect place for the synergy of my gifts. For me, it is simply teaching and encouragement. It is no wonder I am crazy about what I do! It's such a perfect fit for me.

I did fight against some of this in me at one time. I thought I wasn't a good helper to anyone. I thought I wasn't wise enough. I made too many of my own mistakes. I thought, *"I can't write like so and so."* However, God has always brought me back to the place that excites my spirit. This allows me to give all of myself to both the responsibility and the goodness. But I had to respond. L had to train.

Even today I still have to be open to growing and learning. I have to keep responding. What is it that calls to you?

"At that very time, He rejoiced greatly in the Holy Spirit, and said, I praise You, O Father, Lord of heaven and earth." (Luke 10:21)

FEBRUARY 7

"Trying to find proof of God is like tearing a piano apart trying to find a tune." – Adrian Rogers

OUR ATTEMPTS TO find God often leave God out of the equation. We try to build a life believing in God while living however we wish. When something goes wrong, we blame Him for not being who He said He was or for not doing what we think He should.

Proving God is never really worth all the fussing for this simple reason: To know God is an act of choosing to believe in someone. It would be like me trying to prove my husband Dan. Ultimately, you can choose to believe he exists or live pretending he doesn't. We can argue till the stars fall, but it will still be a choice of faith.

Tear the piano apart if you wish. Lord knows you aren't the first and won't be the last. Try to find the tune outside of faith and you will be more frustrated than when you started. On the other hand, if you just jump in and play, your life song will be in the harmony of faith. That will make all the difference.

"Become imitators of us and of the Lord, having received the Word in as much tribulation with the joy of the Holy Spirit." (1 Thessalonians 1:6)

"The world is grand, often big and astonishingly beautiful; frequently thrilling." – Dorothy Kilgaleen

GRANDPA TAPED A beautiful show the other day. I think it was called Genesis, but I am not sure. The photography was breathtaking; the stories left you wiser and more fascinated. For several weeks after, the grandchildren asked to watch the *"ocean and sky"* movie. Yes, it was astonishingly beautiful. Thanks to channels like National Geographic, we are privy to the wonders of our thrilling world more than ever.

If you don't watch too much news and too many political media alerts, you will find that the world is quite an amazing place. Even if you do see too much news, you still might just find the world is something of interest wherever you go. We have a blast taking the grandchildren to all kinds of mountain spots where they discover, for themselves, the amazing world God has given to them.

But we, too, find places of untold beauty. How many pictures l have from the times my hub has yelled to stop and get my camera is a matter of debate. Smile. He's not above waking a child to run and see the moon. He has kept a child-like wonder himself and there is always something fascinating in the world. He will stop breakfast so everyone can bend an ear to hear the mourning dove.

Today, pretend you are the National Geographic Reporter. Look specifically for things you might ordinarily miss. Ask God to open your eyes to the wonder of His gifts in all kinds of places. Don't be surprised if you find yourself engaged in an epic wait. The world is incredible. Unwrap your gift today and enjoy the blessing! It makes us infinitely more aware of all that is ours. Practice grandstanding.

"See what great love the Father hath lavished on us." (1 John 3:1)

FEBRUARY 9

"Sometimes, you have to stand alone; just to make sure you can."

ONE OF THE hardest things to come to know is what I call the *"Nobody Cares Law."*

I have people come to me who desperately feel they need help. They want their friends and family to be there. Sometimes, and even usually, some people are there for you. But, as a divorced man once openly concluded: you don't feel they are there when you need them. They don't call or check up on you. Lf you call and leave a message, it's a week before they call back. Or you want to go out and they don't want to go out. Or they call and invite you out and you just do not want to go.

All these things can easily add up to a feeling of *"Nobody Cares."* It's really not that nobody cares. It's just that we all have so much of our own stuff to take in and we often appear less than caring. Can you receive that? There comes a time we must learn how to stand on our own, just to make sure we can. Thank those who come and go and give what they can give. Then go on and be of whatever use you can be to another. Dropping the expectations will do your heart good. Learn to depend on yourself.

"He gives strength to the weary and increases
the power of the weak." (Isaiah 40:29)

FEBRUARY 10

"Night never had the last word. The dawn is
always invincible." – Hugh B. Brown

I think of the parents of the little girl who was murdered on her way to school. I think of the father of the shooter at the cinema. I think of the terror we all feel, when evil comes upon us in that hammer drop of a day. I know the dread of night when business is left undone.

My tiny four pound infant son died in the hospital.

The night calls were fearsome. I know the dread of a morning where you have been told it isn't over and it isn't good. But thank God, that if we can gather the fight in us, through the power of His might, we can take hold of the morning. We can find the resilience to endure. The bright light can spur us onward to breathe beyond the dark nights of our soul.

Evil exists. Terrible nights can come. Pain is hard. So, we must be harder and braver and grab the invincible dawn. Today, we may win. It is a hope worth fighting for no matter what happens.

"Lord my God, I cried to You for help and You healed me." (Psalm 30:2)

FEBRUARY 11

"May you never forget what is worth remembering and always leave behind what is best forgotten." – Irish Blessing

THERE IS A Rascal Flatts song called *"Ellsworth Kansas"* about a couple who are experiencing age and perhaps Alzheimer's to a degree. They seem to recall their meeting, the autumn, the leaves, the love, the going off to war, and the coming home. They may not know about today, but their eyes light up at the best moments of their life.

Likely, many of us will choose to forget some things and others will go with age. But we will always remember those times that were the best for us. So, make sure you keep a steady supply of those best things. When l take someone through rape recovery and there are details they think they should know, I encourage them to let go. Unless there is a specific need to know, God may well equip us to forget. That can be as much of a gift as remembering the goodness. The key is to know the balance; to tuck the best away, but readily available, to let the forgettable be more space for more love.

Know what to take and what to leave behind.

"I press on toward the goal of the prize of the upward call of God in Christ Jesus." (Philippians 3:14)

FEBRUARY 12

"Truth is the beginning of every good thing both in heaven and earth;
and he who would be blessed and happy
should, from the first, be a partaker
of truth, for then he could be trusted." – Plato

IF YOU'RE MARRIAGE began in adultery, then it began in deception, and you will never experience trust in your partner the way you should. There will always be a place of deceit that marks areas of your marriage with a scarlet letter. A quiet unrest will mark your days.

You deceive yourself if you imagine your partner will cheat on them, but not on you. The numbers are not curious on this matter. It has become quite common, which goes to show how wisdom and discernment have shrunk. Divorce rates for second and third marriages are clearly marriages at risk, much higher than a first marriage.

We must stop kidding ourselves. God is not mocked. You reap what you sow. Let me make this perfectly plain. If you sow compromised truth, dishonesty, or secret lust, that's what will be harvested in your life. If you cannot trust each other from the day you get married, you don't have true love.

You have deception. That's all.

If you are contemplating this kind of a relationship, you need to contemplate why. I have never known anyone who has said they wished their love was built on mistrust and deceit. Never compromise truth.

"If we claim to have fellowship with God, yet walk in darkness,
we lie, and do not live out of the Truth." (1 John 1:6)

"Do not spoil what you have by desiring what
you have not; but remember what
you now have, was once only among the
things only hoped for." – Epicurus

WE WERE LIVING in a part of the country that had good people – but not much else. We had made a trip to Colorado the first week of September…and we fell hopelessly in love with it. I came home disgruntled and unhappy wishing we could live there.

I yelped at God for weeks before I finally surrendered to the time and location of HIS choosing. I learned to love it. Just a few years down the journey, we were packing for New Zealand. Colorado wasn't even a consideration. Instead of New Zealand though, we ended up pioneering some work in Papua, New Guinea.

Returning stateside, we soon landed…in the place I had hounded God to go years before: Colorado.

Smile.

Through it all I learned a lot about myself. I was guilty of missing the blessing of where I was put because I had decided I wanted something else. I now know the gift of contentment. I found it in the place called home for over 15 years; in one of the smallest houses we've owned. I found it in the simplicity of life. I now refuse to spoil this goodness by wanting something else. When you get there, you will know what I am learning: I could not ask for more.

"Take care and be on guard against all covetousness, for one's life does
not consist in the abundance of His possessions." (Luke 12:15)

"Redemption and intimacy reign together."

THE DEEPER A redeemed person grows, the wider their intimacy becomes. It draws in others. It wants others to know this redemption is no small thing.

Redemption rocks your world.

While we often hear we have no need of a Savior and that redemption is a worthless ideology, it is just a ploy to keep us from the glorious truth. While we hear that we are not sinners and that we only make mistakes, we ache inside and wonder why our peace is short lived and our forgiveness is a struggle.

It is the enemy again.

After all, the enemy believes in God, so why would he mind if you did? Because when you do finally believe in truth that transforms, the enemy is seen for who he is and not what you once thought.

Redemption pays the price for those things we have chosen that are against the divine law. Grace is a haven of God's riches at Christ's expense, not ours. Redemption is the power of the Resurrection. The Resurrection, in all its birthing, gave eternal life. Redemption gives us a choice.

"For if by one man's offense, death reigned by one; much more they which receive abundance of grace and of the gift of righteousness shall reign in life by one, Jesus Christ." (Romans 5:17)

FEBRUARY 15

"Joy gives away the given."

I T WAS A little church in the middle of nowhere. It was our first time to visit so we sat in the back. We had a wheelchair and a six year old, so we needed to be near a door. Someone said something about the pianist not coming. Dan told them his wife plays. So, I did! It was a wonderful blessing for me and it seemed so for them as well. But how many people do you know who would do such a thing?

Don't waste the gift. Your gift doesn't have to be fantastic to still be useable somewhere.

Everyone has a few gifts. I can sing a little, play piano, organ. I can write. I can cook a little. I can create. I can clean. I can design. I can organize. I can drive. I can read. I can hug. I can solve problems, see into the depths of a troubled spirit, and inspire people. Yep, I can do a few things. But if I don't use those gifts to bless other people, it would be the same as if I took them and buried them. I might as well not have them. What is their value if I am not using them for the highest good?

I may not be the best pianist or the best-selling author or even the best car driver, but what I am is exactly what someone else might need. They won't care that I haven't been on TV or traveled the world or can drive 85 miles per hour. They will care that I have used what I have been given to bless them. My dad used to say, if you don't use what God gives you to bless others, God reserves the right to take your gift from you.

Somebody needs what you were already given.

"Each of us has received a gift to use to serve others." (1 Peter 4:10-11)

"Joy doesn't live in the falling down."

PEOPLE CONSISTENTLY OVERESTIMATE how awful they feel or are going to feel. Most people actually keep those awful feelings close enough to their surface so they can grab them when they want to.

"Time to feel awful!" they say to themselves.

Often, the biggest reason for feeling awful, aside from **choosing** to feel awful, is disappointment. For example, you won't ask that girl for a date because she might disappoint you and you can't bear that. You won't ski because you might break a leg, so you spend your life talking about how you are unhappy in your dating and you're sad you can't ski. So, look at your list...think about the disappointment.

Remember when you were one year old and you wanted to run, but you were barely crawling, your feet never leaving the floor! Run? Why try? But you didn't think that at all. You just grabbed hold of something and tried standing. Then, boom – you fell down. Then you just grabbed that table leg again and stood up. You must have done that a hundred times. Then one day, you walked. The next few months you ran. Falling was just part of walking.

Quit living in the falling down. This falling thing is just a part of a growing life. Challenge yourself to just do it. If you get disappointed, learn to be excited you tried. Never underestimate your potential for feeling fantastic, and Jesus is the Love of all Life!

"The Lord helps the fallen and lifts those bent beneath their loads." (Psalm 145:14-16)

"Where is home for you?" A stranger asked a
fellow traveler, "Wherever she is"
Came the reply as the man pointed at his wife." – Unknown

D AN AND I have moved a lot; about twenty-one times. We always told our daughter that home wasn't a place. It was a state of mind. In fact it wouldn't even feel like home, no matter how grand, if the people you love the most weren't there.

Life is for sharing.

We have made all kinds of places home because while a house may hold a home, a home is the makeup of the people connected there. Even when you say you are going to return "to the old home place," you know that you mean the people in that place. Dan and I have always felt as long as we had each other, anywhere could be home. That's what true loves bring to the whole of life. It's easily moved and can go everywhere you go.

When you find the love of your life, you've found your home.

"Unless the Lord builds the house, they labor
in vain who build it." (Psalm 127:1)

FEBRUARY 18

"Be Happy! It's one way of being wise." – Gabrielle

HAVE YOU EVER considered this thought? Being Joyful is a choice. It's a wise choice. The Great Physician says that depression is rooted in an anxious heart.

Thankfulness is the key to abundance. To revive an anxious heart, we may be wise to focus on more joy...**through thanksgiving**. If that sounds too simplified for those who feel overwhelmed, remember that it is truth that transforms us from night to day.

Joy keeps us focused.

Joy gives us purpose.

Joy creates more joy. Choosing Joy creates well-being in our spirit. All these things are wise. That is what God was telling us throughout the book of Philippians. Philippians is a book of instructions that lead to joy.

"Rejoice in the Lord always, and again I say, rejoice!" (Philippians 4:4)

FEBRUARY 19

"True godliness doesn't turn men out of the world, but enables them to live better in it, and excites their endeavors to mend it. We have nothing that we can call our own; no, not ourselves; for we are all but tenants, and at Will, too, of the great Lord of our selves, and the rest of this great farm, the world that we live upon." – William Penn

HISTORICALLY, WILLIAM PENN was in the business of saving people from uselessness. The fact that he saw the world as a great farm is of interest to me. I live among farmers. While I could not begin to imagine how to run a farm, I know the work is hard, deep, wide and all consuming. They recognize the goodness of God in the rain and the wisdom in the almanac as God's order.

So, you and I can see ourselves as useless or we can see ourselves as farmers in the world's great farm of life. If we become open to farming lessons, I believe we can nourish others, be positively busy mending fences, and shoeing and smithing the needs around us.

"If any would not work, neither should he eat." (2 Thessalonians 3:10)

FEBRUARY 20

*"Real love is when you go through the toughest storm and find yourself
still holding hands when you come out."* – Victor Hervey

USUALLY YOU FALL in love in the good times. Maybe
you are young and still have all your teeth. Maybe you just
backpacked Europe and the time was perfect. Maybe you had finished
your last thesis and wanted a family. I don't know. For us, it happened
in college where we thought we knew everything and thought little
could go wrong.

A few years down the pike and we didn't know if anything would
ever go right again. It has seemed much of our love's learning has been
out in the saddle, in the North Forty in the blizzard and the famine and
the peak of wildlife season. Sometimes, holding on to each other was a
blood, guts and sweat kind of thing. While some face the battles within
their own love, we faced battles of life we never imagined.

Everybody gets a storm. How you get through the storm is how you
win the peace on the prairie. There is a love that is stronger than any
storm. Grab hold of it and cowboy up. The best is yet to be.

*"Who no eye has seen, what no ear has heard and what
no human can conceive is the things God has prepared
for those that love Him."* (1 Corinthians 2:9)

FEBRUARY 21

"I am aware that I am less than some people
prefer me to be, but most people are
unaware that I am so much more than what they see." – Douglas Pagels

GREAT THOUGHT, ISN'T it? I have always loved, enjoyed, and have been fascinated by people. I like finding out why they do what they do. I am captured by their stories. I like the different colors, cultures, customs, traditions, songs and religions of people. I have been blessed by knowing generous lovers of life, campers of comforters and victors of the overwhelming. There are some who have caught my eye in their deepest sin while I have stood with others in their greatest joy. I have listened to dreams and fears, hopes and yesterdays bound in love.

I find, on a nearly daily basis is that people are precious. There are so much more of us to know on a deeper basis than ever. I know I have failed a great many in some way. I am aware there are things we all keep in journals and under the bed boxes. I often watch people and wonder what their story might be. May we all get to know each other as deep as we do wide.

"Since you are precious and honored in My sight, and because I love you,
I will give people in exchange for your life." (Isaiah 43:4)

FEBRUARY 22

"When I pray for another person, I am praying for God to open my eyes so that I can see that person as God does, and then enter into the stream of love that God already directs toward that person." – Phillip Yancey

P RAYER, FOR ME personally, is one of the most incredible, most precious blessings of life here in earth. You just speak from anywhere, at any time for any reason and you can have a direct, immediate connection to God. He does say sin can block our conversations, but He will always listen. He is, after all, God.

I believe prayer has often become a careless list of wants and junk. But prayer is so much more than requests. God says He welcomes our requests; but, for our benefit, we need to praise and be thankful. For our benefit, keeping our life cleansed opens us to more blessings. We need to recognize that asking less and *"being"* more is the real treasure of the process of prayer. After all, God already knows the list. We often treat Him like He is slow or too old to catch on to what we are saying. But He knows. I find the more I pray with thanksgiving and praise, the less anxious I am; the more profitable my praying. Frankly, I don't want to miss a single blessing.

"This is the confidence we have in approaching God, that if we ask anything according to His will, He hears us." (1 John 5:17)

FEBRUARY 23

"An empty swing is not an empty life." Ann Stewart Porter

WE LOOK AT things from time to time in little more than marks of time. I was a child. I am no more. I had a child. I don't have a child. I had a mate. I don't have a mate. If we can take a moment to transcend the precarious ticks of our time, which tells us very little, we can see. Time is often just a traduce in our lives. We don't lose our childhood. We live it out in some way, almost daily.

Our children don't leave us. They are around us. Our mates are not gone from us. They are just not present in this world in their human form. Life is more theophany than we take to heart. Emptiness is the emotion of releasing and letting BE what is, so there is room for being filled with other parts of life. That way, we can take on more and more of the eternity of God's goodness in our fullest living.

Push your cerebral heart swings as you pass by them. Take a moment to swing. But never become a friend to the *"had"* family. It's all still yours, for what was given and taken away always leaves a gift for us to unwrap and enjoy. Be it the passing of time or the passing of life, there is no empty life. Let everything that had breath in your life breath through you. Eternity is a way of life in the Master Timepiece.

"Let everything that has breath praise the Lord." (Psalm 150:6)

FEBRUARY 24

*"Relatives share the same bloodline, but FAMILY shares
your successes, pains, ambitions, celebrations, failures, values,
love, and so much more. I realize that many friends
have become family and some relatives just are not."* – Gaye Miller

B LOOD IS THICKER than water. Ever hear that? Or blood runs deeper and truer than anything else. But…what about that very sick father who has sex with his daughter, ruining her sexual health? What about the controlling mother who has emotionally crippled their son? What about absent siblings?

Blood can be hard. Blood can rip out your soul and throw it back into the arena. Blood can damage and steal and break every bone in your heart. At some point, we come to know that not all blood is family. Some of us desperately need to redefine family. Family is not always bloodlines and shared names. I think it might surprise us someday to find out how much blood flows between us, that in some ways, we are all related.

I am learning some blood is not family. I see many suffer needlessly because they didn't get *"the package"* the way it should have been. It's okay; GO find a family. Love them like family. Call them family. Live joyously. Sometimes, you have to color outside the lines. And that is just fine.

*"He who brings trouble on his family will only inherit the wind and
the fool will be a servant to the wise."* (Proverbs 11:29)

FEBRUARY 25

"The seeds of greatness are sown in ordinary soil." – Leah Griffith

S O, YOU ARE ordinary.

Hum.

Ordinary in looks or intelligence or health or wealth or what exactly? Where do we think greatness starts? Do people get up one morning and decide they will be this great person? If you choose great people you know, look way back in their life. It's likely that you will find a lot more ordinary than extraordinary. You will generally find humble beginnings.

Many are home grown, salt of the earth. Most people start off by being born. (Surprising isn't it?) This is quite extraordinary, but not in decisions of their greatness. Greatness is a habit of planting and being, digging and sowing, doing things most people would not do. Most of all, greatness is more common than we believe. It's not the well known or wealth endowed or those of uncommon grandeurs. True greatness has cost more work than anyone might see, and it's a daily cost. It is an everyday commitment.

It is a deep, in grounded belief system. It is a determination no storm uproots. It may never be considered greatness here on earth. So do not worry that you are just a common, ordinary person. That is part of greatness.

"Humble yourselves before the Lord and He
will lift you up." (James 4:10)

"Human things must be known to be loved; but Divine things
ust be loved to be known." – Blaise Pascal

WE HUMANS ARE always trying to make the divine too *"earthy."* We don't see faith, can't touch love, can't smell grace…at least not like you hold a carrot or a baby or pet a horse. I've heard people try to explain the mysteries of God. I have noticed humans create gods that fit their perspective of what they desire in a god. Most often, that involves a god who allows us anything we would desire or think we want…more tolerant than a god could ever be.

Why is it we feel obligated to change the divine, rather than receive it and enjoy the relationship? Once you choose to love divinity, it opens up to you like an all-embracing world. You can hardly escape the overwhelming joy, peace, and comfort simply because you don't wish to leave. It doesn't make sense to leave the home you looked for all your life. I hear people tell me they don't believe in God and all that stuff. They make it mystical and pretentious. And frankly, I can't tell them how awesome it is to be who you are in the divine.

The more you love the divine, the more it embraces every fiber of your being. The world didn't give it to me and the world can't take it away. Know the love divine.

"We declare God's wisdom, a mystery of God, which He
destined for our glory before time." (1 Corinthians 2:7)

FEBRUARY 27

"Nothing is more overwhelming than God's grace."

B EEN THERE?
"Where your tears were your food, because the pain was so deep, the spirit so disturbed, the silence of God such a dark ricochet in the pain?" I am truly thankful this Psalm was included…and not under Lamentations, but in Songs for the Spirit. Songs for congregations and people in pain, who still wish they could worship and feel the old joy they once took for granted.

I am thankful because I have been in that dark place, the underground of my spirit. I have been there, weeping through tons of tissues and wearing my grief as a life song. If you read this little Psalm, you will find that the writer knew grief, but even greater, he knew where to go. He says this time has made him thirsty for God, that he trusts God, hopes in God, will listen for the deep calling the deep, will praise Him, will see God's loving kindness, will know the help of God's presence, and will remember the good times with God.

Where you are today might be the place God has chosen for you to know Him in the deepest ways. Let it be, as the Psalmist says: *"A prayer to the God of my life."*

"My tears have been my food day and night. While people say to me "Where is your God?" (Psalm 42:3)

FEBRUARY 28

"For the rest of his life, Oliver Twist remembered
a single word of a blessing
spoken to him by another child, because this
world stood out so strikingly, from
the consistent discouragement around him." –
Charles Dickens, *Oliver Twist*

G ROWING UP IN my family meant you could not attend movies. So, when my teacher at school announced we would be going to the theatre to see Oliver Twist, I didn't know what my parents would do. To my delight, they approved. So, the first movie I saw on the big screen was Oliver Twist; the story of the plight of many orphans in the 1800s in England.

To this day I remember the soulful voice of the song *"Where is Love"* and I adored *"I'd Do Anything for You."* I nearly cried at the sadness. I rejoiced in the kindness. It is a powerful story everyone should see. What has always stayed in my heart is the power of kindness, how it can change deep pain into bearable days; how it teaches others to be stronger and overcome.

There are Oliver Twists everywhere; people in need of kindness. It's a classic story. Kindness is the classiest thing anyone can ever do.

It still stands out because of the discouragement around us. Blessings are remembered for lifetimes. Maybe we can remember that. Be kind.

"The fruit of the Spirit is love, joy, peace, patience, kindness,
goodness, faithfulness, gentleness, self control; against such things
there is no law." (Galatians 5:22-23)

MARCH 1

"Great grief makes sacred those upon whom
its hand is laid. Joy may elevate.
Ambitions glorify. Only sorrow consecrates." – Horace Greeley

GRIEF IS OFTEN *like mists on the mountains. Give it time to let the sunshine through. Grief comes; intense and overwhelming. It bends up inside us and sits; rather stubbornly some days. Some days you rise up feeling the weight of the world, or there is some grief you feel has chased you all night.*

Sometimes, you so want to be done.

But "done" is an itchy thing. Like today, Dan and I were eating at a favorite place. In walked a gal with a wheelchair and a little girl just like our Rachel who died a few years ago. We both ate with tears in our eyes. It seems so long ago and yet so close to us. We have traveled onward, but the moment jerked us back to that time of loss. There's not much to do really. It's more a matter of *"Being."*

Be patient with yourself. Be kind to yourself. Be thankful for what you have. Be mindful of others who need what you were given. Be quiet. Be spiritually leaning into the growing. And wait. Grief carries no watch. Grief comes in waves. Grief is conforming and transforming. There's so much work going on, it should not surprise us, that it takes so much time and energy. And truly that's okay. The sunshine doesn't have a watch either.

"Praise be to the God and Father of our Lord Jesus Christ, the Father of compassion, the God of all comfort, who comforts us in all our troubles, so we may comfort others." (2 Corinthians 1:3-4)

MARCH 2

"Cold words freeze people and hot words scorch them, and bitter words make them bitter, and wrathful words make them wrathful. Kind words also produce their own image on men's souls; and a beautiful image it is. They smooth and quiet and comfort the hearer." – Blaise Pascal

WE HAVE SO much power in our words. Lf you think that is not true, think of something someone told you long ago that keeps ringing in your head. Sometimes, it's so small and wouldn't mean much to another, but it's there.

A co-worker I once had was a beautiful looking lady, but the moment she opened her mouth, you just weren't sure what had gone awry. She was catty, sarcastic, cold, pressing with a pinch of anger. I never knew her well enough to know her well, but who would? My goal was to stay away from her mouth. Is there someone like that in your life? Or are you that someone? It's like that old saying that if it takes more muscles to smile than frown, then why are we still frowning?

You will likely have opportunity to speak into someone's life today. You can speak bitter. You can speak arrogance. You can speak anger or block an open door with cold, crinkly words that disengage. Or, you can let love pour out, fill up and overflow. Make your words comforting, an unruffled expression of kindness. Someone needs that word today.

"The one who guards his mouth preserves his life." (Proverbs 13:3)

MARCH 3

"Our chief want is someone who will inspire us to be what we know we could be." – Ralph Waldo Emerson

P EOPLE COME AND go, in and out of our lives, leaving us in a perpetual cycle of growth. Some have left us wounded in the battlefield. Some have watched us bleed and traveled on. But some have seen in us what we could not see in ourselves, or what we saw inside a place we dare not let another go. They step in and challenge what we once thought. They make us believe it is possible for us to be that picture in our mind that no one sees but us.

I have a talent for piano. Not a gift (and there is a difference.) A Music Director believed I could play with a symphony. I was terrified and I refused. He wouldn't take my no and his yes became a thing I look back on with great pride.

I had parents who believed I could teach long before I had a classroom. I had a husband who has seen me as an author long before I saw the first book in print. I had a dear friend tell me I needed to be a counselor and that I had a gift. I had a Drama Director who wanted me to play for a Broadway Musical. I fought it all the way to the piano bench. I thank all these people who have seen in me remarkable things. These people inspired me.

Today, look around for someone who needs your challenge to rise above their own mediocrity. If someone challenges your thoughts, take it as a chance to see that you waiting to be seen. Inspiration makes us be what we want to be!

"Let nothing be done through strife or vainglory, but in a humbleness, let each esteem others better than themselves." (Philippians 2:3)

MARCH 4

"Do you consider yourself a blessing or just another person?" – Jonathan Anthony

I LOVE THAT QUESTION! We adore autumn and take time each year to go see the paintings God has given us. We always love the mixed colors, the mountainside of pure golden aspens, all tingling and swishy. But if we turn a corner to see that bright flaming red maple or that mammoth orange oak, it just stops us in our tracks.

That's what a Blessing of a Person is like!

Every life is a blessing, but if you don't know you are one, you may grow up just blending in and looking all normal and doing good things. A person who has decided they are a blessing turns the ordinary upside down. They seem extraordinary. They have an unmistakable life statement they live out. They have a slight glow they don't see, but you do. They don't try to take the spotlight. In fact, most are kind of terrified of that light. Then again, they aren't pretenders so if they need to step onto a stage to get the blessing done, they will be there.

Wherever you may be today, ask yourself that question. Then go out and be a Blessing!

"I will bless you so you be a blessing." (Genesis 12:2)

MARCH 5

"If I can put one touch of a rosy sunset into the life of any man or woman, I shall feel that I have worked with God." – Henry David Thoreau

P EOPLE WHO WORK with God touch other people's lives. Why – because people are so valuable to God. You may not be able to create a sunset, but there is something you can create.

We were designed in the image of God. He gave us tools to bless each other. God is too economical to give you things just for you. Besides, He knows when you are giving your life away; you are getting the blessing back in your own life.

Take your opportunity to work with God today. I know. I'd like to send a rainbow to someone or a fresh pile of snow or a sunset glow. While I am not God, I can be there for them and give them what I have. I know I have some people in my life who are giant sunflowers, a gentle rain or sunshine to my soul. Maybe they didn't know it, but they partnered with God to bless me.

Reach out and touch somebody. Go work with God.

"We love because He first loved us." (1 John 4:19)

"Let's not forget that the little emotions are the great captains of our lives and we obey them without realizing it." – Vincent Van Gogh

EMOTIONS. HOW DO you control them? Distract them? Hide them? Drown them? Actually, if you want to control emotions, you have to confront them and redress them. Emotions come up constantly. They can easily be left as guides in our lives unless we use them profitably.

How do we do that – first, think small; really small without applying words like *"forever" "always"* or *"never."* For example, you cut your toe on something. If you say, *"I am so stupid"*, you give too much power to that emotion.

Next, hold that emotion accountable. So you are frustrated you don't have a job yet, but you are still able to see and hear, aren't you? Then just note that.

It gets more automatic with practice.

Then address the emotion. Why is it here? Is it really all-consuming or just a moment thing? Do you really need it?

Lastly, redress the reality. You stubbed your toe.

Done.

Ouch.

Over.

Onward.

No job yet? Coming. Just a matter of time. I personally use spiritual conformation. **How can this be a fruit of the spirit in my life?** It has blessed me in wisdom I never knew. No fight or flight responses. Just a wait a minute. You have to be willing to practice the process; then it will happen with more clarity. Live emotionally strong.

"There is no fear in love, but perfect fear casts out love." (1 John 4:18)

MARCH 7

"To keep the heart unwrinkled, to be hopeful, kindly, cheerful, reverent; that is to triumph over old age." – Thomas Aldrich

HUBS AND L have flipped through these ideas of getting older. Since we aren't getting any younger, we tend to want to slap people who say that 50 is the new 40. When hubs and l get done with our snap, crackle and pop and l don't mean cereal, we sigh at the thought of years to come. Neither of us is counting on leaving just yet, although you never know. Uncle Gene went to bed with a cold and never woke up. Uncle Roy went to the bathroom and died sitting up on the toilet. So, who knows? But for now, we have mutually decided that whining is optional, not all that attractive and of little value.

We've liked the sound of unwrinkled hearts. We both look in the mirror and think something's gone wild. And nobody is going to buy *that* video. Together and alone, we are choosing to be hopeful, staying kind, live laughing and keeping ourselves in awe of all that is, even the crazy things. Grow old with us; the best is yet to be.

"So, as those who have been chosen of God,
holy and loved, put on a heart of
compassion, kindness, humility, gentleness
and patience." (Colossians 3:12)

MARCH 8

"If you would lift me up, you must be on higher ground." – Ralph Waldo Emerson

THE HIGHER GROUND is a place of adventuresome joy, tale-tell signs of extravagance, awe and the celebration of our highest calling. Whoever you allow in the realm of your influence will dream with you or make you more fearful. Whoever allows you in their realm of influence will be encouraged and inspired or wanting for it.

What kind of person do you choose to be today?

Years back, I was up for one of those "got to have it" jobs. I had to do that Mission Statement of my life. Know what's still on my résumé? I am here to live in the double blessing of being salt and light, to bless and inspire. That requires I cover ground that others might never see. That requires bravery, consistency, preparation and strings tied to eternity. But I love it!

I didn't take the job, but it so helped define my life work and true calling. It made me unafraid to climb the highest heights and reach back for others excited at the goodness. It is very fulfilling and satisfying even on days when we all fall or miss a step or hang in the balance wondering what to do next. Higher ground is a great life! What's your life mission?

"Whoever sees the world's goods and sees his brother in need and closes his heart against him, how does the love of God abide in him?" (1 John 3:17)

MARCH 9

"Joy sees what others cannot see."

"**HEY LADY, THE** line is over here!" Nobody moved. The cashier looked at the lady in front of her.

"Lady, you are butting into line." Then she looked at the cashier.

"She got in front of me. It's that lady and then me and then her!" What she didn't see was the Seeing Eye Dog at her feet just around her side.

Nan was a speaker. Every week a gal came and sat on the front row and half way through, she closed her eyes. Finally, she asked the organizer about the woman. She had a medical condition that kept her from looking at the bright lights. Another time, I was the speaker. I was sure one gal hated me. Imagine my shock when her boss came in and I heard her say: *"You are going to love the speaker. She's fantastic!"*

Before you cut somebody off in traffic, tell someone off, make a judgment call, or treat someone disrespectfully, just take a few minutes and wait. Think about why they might have chosen their behavior. If you can, let it go. If you must address it, remember that kindness is never over- rated. The taste in your mouth will be sweeter if you have been wiser.

"A new commandment I give you, that you love
one another as I have loved you.
By this, all will know you are My disciples." (John 13:34-35)

"You have the ability to change a person's life, don't waste it."

I SEE A LOT of waste in the world. From our government down to our households, we are a wasteful people. Perhaps, until we realize the material waste, we will not value our worth to each other.

I believe in personal responsibility. I believe we are responsible to care for those who come into our personal realm of influence. I believe we can make a difference in another person's life in a negative or positive way. Because I believe these things, it holds me accountable for what I write, what I say and how I love. While we can get angry over all the other wastes we see around us, we are hypocritical if we are not speaking life into others. Our actions either silence our words or hand them the megaphone.

You may be tempted to say that you are just a parent or a whatever, like it releases you from the big thing of influencing another. It doesn't. You are a valuable human being. What you offer to those around you is of great worth. While you may not believe it, it is true. Quit taking yourself for granted. Somebody needs you.

"Be devoted to one another in brotherly love, give preferences to one another in honor." (Romans 12:10)

MARCH 11

"Maybe the end of the road is exactly where you should be." – Ann Stewart Porter

SOMETIMES, AN END of the road is just what you need. It's not healthy to know everything all the time. It's not wise to pretend you aren't human when we all know you are. It's not practical to always think you will arrive exactly where you want to be. Roads of life are made of bumps and turns into great unknowns. Sometimes, you go up. Sometimes around, out, through, and yes, down. So what is the big deal about having that stunned moment of lostness?

This is often the very place you stand most in awe of and lean into as you grow.

Now, that you are aware, you can sit for a while. Be anxious for nothing. Give some thanks. Pour out your heart. This place might not be as you wanted it to be, but if you wait long enough in the dark you just might see something really spectacular. Try saying out loud that you are trusting the God of roads and sunrises to make good use of this time in your life. Appreciate those ends-of-the-road days. They are often such sweet beginnings.

"The secret things belong to the Lord our God." (Deuteronomy 29:19)

"Live while you are still alive."

"**B**E CAREFUL," WE say, like a signature underlining our breath. I am convinced they don't hear it. Equally convinced there is a reason. It is more for me, than them. I am certain my parents must have said it a dozen times. I never remember hearing it. It was a fly on my ear. I never knew it was there.

Just when I had learned it well myself; how to say it, when to say it and even why, it flipped on me – like when you hold a pen and it somehow gets engaged in a warrior moment with your finger. You, scrambling like some fool to catch it before it falls. It's upside down by then, with a smirk in the air.

What if we said *"Be uncareful"*?

Same tone.

Same tag.

Just a turn about of fair play.

Suppose they asked what l meant? L guess I'd say to cast away the cares of today. Let it come. Befriend it. Beguile it.

Bubble wrapped living can be for some other visit. Today, bring out the best china in your life of do's and don'ts, pluck the chords for a fanciful song and pray for joy. Who wants to be so careful, they forget to live?

"In Him we live and move and have our being." (Acts 17:28)

MARCH 13

"All that the Father giveth Me shall come to Me; and him that cometh to Me, I will in no wise cast out." – Jesus

I BELIEVE GOD SENDS things to us. I believe He particularly sends us people. I believe these things and people create in us the good He wants to do in our lives. We live in a world where things and people are often thrown away. There are over 210 million orphans in the world today! We change and we simply get rid of what we think we no longer need. Or choices have left us in a number that burns holy shame into our materialistic pockets.

But what if today we began to look at everything as such a gift! From the fresh peach at the farm stand to the teacher with a stern voice. From the broken shoelace to the child who came in two hours late last night. From the gift you can't imagine using to the person you can't imagine loving. What if you held out your hand just far enough to know the goodness of that gifting? What if instead of another battle or an aggravation, you accepted the moment as a gift?

What if you could say to yourself that you will not turn it away, but embrace it.

Even the grief.

Even the pain.

Even the person who hurt you the worst.

You will seek out the wonder of it. What if every orphan could feel the awe of being loved, fed, and clothed. What if you could actually discover the reason God gave you that gift? Are you willing to open your hands, your heart and your mind? God wants to give you some beautiful people.

"As each one has received a special gift, employ it in serving one another as good stewards of the manifold grace of God." (1 Peter 4:10)

MARCH 14

"Our parents, our children, our spouses, and our
friends will continue to press every
button we have until we realize what it is
that we don't want to know about
ourselves yet. They will point us to our freedom
every time." – Byron Katie

I SMILE TO MYSELF reading this. How true! There it is, out in front of God and everybody the *"we"* we don t want to see. I often tell young parents that if they want to know their own worst weaknesses, watch their child at play, because they tend to mirror their parents faults.

Look at yourself. Friends who make us wonder about ourselves are the best kinds of friends to have. They challenge us and cake us with our own mud at times.

Spouses? – the ultimate wisdom, really. If you learn nothing from them, you are ruined in your own demise. Your freedom in growing as a beautiful person is through the doors of the ability to surrender. Even the word *"repent"* means to surrender and turn-about face. When you encounter that particular part of you, standing outside of you, take a moment of actualization. Are they rebellious? Where are *you* rebellious? Are they inconsiderate? Where is that in you? Growing up can be a most beautiful thing, but prepare for it to really annoy you before you get there. Grow beautiful.

"The things you have learned and received
and heard and seen in me, practice
these things and the peace of God will be with you." (Philippians 4:9)

"I have learned now, that while those who speak of life's miseries usually hurt, those who keep silent hurt more." – C.S. Lewis

GRIEF HAS BEEN a part of every life I have ever known. I see it spread like wildfire. I see it turn aside and hide. I see it cleanse and magnify a life once so forgotten. I see it touch a place in me that nothing else could reach, but those who grow the quickest, (as if grief were at all quick, that is), are those who tend to mouth their grief.

Sometimes you can spit it out discreetly in your napkin, without anyone being the wiser. Just as often, it will be that weird spill that you can't really justify. You just sit in it; the fall, the pain, the humiliation, the dire call to get up, the inability to move without awkwardness. (I told you I knew).

Talk to those who listen and those who don't. Talk to those who care and those who are annoyed. It requires attention and you are the care giver of its need. It is healing to speak of grief. Lord willing, you will feel the quiet stop in the under still. You will find the talk is less pushy than before. The intense emotion has calmed. Keep on keeping in. You are bound to find the blessing.

"Blessed are those who mourn, for they shall be comforted." (Matthew 5:4)

MARCH 16

*"Sometimes our light goes out but is blown into
flame by another human being. Each of
us owes deepest thanks to those who have rekindled
this light."* – Albert Schweitzer

SEVERAL TIMES THIS past week people told about one place
or other in their life where someone came along side and made
a difference.

I love to hear those stories. They remind me that while there are
dark places in our shining, these may be just the opportunity needed
for another. You have heard me say it often. I will continue to do so.
We are here for each other. This world is not for us to gather toys, do
battles and build houses.

As needful as a job is, the reason anyone should work is to be
a blessing. You simply can't bless others without getting it all over
yourself. I have been so full of gratitude for people who love me today.
I can't begin to list the encouragers in my life. I know God sends each
and every one at some time to remind me to keep the Light shining.
I owe so much to my husband, my daughter, son, parents, grands,
sisters, neighbors and friends. Seldom a day passes without knowing the
blessing of someone's generous love. It truly is like lighting the flame.
We are often so mad at the human race, that we forget how awesome
we are for each other.

Be awesome for someone and fan the Flame.

*"I remind you to fan into flames the gift of God
that is within you."* (2 Timothy 1:6)

MARCH 17

"Instead of complaining that God had hidden Himself, you will give Him thanks for revealing so much of Himself." – Blaise Pascal

MY HEAD WAS so full today. Dealing with a bout of flu and having it affect so much of my health issues; I got cranky about the whole of being old and of losing myself as I once had been. I missed my children who are up there in heaven, maybe with some envy. I soon resorted to a creepy- kind of complaining that I despise; the kind where I put up walls and accuse God of stupid human tricks.

Because He and I have been together for so long, I know He lies down beside me in my grievous taunts. I know He holds me in the mist just as in the sunshine. I know He gives me songs in the night. When I am able to fall into gratitude, I fall into glory. I find myself thinking amazing thoughts, like falling in love! I find myself so excited about what He is doing that I can't contain the magnificence of being connected.

He reveals more to me. I walk and talk with Him as though a dark day had never come. A spontaneous centering comes over me. I can't quit thanking Him for all the blessings surrounding me. Everywhere I look, He reveals more. It's like a walk in the crisp clarity of morning.

If you haven't quit complaining, you are going to miss the centering, the intimacy, and the thanksgiving. I am so in love with Him.

"God has revealed things unto us by His Spirit, for the Spirit searcheth all things, yes, the deep things of God." (1 Corinthians 2:10)

MARCH 18

"If you can't see the flowers for the storm, try bowing your head." – Ann Stewart Porter

STORMS CAN BE scary things. They can take you into turmoil before you know how you got there. They change your focus. The fear may paralyze you. Often the world is so incredible, but we miss the beauty, the fullness, the growth because the storm has captivated our spirit.

I love watching a storm on a lake, but not in a boat. I like standing by the picture window where it's safe. I remember watching a storm at camp years ago. We heard a flutter in the fireplace. There was a beautiful little sparrow. Dan named him Quigley and we nursed him back to fly away in just a few days. I couldn't say I wouldn't have tried to find a place to hide either.

Storms can make us feel like little tiny wounded birds. But if we take a moment to bow our heads, I believe it sends a message of trust to our Creator Redeemer. I think He responds to our heart in faith, in listening, in honoring His place in our storm. I think we can see better if our focus isn't on the storm. **Perfect peace is all about the focus**.

"You will keep him in perfect peace whose mind is stayed on Thee." (Isaiah 26:3)

MARCH 19

"When you have listened to your soul, little else will matter."

MY DAD USED to say, *"If you can do anything else besides preach, go do it."* His soul desire was to preach. He was a little, gangly 14 year son of a man whose knowledge of God was in his bottle of drink. But Daddy was called to preach. He left his Dad's store and money to become a preacher. He lived on peanuts and bananas to get his education.

He's been preaching for some 67 years now.

Mama had her sights set on being a Bible Professor, something the 1940's man population wasn't much interested in. On top of that, her Daddy was dead. Her Mama was dirt poor. But she stood up in her little country church and asked them to pray that she could find a way to go to go to college.

Mama became the first woman to get her Bible degree. She taught Greek and Hebrew for over 40 years. It's in her soul.

I know I may never have that million dollar writing contract I dream about, but it doesn't really matter. I saw a course on how to write for money. How dull must that be!

All I know is a long time ago, before I could even write a single page, I wanted to write. My soul had spoken. My life became full of stories. I cannot ***not*** write. It's what I do. It's who I am.

What's in your soul?

"What good will it be to someone to gain the
whole world yet forfeit their soul?
Or what can anyone give in exchange for their soul?" (Matthew 16:26)

MARCH 20

*"When God wants to give, the hands become too
small to hold the gift."* – Congolese Proverb

HAVING HAD A day so full of goodness, it strikes a chord in me when I think of my hands becoming too small to hold God's gifts. Yet, it's true! We each must know it when we see our babies being birthed, our children smile, our loved ones laugh and when our own courage is beyond the strength we have in ourselves.

A few years back, I wanted to show the grands the elk that often grazed through the mountains. For the life of me, we couldn't spot a single one. I remember praying rather earnestly for just one, just one elk for my grands to see. We rounded the corner, to a colorful open field and to our delight there stood about 300 elk!

It was fuller than we had ever seen a field. There were all shapes and sizes and it was truly a breathtaking sight. The hills were literally covered with elk. I remember thanking God that He was so generous, so extravagant and such a giving Father. I felt that again today as my husband took my hand and looked me in the eyes to tell me, *"I had a wonderful day. You are so fun to be with!"* and I thought I could not ask for more.

My hands and heart are way too small to hold such goodness. May yours always be too small as well.

*"Praise the Lord, my soul and do not forget
all his benefits."* (Psalm 103:2)

MARCH 21

"The winds of grace are always blowing, but you have to raise the sails." – Ramakrishna

THERE'S A FUNNY story about a mean old Buddhist woman. She had been chanting and following rituals for many years, but it had never changed her. Finally, a man asked her if it made her mad that her works did not seem to bear fruit. She said she was mad indeed! He replied that if she was mad, didn't she think Buddha was even madder?

Smile.

Oh, I reckon we all know folks who can quote the Bible all day long, but they get tripped up right about the practicing part of being a believer.

I saw a little boy scout this week who was selling door to door. Listening to his conversation, I thought it was cute when he said he didn't want to wear the uniform. He just wanted to do the fun stuff and see his friends. I think I know some Christians like that. They want the getting, but they don't want the giving. Apparently, the Buddhist lady was in the same boat.

You see, a life of grace isn't about some perfect wishful performance. It's about receiving the gifting, becoming intimate, falling in love, and having a gratitude that overflows.

As funny as some of these pretended intended can be, the sad thing is that God speaks of a time when, if the walk was all talk, He would say *"Go away, I never knew you."* We might even fool a few common folk down here, but our Uncommon God knows our deepest heart.

Nobody fools the Real. Raise your sails with love and light. We need to see your grace.

> *"Then I will say to them, 'I never knew you, Depart from Me, you who practice sin."* (Matthew 7:23)

MARCH 22

"Your life moves in the direction of your heart."

WE MOVE IN the direction of our current dominating thought.

That should scare some of us.

It should motivate us to change what we are thinking and saying and believing! A thought provoking life is one aware of the focus of that life. You might notice we have themes for our dominating thoughts.

"When it rains, it pours."

"I can't do anything right."

"I've never been good at..."

"I am too busy."

"I will never get out of this mess."

Have you ever seen a pattern of what you say X about, and what actually is? This is not just a coincidence. **God clearly says over and over that we create out of our belief what we speak.** For some strange reason, we don't seem to think that includes us or we don't know if we can really have that affect on our own lives.

This week, begin to change all the negative values to positive. When you hear yourself speak *"death,"* turn around and speak *"life."* See what wonderful fruit you can create. It would appear that this thing about the words we think, speak and act upon is indeed a matter of life or death!

"A good man brings good things out of the good stored up in his heart
and an evil man brings evil things out of the evil stored
up in his heart. The mouth speaks what's in the heart." (Luke 6:45)

"Just because you don't see it doesn't mean it isn't coming."

THERE WERE TWO thousand children to feed and no food. Fervent praying had seemed to yield nothing of substance. But, as was their usual custom, the table was set, prepared for mealtime. The bowls and plates were empty, but the faith was full. George Mueller, caretaker of the orphanage, led them in prayer, not asking, but ***thanking*** God for His wonderful provision of food and drink.

While he was praying, there was a knock at the door. A nearby baker felt God had told him the orphanage needed bread. He had gotten up at two in the morning to bake bread. Could they use it? He had no sooner left than a milkman knocked at the door. His cart had broken down. Repairs meant the milk would likely spoil. He wanted to know if Mr. Mueller would be so kind as to use the milk quickly before it could spoil.

That was the very common of the Mueller's uncommon life. No one was to know their needs except God. What a life; a life that George claims, was exciting and rewarding.

People sometimes say prayer makes people lazy. That's because they have no idea the business God runs from the basis of that which they cannot see. Prepare the table.

"Do not be anxious about anything, but in every situation, by prayer and petition, with thanksgiving, present your requests to God." (Philippians 4:6)

"Give me the love that leads the way, the faith that nothing can dismay, the hope no disappointments tire, the passion that will burn like fire. Let me not sink to be a clod; make me Thy fuel, Flame of God." – Amy Carmichael

SEEING THE SPECTACULAR autumn colors, I think of how these wondrous trees serve us as fuel. I think of sitting around a fire pit, fueling it to burn. Us, with sticks of marshmallow spoofs waiting our turn to roast. Fueling our warmth, our memories, nourishing us in basic needs and overflowing goodness.

To think of being a log cast in the fire, to have no care of recognition, place or need. Just to be fuel, useful, passionately alive. What a prayer! A love that leads the way. How amazing. An unsurprised faith! A non-disappointable hope?

The imagery of the fuel. To not lie as a worthless piece of ground, a clod that grows nothing, but to be burnt up with usefulness. Could I dare pray that way?

"For our God is a consuming fire." (Hebrews 12:29)

MARCH 25

*"See if you can find a way to love, the way you
really want to love."* – Ann Stewart Porter

WE ARE OFTEN in a state of anxious love. You know it by the feeling that you aren't doing love quite right. Maybe it was knowing your parenting skills lacked something. Maybe it was knowing you had not said what you should have said to your mate.

A while back I found myself wishing for the kind of love I wanted to give. As I relinquished some bare facts of the event, I considered loving more wildly. I would take out the emotion of expectation and anxiety. Instead, I would just love fully, like I wanted to love.

I told them it did not matter what they had said, what I felt or what could not be changed. I would love them no matter what. In fact, my words were that they could not stop me from loving them! How's that for surrender? There is such a sweet freedom in that. I would not feel this. It excited my spirit so much, I hardly needed more. I no longer cared what they might say or do.

I just loved. Whatever's been messing with your love lately; love the way you really want to love.

*"Love never fails. These three remain: faith, hope and love,
but the greatest of these is love."* (1 Corinthians 13:8)

MARCH 26

"Ninety percent of learning comes through encouragement." – Kevin Thomas

THROUGH ALL THE years I have been in the educational systems, I never failed to see encouragement lead students toward a higher standard. I have had some very troubled students.

Ethan was such a young man. He was a huge boy, tall and muscular for his age. He was also Native American. He had been rescued by a white missionary, but his heart had been broken a long time. He was a smart boy and I told him so, but he insisted he was what people usually called him *"the big dumb Indian."* I explained we would not be using those words anymore, that he was now an Honor Roll student. I also told him I loved him and believed he was special.

He had come to me as a D student. He left an Honor Roll student.

Later, when he was in his twenties, I called his Grandma to check on him. He answered the phone. I identified myself asking if he remembered me. *"Yes, Mrs. Porter, of course I remember you! You were the only teacher who ever loved me."* And I cried. Those were his first words. That was the day I learned how badly I wanted to be an encourager in my life.

Never stop loving. Someone is learning more than you know.

"Anxiety in a man's heart weighs it down, but an encouraging word makes it glad." (Proverbs 12:25)

MARCH 27

"And who, being worried, can add a single hour to his life?" – The Bible

S O WHAT ABOUT this little question God poses to us? Did God know that if we got that extra hour, we might use it for worry anyway? I kind of get a kick out of God's sense of humor. Like: So you really think if you think long enough on something, fretting and fussing about it, you get an extra hour? That's funny.

You can worry anywhere. It doesn't matter if you have money for a second house or if you are going hungry. I believe that is what God was really trying to say. Worry will add nothing to your life. Worry is useless. Worry is nonproductive. Worry is a lack. Worry is a deficiency. Step outside your worry. Give it up. Let it go. Choose trust over worry. If God gave us the ability and instruction not to worry, then a thousand voices can't tell you it isn't so or it can't be done.

It may take plenty of attention, but it can be done. Do the math. If you don't worry, you could actually add an hour to your life!

"Therefore do not worry about tomorrow, but
tomorrow will worry about itself.
Each day has enough trouble of its own." (Matthew 6:34)

MARCH 28

"Love all of God's creation, the whole of it
and every grain of sand. Love every
leaf, every ray of God's light! Love the animals,
love the plants, love everything.
If you love everything, you will soon perceive the divine mystery in things.
Once you perceive it, you will comprehend it
better every day. You will come at last to
love the whole world with an all embracing love." – Fydor Doestoyevski

JOY IS RECOGNIZING that we have been blessed to be givers of love! Do you even begin to fathom the enormous privilege and responsibility you hold in your hands? It is likely not, because love is tossed around like an old shoe.

We don't know how to love everything anymore. We try to tolerate anything (which by the way, takes away from our wealth of true love), and we steal from ourselves in ignoring the love of creation. Perhaps it is time to sit down with our two-year olds and go from plant to bloom to animal to grass; speaking of love.

For as you and I know, opening the door to love, opens up the mystery of divinity given freely to us. Let your love grow.

"Above all, put on love, which binds everything
together in perfect harmony." (Colossians 3:14)

MARCH 29

"Find your own Calcutta." – Mother Teresa

SOMEONE ONCE WENT to Mother Teresa wanting to be an imitation of her. She told them to find ***their own*** Calcutta. Find *your* place.

Find where you are supposed to be. Everybody has a place and a purpose. Everybody.

Only a quarter of Americans volunteer in charitable ways. I don't know about other countries, but that should give us food for thought. That leaves plenty of us to work and plenty more work to be done. The causes are everywhere. You need never utter the words *"I'm bored"* ever again.

There is too much to do. A great side effect of giving is that it's always a *"back at you"* kind of thing. Be selfless, if only for selfish reasons. The more you find your place, the more joy you will experience in your life. Helping others is a real healthy boost to everyone, but especially your own self. Many people find their place inside their calling. Many find their challenges are growing places.

Go find you own Calcutta. God has need of you.

"For what we proclaim is not ourselves, but Jesus Christ as Lord, with ourselves as your servants for Jesus' sake." (2 Corinthians 4:5)

MARCH 30

"We can't always build our youth a future, but
we can build our youth for the future."

I T'S AUTUMN AND soccer season.
Hundreds of kids chasing after a ball.
Hundreds of family screaming and clapping.
Coaches yelling directives and *"good play"* for miles.
Sunshine, green grass and the chatter of community.
Proud peacock Pappas.

A lot of life is happening here in these fields of green. People are learning the fine arts of team work, personal responsibility, tireless giving, a willingness to be the best, listening, watching, courage, strength, receiving and enjoying the pleasure of appreciation, of knowing the value of giving their all, and so much more.

We give them these things as a labor of love, making all our lives richer. It happens in dance recitals, band concerts, karate class, debate contests; all kinds of places where people are taught things they will take and use throughout their lives.

It's wonderful to know we have the opportunity to build magnificent people, leaders, lovers, parents, teachers, community servants: all from the soccer fields of Saturday morning. Hope you are out *"building"* somewhere today.

"That the generation to come might know,
even the children yet to be born,
that they may arise and tell them to their children." (Psalm 78:6)

MARCH 31

"All that we send into the lives of others comes back into our own." – Markham

IT MAY NOT come the way you are expecting, but it comes. It has taken me years to be able to gain enough understanding to know that when you send envy and complaining into other's lives, it comes right around to your back door. If I am impatient, dishonest or angry with others, I meet those three fellows just around the corner. If I am unforgiving, selfish or prideful with another, before I know it, these things are sneaking into my life in one area or another. But I also find the more joy I express, the more gratitude and love, the more I find it finds me!

This isn't just some positive guru, mystical thing. This is the Scripture saying *"Give and it will be given to you. Pressed down, shaken together, and running over. For by your standard of measure it will be measured to you in return."* (Luke 6:38)

I have struggled for years thinking of this only in terms of money. Living in divine order means a different standard of measure for your life. The more peace I give to others, the more blessing, understanding, wisdom, generosity, healing, abundance...whatever, the more God is going to bring that measurement back to me! That's an amazing revelation, one worth learning and living. What are you giving?

"As you would that men do unto you, do to them likewise." (Luke 6:31)

APRIL 1

"It is wonderful what strength of purpose and boldness and energy of will are roused by the assurance that we are doing our duty." – Walter Scott

MOTHERS SAY IT. Dads say it. Even teachers and grandparents say it.

"Do it because I said so."

Do it because it is good for you to do it. Do it because it's good for others. You get older and there's your duty to vote, to be *"a good this, a great that."* It can boggle your mind some days.

But I believe Walter is right. When we know we have done the very least of our duty, there is a sense of pride and kingly boldness. It's hard to describe to a world that seems to chase the badness. I feel like the proverbial geek. Still, I have experienced enough of this dutiful energy that I know how it can infuse a life, a home and beyond.

Rather than the constant drone of drama, why not grab some duty that needs doing. Clean up the litter of life one piece at a time. Be a faithful man. Be a good mother. Be what you say you are. Help another in a dark place. Play with a child. Visit those who cannot travel.

I believe doing your duty makes you want to do more. I believe duty energizes things. Let us not hesitate to do that duty in our life with uncommon strength and joy. Make a difference.

"The conclusion, when all has been heard, is to fear God and keep His commandments. This is the duty of all people." (Ecclesiastes 12:13)

APRIL 2

"Just because you think it, doesn't mean you think it right." – Natalie Sarters

NATALIE HAS A funny way of saying it as it is, doesn't she? That's my granddaughter.

I can't imagine where she gets that expressional freedom, that "hit it on the head" thing from, can you?

I correct myself more often these days. I say something and the words I spoke stick out their head to look at me, to beg the question of their truth. I have to apologize. That is not true, I speak. Then I rephrase it to be true. It can be as *"small"* as "I can't believe I am so stupid!" to "I will never be…" I have been much better at correcting others in this vein.

Sad, but true.

I have learned it is easy to get in a pattern of negative dotted lines. You barely recognize it until you ask God to help you see it and change it. It's easy to let things go. Maintaining a thought life of integrity can be tedious. Then life comes and writes over the dotted line making it more permanent in your spirit.

I have taken on the position as the great eraser. Erase and rewrite. It gets better. I get better at doing it. Someday, I may even be the "writer" I really want to be. I mean thinker. If you can think it in your mind, you will write it on your heart. You must determine to be kind for God wants to do His part. **Remember that as you think you are, it's the setting of the bar.**

"Let the Holy Spirit renew your mind." (Ephesians 4:23)

APRIL 3

"If you would live in victory…you must refuse to be
dominated by the seen and the felt." – Amy Carmichael

AMY IS ONE of my long-lasting heroes. Her life is a record of many lessons learned and generously shared. From the time she bucked her mission organization and went as a young, beautiful single woman to India, she had learned much about the emotions of making ones way against the voices of others.

While she ran the orphanage, she fell into a hole. It crippled her. Much of what was written after that fall is what we know of her teaching today. It is a much deeper writing than most, requiring regular self-evaluations. She often addresses emotions as mists over the mountain, things not yet crucified in us, things that keep us from victory that should be ours.

With so many emotionally unhealthy people today, it would hurt none of us to understand our role in emotional control. While society claims you can't help what you feel, Amy challenges us to question it and to refuse emotional domination; walking by just our own sight, and what we are told – to become courageous and strong in our grace living.

Let no emotion dominate your spirit. Grow stronger.

"He that hath no rule over his own spirit is like a city
that is broken down, without walls." (Proverbs 25:28)

APRIL 4

"The only faith that wears well and holds its color in all weathers is that which is woven of conviction and set with the sharp mordant of experience." – James Russell Lowell

FAITH THAT WEARS well, in all kinds of weather, is in short supply.

We are mostly circumstantially driven people. This is why God always calls us on it. He wants to see what kind of faith we are wearing.

Once I sat in a car while my mom was shopping, and I saw a truck hit a boy on a bike. It frightened me so much it took away my desire to learn to drive. I had to practice developing my skills outside my emotions. I had to overcome what my mind was telling me. I had to be fully convinced in my heart I would not kill someone with a car. I learned to drive well, in all kinds of weather, but I had to be diligent in that venture.

You may have to develop faith in the same way, outside of what your eyes see, what your mind computes, what your emotions speak and be fully convinced in the growing experiences.

Like anything, it's a choice. If your faith isn't good in all kinds of weather, it's time for a new faith.

"As servants of God, we commend ourselves in every way, through great endurance, affliction, hardships and calamities." (2 Corinthians 6:4)

APRIL 5

"Choose your joyful peace."

M RS. GILESPIE IS not making vegetables anymore. The children didn't eat them well anyway, but last Thursday was the last straw…or should I say "last pea."

They had already eaten the first half of the frozen peas bag without incident. However, the second batch that came piling out had a small green frog the size of a silver dollar. He was frozen and missing a leg or two. Those were never found and this mother of three wonders which one might have unknowingly eaten them.

Still, now that it's done, they are done too. The unexpected frog in the peas has caused some undue trauma. To take care of that, there are no more frozen vegetables at the Gilespie household. Since this wasn't me, I can laugh long and hard. I can also understand their angst and eventual solution. It will certainly make me look over my frozen veggies tonight.

Of course, the fact of the matter is, we get frogs in our "peace" all the time.

Peace that stays focused can be a rough assignment, especially when frogs appear. Not to mention missing limbs! The frog doesn't have to be so big; in fact, most of them are not big at all. But it has set precedence for the rest of the day, the career, the whatever. Be mindful that frogs are, above and foremost, just a frog. If you want Peace, you better be okay with frogs coming in and out of your life.

"Thou wilt keep them in perfect peace whose mind is stayed on Thee, because he trusteth in Thee." (Isaiah 26:3)

APRIL 6

"You can't let it go if you are still holding on to it."

IT WAS A bittersweet September. Our grand twins had just arrived in life. They were mesmerizing. We were learning the two bottle step and knowing they would soon be gone. A fifteen hour drive, just south of the Canadian border would separate us. We could hardly imagine.

The last night there, we put two-year old Dylan to bed; he stood in his crib like a tiny angel, playing with his toy and thinking we would be here forever. We would be gone by morning. We hugged him so tight that it's amazing he is breathing today. The smell of him stuck to us and we blew one more kiss through the crack of the door. Dan stumbled to the top of the stairs and fell into a crumpled cry, deep and soaking. Then so did I. How could we possibly let them go?

I can still remember these emotions today as though still in the moment. These were hard days, days of learning how to cast our cares upon the Lord. God is faithful. The joy is in knowing He still cares for you.

Trust is part of Joy.

"Casting all your care on Him for He cares for you." (1 Peter 5:7)

APRIL 7

"Hopefully joy changes life."

C ADEN WALLABY HAD advanced cancer. He had heard about a miracle drug and was begging his doctor to inject him. The doctor finally gave him an injection of Krebiozen, a now discredited cancer drug. Wallaby so believed in the healing power of this drug that he was released after three weeks, apparently healed.

Shortly after that, Wallaby heard the drug was worthless. He lost hope. His tumors returned.

Realizing the power of his patient's belief, the doctor told him there was a new, improved active form of the drug. He used a fresh water placebo. The tumors melted away, more dramatically than before! The water injections continued. Wallaby stayed symptom free. Several months later, he read a publication telling him how worthless the drug had been.

He lost hope again. The tumors returned. He soon died.

The mind can control the body in startling ways. The mind will respond to expectations. There is power in the mind. For those willing to try and find out how much a body will respond, you may well experience an awakening in your spirit. If a man could use his mind to heal his cancer, just imagine what we could do!

"If we hope for what we do not see, we wait for it with patience." (Romans 8:25)

APRIL 8

*"Do everything with so much love in your heart that
you would never want to do it any other way."* – Amrit Desai

WHAT A BEAUTIFUL thought. We talk of love in terms of relationships mostly, but love is good for all of our living. When we begin to live lovely, we see things we never see walking outside of love. We begin to develop wisdom that excites our spirit.

Love is the fertility of life. It births depths of untold joys. It simplifies the complicated. It yields benefit, rewards and delights the soul with delicious goodness.

Love is a refuge, a hope, a passion cut from the divine, like a kaleidoscope diamond. Precious and beautiful, priceless and incomparable, love changes us.

We begin to notice things we did not know existed like hurting ones, sad ones, broken ones and those who are too fearful to even think of love as a way of life.

Your spirit is ignited to touch others, to serve another, to believe for greater things. And then you find it does you more good than the finest fairy tale. The happier ever after is just getting started when love unfolds in your life.

"Let us not love in word or speech, but in deed and truth." (1 John 4:18)

APRIL 9

"Chisel out some joy and grow from the choices."

BILLY WAS IN 8ᵗʰ grade and a self-described delinquent. He had waited until the last day of metal shop to start a project. That project would be his grade for the entire class. The easiest project was a screwdriver.

So, he shoved a steel rod in the fire, smacked it with an anvil and flattened it more than desired. Oops. There was no time to start over. It was bad and he was skunked. The teacher sarcastically gave him the award for having the best project of the year: a chisel!

While it wasn't meant to be a great lesson, Billy learned that if you go with the flow, use your strengths and let it be, it might turn out better than you deserve.

Too many of us are chisels who think we have been messed up so bad, there's no hope for us. We can't do *"that,"* so obviously we are good for nothing. We spend our lives turning down opportunities because we wanted to be a screwdriver and we are a chisel.

Maybe today you can go with your strengths, learn from the flow, and award yourself the pleasure of knowing how amazing it is to be you!

"For I know the plans I have for you says the
Lord, plans for prospering and
not to harm, to give you a future and a hope." (Jeremiah 29:11)

APRIL 10

"Joy sees remarkable things."

TWO EIGHT-YEAR OLDS were talking about glasses. One asked, *"Wouldn't you hate to wear glasses all the time?"*
The other said, *"Nope, not if I had the kind Grandma wears. She sees how to fix a lot of stuff, she sees cool things to do on rainy days, she sees sad people and helps them be happy, and she always sees what you meant to do if you haven't done it just right yet. I asked her one day how she could see stuff like that. She said it was the way she had learned to look at things. So, I guess it's her glasses."*

Maybe we all could use Grandma's glasses. Maybe we could use our eyes to see WITH instead of just through. Maybe we could catch the vision that ignites our compassion or gives us the insights to know a child's heart.

Evie told me yesterday she was thankful for dusting because it reminded her she had a home. She was really using her eyes in the right way. While it isn't a pair of glasses that creates true vision, or even age, it is our desire to want to see what matters most.

Maybe today we can be thankful we have eyes; and if we can see through them, be mindful to see with them as well.

"For we live by faith, not by sight." (2 Corinthians 5:7)

APRIL 11

"Don't ever lose your sense of wonder."

A FEW YEARS BACK, we sat in a huge church on Palm Sunday, watching as a donkey came down the aisle. The children were in Bible "towels" garb and waving the palm branches per instruction. Most of us had not seen animals in our worship services, least of all a furry donkey with fat teeth. But there he was, with some people praying he didn't leave his own gift on the nice carpet.

This is where Jesus decided to show up...on a donkey He borrowed from some guy on the street. It was time to announce His coming as a King, although that wasn't going to look anything like anyone imagined. When He came through town, the "Hosannas" weren't because all the people believed in Jesus being Who He said He was, but simply because they got to be part of the procession.

They wanted a Deliverer...a new "President," somebody to make life easier, and maybe, just maybe, this Jesus on this borrowed donkey was the answer.

But who wanted a King on a borrowed donkey? (Wait till they find out His way of taking over involves a Cross and a sacrifice.) But doesn't that sound familiar? People only interested in what's in it for them? Knowing who you know can make a difference in what you know.

Why don't you "branch out" this Palm Sunday? Get to know the joy of knowing the real Jesus. You will never lose your wonder.

"The Lord is my Rock, my Fortress; my Deliverer in whom I take refuge."
(Psalm 18:2)

APRIL 12

"One day in the country is worth a month in the city." – Unknown

I'M NOT A city gal. You can have the bright lights, never sleep, clubs and party life. It holds no appeal for me. Never has. Thankfully, I married a man who is also not the least bit interested in city life. For us, it represents busy life, crowds and crime.

You know none of that happens in the country. Smile. I have friends who love the city and despise coming to my country home. I know manicured subdivisions really turn my mother on and old *"always needs work"* houses feed my sister's creativity.

We love fresh air, the low "moo" around supper time, the way the grass feels while we swing and the expanse of blue skies that look like an ocean upside down, fire crackling in the fall. We stand in the awe of in horses in the dusk and steeple bells.

We enjoy jawing on the common ground between our homes. We look out for each other. If you left your garage door open, expect a call. They'll close it for you and hoe up the dandelions. We actually drive over to see the new calves and name them silly names.

We swim in the lake from sun up to sun down. We roast marshmallows, ride bikes and tip our hats with a slight "Good morning." It may not be for everyone, but it suits us and our bare feet just fine. Here's to you and your rich life wherever you may be.

"May it always be prefaced by the beauty of your salvation and the joy of His song. The Lord is my strength and my song; He is my salvation." (Psalm 118:14)

"Do good because it's a good way to glorify God."

WHY DO YOU do good?

I am assuming, of course, that you enjoy goodness.

Why do we love? Why do we do random acts of kindness? What is our motivation for righteousness? I don't know of people who do good works who think it's worthless to do good. Even those who wonder if following God is too hard still know in their souls there is a loving pull toward something that brings good. Few contend they would stop living a Christ-like life tomorrow if they could because it's not a good life.

It is good.

God's delight in seeing us blessed and His work in conforming us to be more like Him may leave us in awe. But we can't deny a life of integrity is worth living. A life of giving, sharing, loving, growing, gratitude, faithfulness, and believing is all worth it.

Really, just look at the alternatives.

But the greatest reason we do life this way isn't for the many rewards. It is simply so that people will notice there is a difference in our life. It will glorify God.

Glorify is the Jesus part of God. So if we glorify God, we are making God's reality here on earth seen, touched, felt, heard and spoken. So our primary purpose for doing good is for others to see the reality of God before them. Let your light shine so others see Jesus.

"Let your light so shine before men, that they may see your good works and glorify your Father in heaven." (Matthew 5:16)

"Nature tops the list of potent tranquilizers
and stress reducers. The mere sound
of moving water has been shown to lower blood
pressure." – Dr. Patch Adams

P SYCHOLOGIST CONNIE LILLAS uses a driving analogy to describe the three most common ways people respond when they're overwhelmed by stress:

- **Foot on the gas** — an angry or agitated stress response. You're heated, keyed up, overly emotional, unable to sit still.
- **Foot on the brake** — a withdrawn or depressed stress response. You shut down, space out, and show very little energy or emotion.
- **Foot on both** – a tense and frozen stress response. You freeze under pressure and can't do anything. You look paralyzed, but under the surface you're extremely agitated.

Which one sounds like you?

I love what l do and sometimes forget that I need time to rejuvenate. My husband is much better at it and has been known to stop me from going extra miles I don't need to go. I am learning. Where will you go today? What will it steal from your health? Don't let the days pass too quickly by before you grab some time to rehabilitate those things that might be lost in the run of life.

Go through the mountains, stare at the clouds, picnic in the park, sit by the stream and let these places speak quietly to your spirit. As you let the wonder in, the health benefits are undeniable.

If you don't take the time to take in the wonder, someday you will wonder why you didn't find the time. And instead of a beautiful place, you may be hooked up to tubes and beds with iron that tell you stress has invaded. Find the time to take in good medicine.

"Find the time to call on God in times of stress. I call on the Lord in my distress and He answers me." (Psalm 120:1)

APRIL 15

"God's surprises always come with God's grace." – Phil Callaway

I DON'T REALLY LOVE surprises. My worst surprise was when I had my first born child. Oh, she was a sight to behold. Her little head was in perfect proportion to her body. She hardly cried and she slept most of the day and night. Imagine our surprise when she began to shake uncontrollably.

It was no surprise something was wrong. But it is a big one when a doctor tells you that your beautiful baby girl will die soon.

She is blind. She is deaf. She is without an entire side of her brain. She will remain a three month old infant all her life and then, she will die.

Oh, what a day that was for us young, numb and overwhelmed parents.

But where God sends a surprise, He also sends grace. We had this amazing child in our lives for 25 years, far outliving all her classmates from any school and the doctor's highest guess for life span.

She went with us all over the world. Together, we touched lives as far as Papua, New Guinea, Mexico and more. Every time the experts looked at her, they shook their heads, often cried, but mostly, just seemed shocked she was still alive and so healthy. They always told us it had to be our love. That sounds right to me.

Love may be the best surprise of all.

"My grace is sufficient for you, for My power is
made perfect in weakness." (2 Corinthians 12:9)

APRIL 16

"Blessed is a people that know the joyful sound."

SIGN AT MAYO Clinic: *"Cancer is limited! It cannot cripple love. It cannot shatter hope. It cannot corrode faith. It cannot eat away peace. It cannot destroy confidence. It cannot kill friendship. It cannot shut out memories. It cannot silence courage. It cannot invade the soul. It cannot reduce eternal life. It cannot quench the spirit. It cannot lessen the power of the resurrection!"*

How powerful is that?

It is true of many a disease or pain that comes our way. We can rise up in joy and knowledge, in wisdom and power to fight the good fight, flee the "cannots" and join the freedom fighters of wellness and wonderful.

While disease and pain may come, we are only touched by it here, and it teaches us things about...there. We are stronger than that which seeks to tear us down. Whether we walk in the joy of total healing or the blessing of maintaining our fight, we can do so with the knowing we are not bound by that which is temporal. We have the authority to walk unbound and full of joy unspeakable and overflowing. Let's use it!

"For God is at work in you, both to will and to do of His good pleasure." (Philippians 2:13)

APRIL 17

*"Never put into your imagination what you
would not see in your life." – Dyer*

ALL THE TIME.
All day long.

Everywhere you go. You are saying things to your body and your body is responding. Just listen to yourself. *"I don't want to hear that"* becomes ear trouble. *"I don't want to think about that"* becomes a headache. *"I don't want to change"* becomes a stiff neck. *"I don't want to see that"* becomes an eye issue. *"I am so tired"* becomes fatigue. *"I can't get past this"* becomes the place you shut down.

Statements are made without awareness, without a thought. Your body will respond anyway. But you can begin to notice this balance and respect it by watching what you say. You can't keep saying *"I'm a nervous wreck"* without becoming one. You keep saying *"I knew it wouldn't go well"* and don't expect it to change.

Begin to pay closer attention to your body messages. Learn how to express even pain and hurt in positive ways. Acknowledge but remove the negativity from its power in your body. Always ask what do I want to see in my life? Speak accordingly.

*"The tongue has the power of life and death, and
those who love it will eat its fruit."* (Proverbs 18:21)

APRIL 18

"It's better to bend than to break." Anonymous

I AM OFTEN ASKED how to have a happy marriage. Since that is a favorite subject of mine and a deep passion, I have had to think about how that might look in practical terms. And it often looks like a tree bending in the wind. I hear women say they have lost their identity. I hear men say they don't want the responsibility of trying to please the unpleasant. I hear others in a fatigued marriage say they don't know what to do. They don't feel as strongly about the other as they once did.

Marriage can be a hard place to grow. The critiques and insights are often shared in a storm that has caught you off balance. Insecurity will breed contempt, depression, fear, and bitterness.

Either way, if you don't bend, you are going to break. It's not unlike riding a motorcycle. If the passenger leans in the opposite direction when you are turning the curve, it could be dangerous. You both have to commit to leaning into each other.

In practical terms, this looks like less critical jabs and more words of thanksgiving. It's about forgiveness and picking your battles with utmost concern.

Finally, commit to the leaning tree, to protect your love and to ride out the storm. Just bend when you need to and you won't break.

"Be completely humble and gentle; be patient, bearing with one another in love. Make every effort to keep the unity of the Spirit through the bond of peace." (Ephesians 4:2-3)

APRIL 19

"Forgiveness is a condition of love." – Anonymous

THE QUALITIES YOU take on from other people are those you're not clear about yourself. Let's say you are fearful about something. You may not only sense other's fear, but have become a magnet for it.

Stay resolved to keeping an awareness about your emotions. Do that so you avoid attracting what you are unresolved about in your own being.

Rage attracts rage. Fear attracts fear. If you allow for resentments and circulating insecurities, you will bring more to yourself. You will benefit from setting a philosophy that integrates giving but also sets boundaries. Unconditional love may come initially, but true love living protects love. You have to have conditions for that.

We have become very confused on tolerance and allowing life without its protective covering. That is why there is an epidemic of abuse in relationships. **We have bought into the lie that love must not have conditions.** So it comes to us in ways that teach us we must have boundaries and boundaries are conditions. The stronger you become in your own conditioning, the easier it becomes to attract goodness. Love is, by its own nature, protective freedom.

See your heart clearly. Protect your loving.

"Be kind one to another, tender-hearted, forgiving
as Christ forgave you." (Ephesians 4:32)

APRIL 20

"Healing comes from knowing you don't have to run from the darkness. You go into it; eyes open, and discover your strength." – Rabbi Don Singer

EVERY WINTER, RABBI Don takes a group of people to the now defunct Auschwitz Concentration Camp to remember what needs to be remembered.

We see human beings who do terrible things every day. We often wonder if we could do what they did. The answer is the one we fear the most. The potentiality of darkness within ourselves is that which we all know is true. Hate will bed down with anyone.

We can become the very thing we hate the most. It is insufferable to most of us to imagine being either sufferer or apathetic guard in a concentration camp. Yet, if we do not take consideration of our small hates, our ingrained violence, our own hideous signs of evil within us, we may well be surprised one day.

Cultivating compassion within ourselves is a vigilant virtue of hope to keep hate from rising up against us. Even in the most painful circumstances, there is great potential for magnificence in the spirit of truth and love. Nurture your spirit.

"Anyone who hates a brother or sister is a murderer and murderers don't have eternal life within them." (1 John 3:15)

APRIL 21

"Love trumps criticism. Use it liberally." Anonymous

WE COULD ALL take a lesson from the weather – It pays no attention to criticism.

I'm not particularly fond of criticism, are you? I don't like how it feels like grit in my teeth. I want to spit it out. I want to rinse out my mouth. I want to taste something more refreshing.

I am of the belief we have too much criticism today. I believe its energy is killing our lives from the time we are small to the time we are tall. We are graded on everything in our lives from how we look, to how we speak, to how much money we have, to how we raise our children, to how we live our lives. We speak of tolerance in terms of religion or skin or things we think another needs to think.

Maybe tolerance ought to start in the mirror. Then let's tolerate our children and all their imperfections. You say they are precious, but you cut them to the quick with harsh critical spats. Can you tolerate the boss or the co-worker who seems bi-polar? Or the guy who just got the position you wanted? Can you tolerate getting cut off by another driver in traffic? Can you tolerate waiting in line?

Where can we love each other deeply?

"Above all, love each other deeply because
love covers a multitude of sin." (1 Peter 4:8)

*"The portal of healing and creativity always takes us
into the realm of the spirit."* Angeles Arrien

WE LIKE TO think an aspirin cures us when, in fact, life is deeper than aspirins. We find that out as we grow older or struggle with our health. Maybe we discover it as a child of molestation. An aspirin doesn't make it all better.

Nothing really makes it all better for some of us. We are far too anxious to allow a creativity to hold our spirit.

Raina was such a girl. Brought to a rescuing place, she lacked the ability to feel, to love, to give. She was as hateful as the hate that brought her to this time. One morning, she wandered into the dawn and saw Sweet Betsy, a beautiful thoroughbred, munching on grass. She just stared, the way you do, when you are mesmerized looking at such beauty and strength. She saw in Sweet Betsy the spirit of beauty, strength and power in wholeness. She began to imagine she was whole. It took some doing, but she was willing.

Mostly, that's all it takes. She became willing to enter the realm of her spirit. The portal of healing always takes us through the realm of the spirit. Why? Because we are spirits living a human experience. We will always find our spiritual realm is our truest home.

Everything is connected to our spiritual *"beingness."* Everything.

*"Praise be to the God and Father of our Lord Jesus
Christ, Who has blessed us in heavenly realms with every
spiritual blessing in Christ."* (Ephesians 1:3)

APRIL 23

"Joy is not a negative energy."

NEGATIVE ENERGY IS all around us. It is often other people's negativity that brings ours to the surface.

How do you keep from absorbing it?

First, walk away from it physically any time you can. When I began to understand more about toxic people, I began to feel stronger in letting them go. I began to see why it was so needful. I have people I rarely meet in person. Others, I simply can't be around for any period of time.

Since I deal with a lot of negativity in my work, I also have to have other things in place. You may find shielding is needful for you as well. Shielding is creating a hedge about yourself that centers you. I believe a spiritual shielding is by far the most effective way to guard your heart.

Be brave enough to limit what you allow into your spirit. Use spiritual tools to strengthen yourself. Stay in a pattern of joy. Meditate on powerful soul feeding gifts. Feed on good words of truth as well as good food. This makes it easier to identify untruth and keeps a physical sense you need.

Next, practice transparent vulnerability. This creates openness that protects your spirit. This is a non-based fear strategy; therefore, you are not as affected by it since negative energy roots in fear. These three things will help you avoid negatives that can be toxic to your life. These three practices can yield great fruit in your life. When you have less to defend you have more to give.

"Rejoice always, pray continually, for this is God's will for you in Christ Jesus." (1 Thessalonians 5:16-18)

"Fill the cup of happiness for others and there will be enough
overflowing to fill yours to the brim." – Rose Stokes

YOU CAN WALK around with an empty cup for quite a while and others will fill it if they can, or drop something into it that might get you through the day.

But if you really want a full cup, you have to fill it up for someone else's!

The more you pour, the more it overflows and the overflow can touch so many more lives than we even know. If I am discouraged, I think of someone I know who is discouraged and I think of some way to encourage them.

If I am hurting, I think of someone I know who is hurting and I try to ease their pain. I have practiced this for years. It has been a good gauge in keeping my balance.

I feel we are often given certain feelings so we can relate to someone else in that position. I have found that filling another's cup often changes the way I look at mine and fills me to that overflow of joy that takes me away from self.

Stay in the overflow.

"Each of you should give what you have decided in your
heart to give, not reluctantly or under compulsion. God
loves a hilarious giver." (2 Corinthians 9:7)

APRIL 25

"Crying is all right in its own way while it lasts. But you have to stop sooner or later, and then you still have to decide what to do." – C.S. Lewis

I FIND THAT PARENTS aren't sure what to do about crying children. I was watching the Dog Whisperer, Caesar Millan, work his magic. Every time he worked with a dog, he kept reintegrating the need for TIME. He kept saying, *"If you take the time, you will get results better for you and better for them."* At this point, I am thinking we need a Child Whisperer!

Most crying is a person revealing a need.

There are other needs besides wet and dry or tired and hungry. But when it comes to a child, that's how we use to gauge the crying most of the time. We do need to take the time to teach our children the value of crying; the reasoning of stopping and going forward, because a lot of people get stuck in the crying.

A lot of people don't know even how to comfort themselves; how to move forward and how to learn from that experience.

Crying is only part of the process.

Often, I see parents treat crying as a weakness. Some won't stand for it. Some punish it. But here's the deal. It takes time to do negative parenting. In fact, it takes more time, more work and more energy. So, why not use your time effectively, positively, and more rewarding?

It's all in the **Time**. If you have taken on the joy of parenting, take the time to make it the best it can be.

"The father of a righteous child has great joy. A man who fathers a wise son rejoices in him." (Proverbs 23:24)

"May those who love us, love us. And those who don't love us, may God turn their hearts; And if He doesn't turn their hearts, may He turn their ankles, so we will know them by their limping." – Scottish Prayer

I HAD TO LAUGH at this prayer. In some ways, it does sound like something we would all like to do from time to time. I am always teasing my hubs about his passionate road outburst. I ask him, *"What would Jesus do?"* He's not Scottish, but he is Irish. His classic answer is that God would strike them dumb and stupid then he laughs and says, *"Oh, He already did!"*

Sometimes, it's hard to be god-like when you are so human.

I believe there is only one prayer God is guaranteed to answer.

"THY WILL BE DONE."

So, when we want to pray for limping, loving hearts, we are wiser to let God have His way. But then getting that through the thick skull of a strong Scot may take a good bit more praying! Smile.

Watch your limping prayers.

"They Kingdom come, Thy will be done, on earth as it is in heaven." (Matthew 6:10)

"How should an artist begin to do his work as an artist? I would insist that he begin his work as an artist by setting out to make a work of art." – Francis A. Schaeffer

A CLEAR VISION OF what you want to do is a work of the heart. Because I wrote a book, many people tell me they want to write a book as well. Usually nothing they desire.

I have people tell me they want a husband, but the evidence doesn't say that at all. I have people who want great children, but they are never there to make that happen.

You see where I am going? I am starting something in my life that has to have a clear vision to become a reality. And I am struggling with that! I get one idea and another distraction pulls me aside. I know nothing can really move forward until I am able to clarify my vision. If I am going to be an artist, I must insist on setting about the work of an artist. I can't say I am a great pilot, yet never fly a plane. I can't pretend I am a Doctor and not see a patient.

Catch a vision. Let it capture your heart. Create your work of the heart.

"Where there is no vision, the people perish." (Proverbs 29:18)

"The branch of the vine does not worry, and toil,
and rush here to seek for sunshine,
and there to find rain. No; it rests in union and
communion with the vine, and at the
right time, and in the right way, is the right
fruit found on it." – Hudson Taylor

HOW DO YOU abide?

It surprised me to discover the word "Abide" comes from the Old English for *"Wait"* or *"To wait in accordance with timing."*

Well now, maybe I don't know how to abide after all! Maybe I am the vine trailing off the trellis, trying to find my own water, looking for my own sunshine.

My daughter has this gorgeous, sprawling vine. Every time I see it, it is more beautiful than the last time. But when I stand and wait for it to grow right before my very eyes, well, nothing appears to happen. I've never seen movement at all.

That's how quietly I want to abide. I don't want to be a twitching, bothersome branch. I want to rest in harmony with **The Vine**.

I want to grow in due season. I want my life, my **abiding** to produce good fruit; fruit that nourishes heals and creates goodness in the world. I want to wait well.

Trust is the harmony of abiding. Abide well.

"Abide in Me and I will abide in you. As the branch cannot bear
fruit of itself unless it abides in the vine, so neither can you,
unless you abide in Me." (John 15:4)

APRIL 29

*"Show me your hands. Do they have scars from giving? Show
me your feet. Are they wounded in service? Show me your heart.
Have you left a place for divine love?"* – Fulton Sheen

T HESE DAYS WE tend to give too little and want too much. I
remember a dad telling me about his 17 year old son looking
for a job. The dad had suggested he try the local burger shop. The son
had said he was too smart for that. He wanted to be a manager at the big
Home Center! The dad had told him you can't just become a manager
without experience. The son thought his dad was crazy. The dad was
exasperated. It would be funny if it weren't so sad.

I am sure you have heard like stories; people unwilling to pay
the price of real maturity and powerful growth. I believe it was Amy
Carmichael who helped so many of India's children to be rescued from
temple prostitution.

As she became famous, people would come to work with her. She
would ask them if they were willing to be lonely, to live in poverty, to
work beyond their resources.

She played no games.

She became a great inspiration to me. Her poem: ***"Have You No
Scar?"*** became the title for my book. Her questions of following after the
hard thing became a clear directive in my own personal understanding
of giving in my life.

Always ask yourself the hard thing and be not afraid of it. It will show you a place of divine love you will not soon forget.

"Be joyful in hope, patient in affliction; faithful in prayer." (Romans 12:12)

APRIL 30

"It is not how much we have, but how much we enjoy, that makes happiness." – Charles Spurgeon

I WENT FOR A visit. The person was someone I don't get to see often. Her home was immaculate. Her guest room was a thoughtful refuge. Breakfast was on the back porch with a fresh bowl of berries every day. Dinner was wherever, but dusk always found us on the back porch in front of the fire.

There we sat and sipped and solved the challenges of the world. There, we would let go of the day peacefully. There we would gently swing, rocking the evening away. It was a perfect ending. Sometimes, it got chilly and while we knew it was late, we didn't much rush going to bed.

These are not wealthy people; but they are rich, for they are enjoying what they have received. The surest way we know someone is enjoying our gifts is by how they enjoy them.

I once had a guest who complained about everything: The stairs were too steep, the mountains made her nauseated…the list was endless.

My sister Sarah is different. When she comes she loves my decorating, her bed, the mountains; everything she treats like a feast! She makes me enjoy it more because it becomes a feast for me, too.

I have to admit it though; I can often be like the first guest. God gives me gorgeous days, eyes to see it; a thousand gifts from dawn to dusk and I manage to complain anyway.

Criticism is the endless list. Enjoying what we have, has nothing to do with our financial positioning and everything to do with our heart's positioning. Enjoy your gifts it's one of the ways God knows you appreciate what's given.

"I am crucified with Christ; and it is no longer
I who live, but Christ lives in me;
and the life which I now live in the flesh, I
live by faith in the Son of God,
Who loved me and gave Himself for me." (Galatians 2:20)

MAY 1

"A silly idea is current that good people do not know what temptation means. This is an obvious lie. Only those who try to resist temptation know how strong it is…a man who gives in to temptation after five minutes simply does not know what it would have been like an hour later. That is why bad people, in one sense, know very little about badness. They have lived a sheltered life by always giving in." – C. S. Lewis, Mere Christianity

I HAVE NEVER THOUGHT of temptation this way! It opened my eyes to some interesting things about temptation. It is a battle. If I fight, I come to know that quickly.

I was watching a Bounty Hunter show on television. He had picked up a young gal and was explaining to her what they caught on tape. He was reading the report and he stopped after it said she was looking around and then took the money in the cash drawer.

He said *"When you were looking around, that was God speaking. He was giving you the opportunity in that moment to do the right thing. Next time, listen when the quiet moment comes at that critical decision; listen and stop."*

Temptation always comes in three areas: power, beauty and desire. That moment of decision always comes. It's easy to do the wrong thing. It takes courage to do the right thing, but the reward is better. I'm still learning from my temptations, but I get stronger when I fight for myself. I get wiser with every right decision I make. I don't want to live in the sheltered life of badness. I want to flow in the goodness. What about you?

> *"The Lord knoweth how to deliver the godly out of temptation, and to reserve the unjust unto the day of judgment."* (2 Peter 2:9)

MAY 2

"But God is the God of the waves and billows, and they are still His when they come over us; and again and again we have proved that the overwhelming thing does not overwhelm." – Amy Carmichael

ARE YOU LIKE me? Do you forget that the very things that overwhelm us are created by God? That they are still His even when they seem like we are drowning in them?

I forget that.

I even treat God like He doesn't have a clue what's happening, doesn't know what He's doing, and I imply He doesn't care. Not always, but too often.

When I am fully frustrated by the thing that overwhelms me, I do not trust. I become defensive and believe it is all senseless. Or I try to explain it to God, as though I could. So that the overwhelming does not overwhelm, I must choose to trust and respect God's authority, timing and love. Otherwise, I will drown in my keen misunderstandings and human calculations. Even when the splash hits hard, it is still God's splash.

"The Lord is my Light and my Salvation – whom shall I fear? The Lord is the Stronghold of my life – of whom shall I be afraid?" (Psalm 27:1)

MAY 3

"One Heart that encourages another heart is double encouragement."

ENCOURAGE YOURSELF IN that which strengthens you. Simple, right? If it were, I suppose all of us would do it. But we don't, do we? We dis-courage ourselves. We dissect ourselves. We take futility to a new level. We become more dull and lifeless, more full of nothingness.

Then, when we are done with all our analytical dialogue, we wonder what is wrong? Were we meant to be unhappy, we ask? Will we never rise like others we see? Do they ever suffer our demise, we wonder? Perhaps they have learned the art of "encouraging themselves" because we cannot always depend on others to know our heart.

David was a king. It's lonely at the top. People don't always know what to do with a king. He was grieving. People don't know what to say when you are grieving. He was strong and a leader. People think people like that don't need their words of hope. He was also in a distress mode. He needed courage. Truth is, we must learn how to en-courage (give courage to) ourselves. If you have not yet practiced this, let today be the time you begin.

Encourage yourself...in the Lord means to learn the value of positively speaking to yourself, of speaking words of faith in God, of knowing how to live dependent on God and to embrace livable, active, useable Grace. Encourage yourself in the Lord.

"...and David encouraged himself in the Lord." (1 Samuel 30:6)

MAY 4

"There are only two kinds of people in the end; those who say to God, "Thy will be done," and those to whom God says in the end, "Thy will be done." Without that self choice, there could be no Hell. No soul that seriously and constantly desires joy will ever miss it." – C.S. Lewis

WANT YOUR OWN way?

Your own god?

Your own rule book?

God will give it to you. He is a Gentleman.

You get a choice. He even gives you time to twist the things He says. If Hell wasn't a literal place, it could just as well be what happens when you finally decide God is out of your picture altogether. With all the great ledger of religion and faith and denomination, it would seem they were often more important than the finality of the two kinds of people C.S. Lewis refers to here.

But the last question we face is the simplest of all: *"Will His will be done in my life, or shall my will be done?"*

To know the Creator loves us so expressly beyond our human ability to understand is enough for me to imagine His will to be a perfect conduit of love and joy, purpose and fulfillment.

To be His or not to be His...I think that has always been the question. That we each get to choose just shows the kindness of His love.

"Wherefore beloved, seeing that you look for
such things, be diligent that you
may be found of Him in peace, without spot,
without blame." (2 Peter 3:14)

MAY 5

"If you would live in victory...you must refuse to be dominated by the seen and the felt." – Amy Carmichael

A FEW YEARS BACK, we had a remarkable Administrator at the Academy where we taught. He was kind, gifted, and efficient and lived a life of example and truth. The kids would come up to him basically to negotiate to get out of their work. He would usually put his hand softly on their shoulder.

He never raised his voice, although he could play Sherlock Holmes in the Community Playhouse like nobody we knew. He would look them in the eye and let them speak. They gave all kinds of reasons he had heard before. Then, he would say *"I know. I know, but you just have to do it. You have got to do it. Now, just go do it."*

He said it slowly as though pushing them up a hill. I don't know if it was the position or the soft hand or the kind reflection or the simplicity of his words, but he was basically saying we can't be dominated by a feeling or a thing that looks at us and scares us. Every single time they would smile and go back and do whatever it was they couldn't do just minutes earlier.

That's how this quote comes alive to me. I have said his words to myself a hundred times. Every time, it works. Trust that your faith is strong enough to dominate your unseen and your fear. Faithful is He who has called you.

"My grace is sufficient for you, for my power is made perfect in weakness." (2 Corinthians 12:9)

MAY 6

"The depth and the willingness with which we serve
is a direct reflection of our gratitude." – Gordon Watts

IF PEOPLE SEE you through the reflection of your gratitude, what is it they see?

So often, I find unlikely people in unlikely places serving. As we talk, I come to hear them say they are here because I know what it's like and somebody was there for me and I just want to give back.

It is true. When you have been somewhere and someone made a difference for you there is an overwhelming whispering gravity to pay it forward.

Giving and Gratitude are twins. They know each other and look out for each other and they bounce off of each other.

I think of going to my parent's house. Their pantry is always full. (Scottish people love a fully packed pantry.) My Dad dearly loves to pack bags of whatever he has for whoever is standing at the door. (Which really does explain an overflowing pantry.)

What are you telling people today? That you don't have enough or that you are so grateful for what you have received? It's all up to you!

"God is not unjust; He will not forget your
work and the love you have shown
Him, as you have helped His people and
continue to help." (Hebrews 6:10)

"No reserves. No retreats. No regrets." – William Borden

B ILL WAS A millionaire by way of his family legacy. He was a student at Yale when he went around the world. He came back and did a great deal of good work at Yale, but always found himself in the hardest places. Eventually, he was drawn to China as a missionary, much to many people's dismay.

He challenged all of us to be missionaries.

It greatly bothered him that America had so much and gave so few to the work of his beloved Chinese. When asked how he felt about his life's work, he left us with those "no retreat" haunting words.

I don't know if l could say this in my life. I have reserves. I have retreated. I have regrets. How powerful to live at some point beyond those or to live in arrogant illusion. But this man spoke them from a life of example. Perhaps this is the reward for choosing to live right, to live beyond yourself and to live your calling.

Perhaps it's worth considering even if you never make it to China. It was never really about China anyway.

"Therefore, I urge you brothers and sisters, in view of God's mercy, to offer your bodies as a living sacrifice, holy and pleasing to God. This is your true and proper worship." (Romans 12:1)

MAY 8

*"The drops of rain make a hole in the stone, not
by violence, not by falling."* – Lucretius

SOMETIMES I FEEL like what I am doing is not making a
difference. As if it was doing no good to do good.

At times, the soft steps of progress are so quiet we can't hear them.
Sometimes we can't even see them.

I remember the story of a famous musician whose music touched
many lives. As a child, he would sit at his Grandmother's piano and play
after he had finished all his chores around the farm.

Years later, while he was touring all around the world, he returned
to his home town and visited his Grandmother's church and one of the
ladies told him how wonderful it was that his Grandmother's prayers
had been answered in him. He asked what she meant. She told him
that all those times his Grandmother had stood with her hand on his
shoulder as he played the piano; she was silently praying the world
would be touched by his gift.

She had brought those constant, soft drops of rain that made a
difference; not only in his life, but in the lives of all those his music
touched.

Don't grow weary doing the quiet, small, constant things. The stone
gives way to the soft rain not because of its power, but because of its
constant faithfulness.

Be someone's soft rain.

*"Let us not become weary in well doing, for at the appointed
time, we will reap a harvest if we do not give up."* (Galatians 6:9)

MAY 9

*"Loneliness and the feeling of being unwanted is the
most terrible poverty."* – Mother Teresa

T HIS IS SO true. Poverty, in any form, is sad and useless in a
world that has so many resources and knowledge. But among
the newest members of our society to the forgotten of the oldest in our
society, there is a growing grief. Sometimes, it is as though the whole
earth were groaning collectively for one another.

I have been extremely blessed to have never experienced too much
loneliness. Most of loneliness has been loneliness *for* someone like my
children in heaven. I can't say I feel unwanted all the time, but there
have certainly been situations where the message was loud and clear
and crushing.

We forget that because we aren't all Nuns, or work in a third world
country, it doesn't mean we don't experience poverty before us. We
do. It truly is around us all day long, in every place we go. Yes, even
church, and certainly, work and schools and stores; even on Facebook
and dating sites and in bars and any place people congregate.

Look for those in poverty today. They will come your way. Be
prepared to meet them, to leave a word of hope or a shoulder to bear
their burdens. We have the joy of loving others. We can give the lonely
and unwanted a moment to find their courage. Love is a terrible thing
to waste.

*"You are the salt of the earth, but if the salt has lost its
taste, how can it be resorted?"* (Matthew 5:13)

*"Gravity may put the planets into motion, but
without the divine power, it could never put
them into such circulating motions they have about
the sun; and therefore, for this, as well
as other reasons, I am compelled to ascribe the
frame of the system to an intelligent
agent...the cause of gravity is what I do not pretend
to know."* – Sir Isaac Newton, 1692

WHETHER YOU BELIEVE I can play the piano is of no consequence to me.

I know I can. I know I do.

If you don't believe me, that is your choice, right? Maybe you have never met me, but you met someone who has seen me play the piano. Is that enough to convince you? Or could they be lying?

For years God has never changed His Story. *"In the Beginning, God created..." is* how the Bible is always going to begin, and whether we believe it or not is of no consequence. Our believing or not believing does not affect the truth.

There is more evidence to support divine design than to prove it is not there. Could it be all smoke and mirrors? When do you believe? Because in the final analysis, you choose something to believe. All of us do. The question has never been *"So, is this true or false?"* but rather *"What do you choose to believe?"*

"In the beginning, God created the heavens and the earth." (Genesis 1:1)

MAY 11

"How is my own life work serving to end these tyrannies the corrosions of sacred possibility?" – June Jordan

THE TRULY SATISFIED people in this old dog-eat-dog world are people who have the beautiful audacity to believe they are making a difference; that what they do matters, that they are leaving the world better than when they came, that the world depends on the divine gifts they are giving.

Sure, vacations are great.

Massive homes and yards full of toys, stuffed garages and spoiled children aren't all bad, but there is way too much waste.

We have the opportunity to make our work a sacred work. We have the privilege and honor of giving to the world the Fruit of the Spirit.

If you find yourself feeling empty and deeply unsatisfied with your work in or outside of your job, you can change that. You can give it meaning beyond itself. You have the freedom to explore spiritual sacred possibilities. Let your Wellspring overflow.

"And some have compassion, making a difference." (Jude 1:22)

MAY 12

"If you haven't forgiven yourself something, how can you forgive others?" – Dolores Huerta

WE MET A man in New Guinea who was absolutely positive God could not forgive him. He was a murderer, an adulterer, a father who had abandoned his children, a thief, a renegade, a drunk and Lord knows what else we didn't know.

Oh, how we loved him. He had been so kind to us. It was like the other side of him did not exist. When he shared his childhood, we wept and understood how he could be so terribly perplexed. He loved us back too. One night, he came to the door, drunk and weeping. *"God could not forgive me"* he wailed, *"I have done too much for too long and I don't think God could forgive someone like me."*

He left worse than he arrived, so hungry for God yet so arrogant for self. You see, you and I can't tell God what God can do. If God says *"I forgive you,"* it's arrogant to say He cannot. It's just as arrogant as saying you don't need a Savior and that you can save yourself.

To refuse forgiveness means you don't receive what God has given to you, out of His great love. You can't receive part of God any more than you receive part of your child. To push Him away because of your emotions is sad and will result in your own deep grief. The greatest disappointment any of us will ever have is in our own selves. But this cannot keep us from receiving the blessing of forgiveness for that is how we learn to forgive others.

"Bear with one another and forgive one another if any of you has a grievance against someone. Forgive as the Lord forgives." (Colossians 1:13)

MAY 13

"Some people talk simply because they think sound is more manageable than silence." – Margaret Halsey

I AM QUITE GUILTY of this, especially in a situation with new people. Professionally, I seem to be able to wait and listen because I see the need to listen to what is *not* said. But with ordinary meetings, I am plagued by that silence between us.

Sure, sometimes I say things of view and hear things needful, but it wouldn't hurt me to practice silence more often. Talking is not more manageable. It is not always the wisest thing I can do. I have practiced being quiet for the day. People ask me if I am sick or if something is wrong.

I have noticed lots of people stand around and squawk quite uselessly. I understand that nervous laugh. That weird thing you didn't want to say, but did. I like being friendly. I like people. But the more I trust you, the more likely I am to just enjoy the silence and not worry about the speaking. If it happens that we have a lovely conversation terrific. If we just enjoy the space we share, I am learning that is just fine too.

"Do not let unwholesome talk come out of your mouths, but only what is helpful for building up the one in need and bringing grace to those who hear." (Ephesians 4:29)

"I pray because I can't help myself. I pray because I'm helpless. I pray because the need flows out of me all the time – waking and sleeping. It doesn't change God; it changes me." – C.S. Lewis

PRAYER IS NOT for the weak. It is not for the coward or the arrogant. It is a connection of reality beyond a world of illusion. It stamps our life with the unseen. Like love, it cannot be seen except in the reflections around us. What we say, what we do, how we give out of that well inside us.

Prayer has changed a great deal of things in my life. I can't deny the miracles I have personally been privy to in my own life. But even greater than the things prayer does is what it produces in me. To talk to an invisible man doesn't bother me so much as talking to an arrogant plainly seen one.

If something makes you a better person, gives you a thousand things that you are thankful for and causes your heart to sing, praise and live in thankfulness, then I say game on! If I die and find out I was crazy, I have lived crazy in divine love and I know I could do a lot worse. Prayer has made me stronger, wiser, more loving, giving and peaceful than anything I know. I pray to a God who is fully alive and connected to me by His choosing and mine.

"Rejoice always, pray continually, give thanks in all circumstances, for this is God's will for you in Christ Jesus." (1 Thessalonians 5:16-18)

MAY 15

"Nothing could stop you. Not the best day. Not the quiet. Not the ocean rocking. You went on with your dying." - Mark Strand

WHEN A LOVED one has seen the heavenly landscape, they are leaving and nothing can stop the going home. They ask for nothing from us. They have pulled away while we beg them to stay a little while longer.

Death is a mystery to those of us still living. They have now begun experiencing a place we can only imagine. The pain pulls the roots out of our soul. All that can be changed will be changed. From the moment we leave their side, we are different. They go on with their dying and we try to go on with our living. Grief is a soul searching, soul changing experience. And then life goes on.

We learn a new dance, a different music, a joy that grief cannot bear.

"And this Word, yet once more, signifieth the removing of those things that are shaken, as of things that are made, that those things which cannot be shaken may remain." (Hebrews 12:27)

MAY 16

"They rise up and call her blessed." – Mothers Day

MY MOTHER WAS the meanest mother in the world. Every morning, she insisted we be dressed with our bed made and chores done by 7:30. Saturdays, we had to clean the house before we could go out to play! Imagine!

Every week, we took turns cooking a meal for our family of eight! Every Sunday, we were made to go to church, but not to sit in pews. Mama made us play piano, sing, teach and do the nursery. During the week, we cleaned the church! Mama had a strict curfew. If you weren't in by 11:00 pm, you were locked out for the night.

Mama didn't put up with stupid nonsense. You had better put your thinking cap on early at my house. She didn't tolerate sloppy anything. Being late, untidy dress, and cussing were all unacceptable. She made us eat breakfast every morning because it was good for our brain. She made us play in the rain because it was good for our soul. She made us learn to play musical instruments because it was good for our spirit.

She led us to God, because it was good for eternity.

If you fell down, you got up. Mama didn't mess with crybabies. She made us serve the adults dinner. She made us read. She made us work hard.

Thank you Mama! I could not love you more!

"She opens her mouth with wisdom, and the teaching of kindness is on her tongue." (Proverbs 31:26)

*"In the fellowship of service I seek to attach a
friend to myself, so that others are caused
to feel unwanted; if my friendships do not draw
others deep in, that are ungenerous
(to myself, for myself), then I know nothing of
Calvary's Love."* – Amy Carmichael

AMY ALWAYS HAS a way of looking at everything from a perspective few ever do.

Friendships are blessings. When we find them, it is meant to be for our good and our growing. But often, as good as I try to be as a friend, I can be thoughtless and eager to feel fine with myself, to the exclusion of another. I expect friends to understand when my time is limited or my choices are different from theirs. But that isn't always how it goes, is it?

Sometimes, we attach ourselves to someone who has a personality we enjoy easily while another, just as precious, feels we are excluding them. I don't want to be that way. I want to be the kind of friend that is true and loyal. But I don't want to be smothering or demanding or all inclusive. Being generous is a mark of true godliness. That includes our choosing friends.

We must enjoy all kinds of beautiful friendships in order to experience a greater generous spirit. Make new friends, but keep the old. One is silver. The other is gold.

"One who is righteous is a guide to his neighbor." (Proverbs 12:26)

MAY 18

"Mothers – the other miracle worker."

L BECAME A MOTHER by choice, by deliberate action, by way of loving a God given man. I had a good idea of what I was doing and why, but I did not know how much it would change ME!

You hold this tiny, helpless beautiful baby in your arms and push the panic button. How will you ever meet their needs? How will you ever protect them as you wish? How could you ever keep them from being hurt? Oh, the endless questions stare back at you. They are so small. They have come out of you. It is a miracle that has no competition.

They begin to grow. You find out you must often do the very things you said you would not do with your child. You think about how to make them the best they can be. Sometimes, you even get lost in them. You learn together. You grow together. You are pieces of each other.

You find out that mostly, what you say carries a great deal more weight in their life than any other being they come to know. Certainly, you are unprepared to be the example they require. They and you are haunted by those sorts of things. And by the need to be connected by the invisible cord left from birthing. But always you and they know: Once a mother – Always a mother.

"Her children rise up and call her blessed, her husband also praises her." (Proverbs 31:24)

"Big backyards, good fences and love make good parenting."

I ACTUALLY HAD VERY few rules for mothering. I believed if I led them to God, He would perfect that which concerned them. I would be the cheerleader, the truth teller and the soft place to fall.

My often guiding factor was how much it would matter ten years from now.

Would I need to be so worried about potty training or when they learned to walk? This helped a lot because a lot of things we mothers worry over, simply need to be over. I did not have curfews because I didn't need them.

Every child is different. My child was very independent and that was fine with me. I adore individuality. I lived out what I said I believed by what I did. There was no double standard or two face jaunts. My daughter once told her Psychology class that my parenting style was like having a huge backyard. Sure, there was a fence and she knew it was for her protection. There was so much area for discovery and exploration; she seldom felt the need to jump the fence. I thought that was a great way to put it.

Always remember, to never forget, that you were once a child, too. It's still a great rule of thumb to do unto others, including your children, as you would have them do unto you. A good fence, plenty of growing room, respect and love make for beautiful, happy and productive children. Not to mention adults.

"Do unto others as you would have them do unto you." (Luke 6:31)

*"If we find ourselves with a desire that nothing
in this world can satisfy, the most
probable explanation is that we were made
for another world." - C. S. Lewis*

OH, HOW L cherish this thought! We, here on earth, carry on as though this here before us, is all there is or will be. We live borrowing pieces of thread of each other to hold onto in the day. We find ourselves discontent and frail with no place to go. We look to those who had opportunity to use their gifts for goodness, but stole it and used it up, trying to die while they were living.

Did they ever wonder why their desire was so divinely deep? Do we? Or do we simply try that much harder to have it all right here where we are today?

God has revealed to us this earth will never satisfy. Earth cannot give me my true identity. It cannot give me my worth. It cannot give me my present peace or eternal tomorrow.

What if there really was another place? How then would you live? We were never made for this world alone. That is why folks leave every day. Live with eternity in view.

*"I do not pray that Thou should take them out of the world, but that
Thou should keep them from the evil one. They are not of the world,
even as I am not of the world."* (John 17: 15-16)

"Write hard and clear about what hurts." – Hemingway

"*MR. PORTER, THIS is Dr. Frakadean at Georgia Baptist Hospital. Your wife has gone into a coma. We are afraid we may be losing your son and your wife. But if we could save one, which one do you want us to save?*" Dan had mumbled to save his wife and drove in a numb itch all the way to the ICU where I lay dying.

It was a hard summer. They had managed to save both of us, but neither of us was faring well. It was a month of Sundays before I was able to leave; not sure I knew what had happened. I had a loss of memory that would need lots of work to recoup, and a feisty beautiful two-year old that didn't recognize me from the seizures that had ripped up my body. Oh, and the profoundly retarded four-year old that has overwhelmed me once, and did so now.

In September of 1984, we had gathered in the office to pray with our doctors about pulling the tubes from our two-pound son's body ravaged by pain. Matthew was born on May 21, 1984. His life was over full of pain. Seventeen tubes from all over his body held him together. His open heart surgery had been a brilliant success. He was a great warrior. But it was all coming to an end.

Mercifully, God took him without our consent and yet, with our knowing. I often write of joy and choosing life beyond the pain. I am not just quoting pretty things to make us all feel better. I have lain in the trenches of the war. I have felt the muddy, bloody incapacitating pain of not wanting to rise again. I know pain. That is also how I know the depth of joy today.

> *"The Lord giveth and the Lord taketh away.*
> *Blessed be the name of the Lord."* (Job 1:21)

MAY 22

"We love people most for how they make us feel."

L OVE COMES WITH feelings.

This is a nice thing because sometimes that's how we gauge our love. How do we feel with this person? Love is also more than feelings, which is good, because feelings change. Love deepens. I have heard people who have hurt other people say things like how much they love the other person, but they felt so belittled or betrayed or unwanted or whatever.

Often people will stop off by the bar on the way home from work (which lasts all night) because, frankly going home kind of worries them. Or they shop endlessly, do the church work of ten people, or find other ways of feeling what they need to feel, other than going home. I have had people admit their marriage fell apart because they knew the other person had to work too hard to make them happy.

So for those who want to be wise and take this to heart here's the secret: We love people most for how they make us feel! ***We love people most for who we become in their presence.*** We love to feel the highest good in us has been found in the worst in us.

Here's to love and all its goodness.

"Beloved, let us love one another, for love is of God and whoever loves has been born of God and knows God." (1 John 4:7-8)

MAY 23

"The soul can split the sky in two and let the
face of God shine through." – Edna St. Vincent Millay

HUMANITY IS MADE in the image of God. That is what His official word says and that is my belief. We are created to be like Him, to engage in a relationship that is unlike any other and also as familiar as a son who resembles a father.

If we truly believe and practice this, imagine what could change around us. Even if your God wasn't my God, if we believed the other to be in the image of our beloved God, why would peace not be simple? Why would murder ever occur? Why would we do unspeakable things against each other if we believed we were made in the image of God? Yet, every day, wars and rumors of wars are devised on the premise of religious character.

Bullying would not survive in a world where children were taught they were made in the image of God. Terrorist and tortures, child abuse and rape gone! Imagine! Try it today. Every time you look at your child in the whiney of their day, at your spouse in the fatigue of life, at the kid with the music too loud and the old man who snarled at you look again. And see the face of God. It's bound to make a difference. Challenge yourself in that.

"Then God said, "Let us make man in Our image,
according to Our likeness..." (Genesis 1:26)

"Drifting in a sultry day on the sluggish waters of the pond, I almost cease to live and begin to be." – Henry David Thoreau

I DID NOT GRASP this concept upon my first read. It wasn't till I was stooping on a rock, the upright fetal positioning of being not by the pond, but the river. The mountain air was crisp and the butterflies rampant. The gnarly trunks of trees hugged rock and dirt and stumps.

It was a hot sunshine that stopped us, and the way of the river splashing against the boulders in the way. We had come to walk awhile, but stopped and lay down on the biggest boulder with a flat spot. It was a feast. Every little flutter was quiet and loud, still and moving, surrendered and triumphed. Engulfed by a Presence far greater than all this goodness, I found us speechless.

Floating in a canyon of engaged sentiment, letting it play in my spirit. And like Thoreau, l find I am almost the BE of my living. I cast off the worries like a child at the door of warmth and light. I quietly embrace the power to BE.

"In Him we live, and move and have our being." (Acts 17:28)

MAY 25

*"Watch the kind of people God brings around you
and you will be humiliated to find He
brings people to you who reveal to you the kind
of person you have been to Him. Now,
you can exhibit to that one exactly what God
did for you!"* – Oswald Chambers

THE THINGS JESUS did for us were not "rise to power" stories. They were stories of a different power. Can you use a towel like Jesus did? Towels are ordinary things. They are mundane. But towels and dishes and sandals are all those ordinary things that reveal that which we are made of, in our deepest will. Jesus took a towel to show His servant heart.

He took the ordinary to do something extraordinary.

This is a message we oft times miss looking for success or someplace we wish to be. I was made privy to this call on two strong occasions I have yet to forget. One was in the service of my handicapped child. I had bent to massage her reed thin legs when I felt God speak clearly, *"You say you want to be a servant? You talk big. But this is service. Can you do it?"* And I did it for 25 glorious years.

The other was a woman who had disliked me for reasons even she said she didn't know. She ended up hospitalized and I went to visit her. I took off her shoes and washed her feet and massaged them. She stared at me in wonder. Her hate turned to love and has remained so.

I want to do what Jesus did with the ordinary. I want to do the unexpected. I want to give back what He has given to me. Breathe servant-hood.

"Since you are my Rock and my Fortress, for your Name sake lead me and guide me." (Psalm 31:3)

"We are not necessarily doubting that God will do the best for us; we are wondering how painful the best will turn out to be." – C.S. Lewis

I FIND MYSELF HERE sometimes. I truly believe God is good, but God is mostly in the conforming business not the comfortable business. He intends to mold and create. Like the pottery on the wheel, that can make me dizzy and lean to the falling side some days.

I never doubt God CAN but I usually question if he WILL. I know He wants what is best for me, but he also knows I humanly may disagree on the best of my temporary pursuits. So, I do wonder what this being like God might mean for me. After all, when He sent His Son, it didn't turn out the way most of us define best here on earth.

I hope I am never crucified. And yet, God asks this of me every day. When will the ego in me die that the divine might live? Am I willing to trust that His best for me may not be revealed on this earth, in my temporary frame? All I can think of is that very old hymn I sang as a child: **Oh for Grace to trust Him more.**

"Whoever pursues righteousness and love finds life, prosperity and honor." (Proverbs 21:21)

"Mistakes are the dues one pays for a full life." – Sophia Loren

F ULL MONTY LIVING will mean you will make a mistake or two or more if you are anything me. I don't like them any more than you do, but if you want to live serendipitously, the mistakes will be the dues you pay.

Granted, some mistakes will cost more than you ever want to pay. Others will be serendipity in the way that changes everything in a positive way. Others will be beneficial for someone watching. Another will be the mark of maturity changing. I wish we could, from early childhood, teach the words: *"I'm sorry. I made a mistake."*

But they rarely hear it from us big people because we think that is a sign of weakness. Or we will lose our place in heaven or something. How nice it would be just to be able to say it with sincerity and release. After all, we all make them all the time. But we get defensive about silly things. We get in fights and don't apologize for days. We look ridiculous claiming something we need to just let go and grow on.

Mistakes mean we're growing, living human beings. It's okay.

"The Lord will keep you from all harm. He will watch over your life." (Psalm 121:7)

MAY 28

"What's your greatest fear?"

I T COULD BE anything. We talk about having no fear, and some believe themselves to be fearless. After you have encountered enough life, you might likely find it easier to be fearless. Or, you might become fearful of everything. Fear shows up in a number of ways, but often and mostly as evidence that has no real basis.

Experience must be changed In order to free the belief. Perfect love casts out fear. This is a truth we don't often use in the struggle to gain our footing in the fear. But one of the areas to see this used well is generally parenting. Consider you get the news you are pregnant. I was terrified to have a baby. It sounded gruesome. I knew pain would be involved. I wasn't excited about that. It just about paralyzed me.

Then one day, l looked around at the millions of people and thought that if it was all that hard, people would quit doing it. I made it through childbirth. Perfect love kicked in when I looked at that beautiful tiny creation. Love cast out my fear.

Whatever fears you have today, cover them up in love. Always use it advantageously or it will use you to your disadvantage. Fear is what you let it become.

"There is no fear in love, but perfect love drives out fear. The one who fears is not made perfect in love." (1 John 4:18)

MAY 29

*"People in judgment don't care about their
own hypocrisy."* – The Good Wife

THERE YOU ARE. I agree. I know, for a fact, when I am judging another person, I am not even thinking about my own hypocrisy. Black kettles, lumbering eyes and all that talk about judging, I am still better at it than I prefer.

I have noticed God sends reminders. They hurt. They sting like a bee and send me back to the person who knows me best and loves me most. But like you, it can feel smug and slightly fun to feel that you are above all that. That's why we get flattened by our own trolley car sometimes.

While we like to justify it as calling things as we see them, we sure hope nobody sees our calling card. Because, ultimately, where you fall is where I stumble. Where I stumble, is where you trip. Leave the judging for the competitions. As the Good Book says if you are judging, it's only because you forgot where you came from and how much forgiveness you needed.

"Why do you pass judgment? Who do you despise your brother? For we will all stand before the judgment seat of God." (Romans 14:10)

"If we do not plant knowledge when young, it will give us no shade when we are old." – Lord Chesterfield

S OWING THE WILD oats, as we like to say, is often just a time we fill our life with regrets. The sins of our youth follow us further down the road, than any we could know. As I grow older, l see more and more old people who have not planted good shade. They have no real offering to others, let alone themselves. They pride themselves on their selfishness, doing it all their way and never becoming attached.

Often l am sickened by the people l know have been given the potential and foundation to be wise, sturdy oaks. They are out there, flipping in the wind like a vine with no holding place. It is as one man said, *"I'm just a seagull. I fly in and dump on everybody and head back out again."* Nine marriages have brought him nothing but messed up packs of people. What a waste.

Let us, who are grown, seek to tell and show our children the delight of being wise and strong in their youth. We all know the value of a good shade tree.

"They will still yield fruit in old age. They shall be full of sap, green and growing. (Psalm 92:14)

MAY 31

"I didn't go to religion to make me happy. I always knew a bottle of port would do that. If you want a religion to make you feel really comfortable, I certainly don't recommend Christianity." – C.S. Lewis

AMEN DR. LEWIS! You want to feel pretty and secure and smart and snappy? Go somewhere else. You want to do what you want to do, feel that your confusion is your happy and take actions that will not come with consequences?

Becoming a Believer is just not going to be a fit for you at all. Christianity is not a Pope, a Bible or a Republican vote. Its original meaning is to imitate Christ. I don't care who you are, that's hard to do. Imitating Christ is not comfortable.

We don't naturally enjoy doing what Christ tells us to do, like dying to ourselves, or giving our life away or loving our enemy. Ultimately, joy is found in Christ, but while we are here on earth, we have to know that because this isn't home we aren't going to be allowed to get comfy. We are only passing through.

Don't get comfortable means you don't wipe your feet on the world's welcome mat and act like them. If you have chosen to imitate Christ, do it well and with love. It changes us.

"You will be hated because of My name, but it is the one who endures that will be saved." (Matthew 10:22)

JUNE 1

"My wife of 57 years was buried today by our son,
she who has longed for him all these
years, and now she is with him. I know they are
embraced in happiness." – Terry Kay

WHEN YOU LOSE one loved one at a time, it is not at all uncommon to want to be with them. But two or more can feel they are having a place to themselves. You then find yourself so lost and hardly breathing. It is as though the reunion has begun without you. And it is a terrible suffocating feeling.

It is hard to wait for our turn to go, especially in our deep pain. We are indeed happy for them, but heartbroken for ourselves. We weep, thinking it could never happen. We weep because one hour later is too long without them in our life. Why are we here and they are there? Having more than a few children in Heaven and Grandparents, other relatives, and friends who made the Journey first, I know this feeling well. I speak of their meeting and playing together as though they were here in plain sight.

I feel the loss, knowing it is the way of life and death. I was blessed to have been part of their life here, and someday, I will be a part of their life there, but some days, it is hard to wait.

"He will wipe away every tear from their eyes, and death will be
no more, neither shall there be mourning, nor crying, nor pain,
for the former things have passed away." (Revelation 21:1-5)

JUNE 2

"Divinity is seeking to be revealed everywhere." – Matthew Fox

WE WAKE UP every day, even Mondays, and there are several things that have to take place for us to even leave the house. Most of us have to open our eyes to see. We have loved ones to hug and feet that need to bear the weight of our body.

We have a mouth to speak. Somewhere we learned to communicate language. We hear birds singing or puppies barking. There are flowers in the yard; dew on the grass and blue skies and sunshine, or rain and thunder.

We nourish our body with food we didn't create, even if it was from our own garden. We have hands that do all kinds of things from tying shoes to packing lunches.

L suspect God has blessed us in a thousand ways before we even show up to work which by the way, is another blessing if we have it, sometimes, if we don't. All day long, all night long, all week long and 365 days of the year, it takes precious little to see the divine work around us.

It begs to be revealed. It is so easy to miss the awesomeness around us.

Today, just ask God to make you aware. Then just try and see if you can keep up with the thanksgiving. It's the most divine way to live.

"Praise the Lord, O my soul, and forget not
all his benefits." (Psalm 103:2)

JUNE 3

"Little things still count."

ONE YEAR I had the honor of speaking to a group of hospice medical staffers. While I was there, the Director handed me the research on the benefits of pet therapy. We all know pets can be good for our health, but when you are dying?

Yes! It can increase tolerance for pain. It can reduce the fears and stress of dying. It provides a confidant that doesn't expect to solve anything. It can even increase oxygen so the patient can even out breathing issues.

There is also what it does for the hormones in your state of being. Oxytocin has some powerful effects for us in the body's ability to be in a state of readiness to heal and also to grow new cells, so it predisposes one to better health. Yes, that is helpful even when death is sure. If you have a gentle pet, take an afternoon and visit the places and people who could benefit from them. I am equally certain you will benefit as well. It's a little thing that counts big.

"Whereby, we are given unto us exceeding great and precious promises, that by these we are partakers of the divine nature, having escaped the corruption that is in this world." (2 Peter 1:4)

JUNE 4

"The two most powerful warriors are patience and time." – Leo Tolstoy

I THINK I AM a very patient person until I have to actually BE patient. I am pretty certain I am the adult equivalent of the "Are we there yet?" child. I like the idea. Sort of.

I think patience is wonderful. Time is an illusion. Put them together and wonderful illusions become places where I can't find a good parking space. I want to be safe while I rest. I know this is key.

I want to be brave. I want to be wise. Yet, these warriors can break me down so easily some days. Every time I wonder how long is this going to take? It seems like I just rang the bell for hurry up and wait!

In the war with patience and time, you win if you can keep distracted in the focus and keep from wanting. Otherwise, you can be down for the count before the match even starts. But don't feel bad. Very few of us are a match for such magical pursuits. Perhaps it's only comforting to know the race is not to the swift, but to the ones who endure. Endure well.

"…to knowledge, temperance, and to temperance,
patience, and to patience, godliness." (2 Peter 1:6)

"While you are on your way to your pot of gold,
don't forget to pick up the silver along the way." – Anonymous

HAVE YOU EVER known someone who is looking for the right person so hard, they miss the terrific people God sends into their life just as good friends?

Have you ever known someone who's working so hard to make money; they forget to make a life?

Have you ever known a family wanting every member to be so perfect, they miss the reality of a relationship?

Have you ever known a person who wastes all their time finding themselves but lose the part of themselves that needs others?

What about the person who takes care of everybody else except the very people in their life, closest to them?

In the pursuit of the good, don't miss the best. In the pot of gold that has caught your eye; I hope you find the silver mixed in well.

"Keep yourselves in the love of God, looking for the
mercy of the Lord Jesus Christ unto eternal life." (Jude 1:22)

JUNE 6

"Love is always new."

HUBS AND I were sitting on the porch watching the sunset and talking of life. Our rattan wicker patio set the family got me nine years ago for Mother's Day, is shedding its wicker. The seats are ripped up. It's looking sad. The wind destroyed the umbrella. We talked about a new one, but funds aren't there.

I suggested we paint. He suggested not. I fiddled with the wicker and found it ripped apart rather easily. He suggested I stop that. Smile. I did until he got up. Then I ripped it all off the table, suggesting he help. He did. We had bought a new umbrella. He got into the renovation pretty well when he saw the iron underneath that looked brand new. We flipped over the cushions. The new side didn't look too bad and no rips anywhere. We cleaned the glass and iron up.

Presto! An almost new looking patio set and a little pride. I laughed that I was amazing. He laughed and said that was why he married me. Funny, how little things we spontaneously do can often be a big piece of our relationship.

Why did you marry that girl? Why did you choose him out of all the others? Keep that in mind as the years pass by, because lots of changes come and go.

Like our patio set, you get a few rips and years pass by and you develop worn spots. Sometimes, you have to find a new way to have your "new." You will find those are the best stories anyway.

Keep your love fresh.

"Be completely humble and gentle, be patient,
bearing with one another in love." (Ephesians 4:2)

JUNE 7

"Leave a trail of thanksgiving."

TODAY, I'M PARTICULARLY thankful for a man born on this day. My husband, Dan is a great blessing in my life. He's easy to remember, but keeping good records of all thanksgiving is not easy.

How do you keep your accounts? If you are an accountant, you write down everything. You keep files marked well. You are ready for the audit, prepared for the scrutiny, excited that you have kept it all for another's view.

Do you do the same with the wonderful work that God does in your life? I admit that I am careless about keeping records. I needed to be reminded because remembering is a good way to stay in the joy!

It was 1988 when I learned how to keep my accounts. I filled over 40 pages with answered prayer. I have ***Thanksgiving Journals*** from then till now. Some better recorded than others, but they are a remembrance of things l might otherwise forget.

It's truly enlightening to fill a book with thanksgiving. You embrace the goodness of the divine more often. You are more aware of that which is given. You love to share the stories of faithfulness and miracles, or of how God has sustained you through the famine, nurtured you in the growing, comforted you in the grief and blessed you through extravagant people. Our lives are so full of them!

Let us exhaust ourselves writing down the goodness and blessings of knowing the eternal. Let's leave a paper trail of thanksgiving!

"O give thanks to the Lord, for He is good; for His steadfast love endures forever." (1 Chronicles 16:8)

JUNE 8

"There is great freedom in accepting what isn't you."

WHAT HAPPENS WHEN you put a cup of water on a log? Well, mine falls off. It has nothing to do with how good the water is or how strong the log might be. It doesn't matter if the wind is still or the sun is shining. It doesn't matter if five people could do it, but you could not.

It just means that didn't work for you.

Sure, you could hot glue it or Velcro it down, but you know that's cheating and proves little but creativity. You could cut the log so it would be flatter and hold your cup. But what if you just accepted the fact your cup didn't sit on a log?

Likely, you could move on in your life fairly quickly with this information. You would save oodles of time trying to figure out the problem. You would save lots of energy because you could let go of the need to know.

I hope you are getting my point. Sometimes, things just don't work out. If you spend too much trying to make it work or too much energy reinventing, you will just find more frustrations. Just move on.

Take the time and energy and put it into a more positive move. Don't get bogged down analyzing and aching for what is not. Really, sometimes there's a real need to let it be what it is, and no more. There's a great freedom in this.

"I wash my hands in innocence and go around your altar, O Lord, proclaiming thanksgiving aloud and telling all your wondrous deeds." (Psalm 26:6-7)

JUNE 9

"The Word of God is the ultimate JoySong." – Ann Stewart Porter

TODAY IS MY Mama's birthday. I have dedicated JoySong to her, because she loves devotionals. She usually reads more than one every year. But Mama doesn't just love devotional books; she loves the greatest devotional book ever written.

She loves the Scripture passionately.

I rarely see her without the Scripture in her lap or nearby. Her love for all things godly is a profound legacy she has left on anyone who has ever known her.

Mama was born to a very poor family. Her father was killed before she was five. She has had a crippling Arthritis since she was three. She's also been a walking miracle of God's power, even after losing her leg. She accepted Jesus at Vacation Bible School. She went on to be one of the first women in America to get a degree in the Bible. She's been a Nurse, a College Professor teaching Greek and Hebrew, a Special Education Teacher and a Pastor's wife.

O how the world needs godly mothers full of the Word of God, loving Jesus and leaving His truth in the hearts of their children. Because she did that for me, I was able to lead my three grandchildren to Jesus early. God willing, we will all continue to touch the future because of a godly Mama.

Today, I challenge you to be a Mama, a Daddy, who loves the JoySong and sings it for everyone you know.

"That the generation to come might know,
even the children yet to be born,
That they may arise and tell them to their children, that they
should put their confidence in God..." (Psalms 78:6-7)

"Fathers are generational curse or blessing."

C AN FATHERS MAKE a difference in the direction of their families? Can fathers change the next generation? Can dads really be as powerful as we think they can be? Consider the Hatfields and McCoys, whose fathers began a family war that lasted 138 years in the Appalachian Mountains. And it was a father who later eventually said "Enough!"

Consider a boy whose father was an alcoholic and abusive, but he never talked about that. The boy came to know God at the age of 14. He lived it out in front of his dad eventually bringing him to know God, along with his mom and most of his eight siblings. He went to college (living on peanuts and bananas) and then graduated school.

He became the preacher he dreamed he would be. He married a classy girl and they had six children. He later became a college president. His six children never knew their drunken grandfather nor saw their own dad drink a drop. Instead of a generational curse, there would be a generational blessing.

I know this is true. He is my father. I am eternally grateful he was strong enough to let God in, faithful enough to believe change was possible, and committed to the highest good.

Be a great father.

"His mercy is for those who fear Him from
generation to generation." (Luke 1:50)

JUNE 11

"Answer me this…is there life after being with you?" – Drucker

MY FRIEND AND I were discussing how, after all these years of being married, we still have those chemical reaction moments. You see them from across the room and something in your heart flutters. You hear their voice or kiss their mouth and it's like the first time they melted your heart.

It was funny because my hubs had just come in after work and sat in the chair by me. He was telling me he had been thinking about our last night together all day. Happily married people don't get all the hooks and jabs about sex and marriage. We just think it gets better and sweeter and we just wink and feel sorry for the players. If it's sweet, it's fantastic. It's really like you didn't know life until that one came into your path. Now, it's just unbelievable. And yes, it can stay that way for years after.

May your passion be incredible always!

> *"May your fountain be blessed and may you rejoice in the wife of your youth."* (Proverbs 5:18)

JUNE 12

"There is no heaven with a little corner of
hell in it." – Oswald Chambers

HEAVEN.

Intriguing, isn't it? This place of perfection and peace. No more fear or crying. A place of paradise and eternal bliss. Ls it any wonder we can hardly imagine it? Heaven sounds like a glorious place.

We yearn for the lion and lamb to rest together. Especially when we can't get our families to rest from fighting. We ponder the love there, like it were a foreign language beyond us, because of the brokenness we stand in, here on earth. Likely, we will not know heavenly insights until we have arrived, and then we can't return to tell a soul.

We can only imagine this dinner with God. We can be certain it will most be like coming Home, the Home where there is no deception, defeat or deafening pain. No hell. Just the sweet embrace of a Father who has called us home And we have finally made it.

"You know the way to the place where I am going." (John 14:4)

"Whenever you fall, pick something up." – Avery

WE HAVE A saying in our house. Hubs started it. I maintain it. It's simple: Don't waste a trip. If you are going downstairs, take something with you. If you are coming up, bring something up. If you drop something, pick it up.

If you can't put it away right now, it will be harder to put it in the right place later. By that time, you will have filled the space with something else.

We're very profound at our house. Smile. Whenever you are going through a difficult time, don't forget to grab all the things you should be getting.

My last horrific descent seemed to be buying a home. But from that experience, I learned an enormous amount of things. We did plenty of falling, but we did not waste the trip. These things in our life happen on purpose for a purpose.

Value that enough, that you don't miss a thing.

> *"For the righteous falls seven times and rises again, but the wicked stumble in times of calamity."* (Proverbs 24:16)

JUNE 14

"Let the lesson begin."

I CAN'T REMEMBER HER name, but it was fourth grade. I don't remember what she looked like or smelled like or how she spoke. She taught us how to keep a Journal and write down words that made feelings. She was strict, but not too strict.

She was strong in English, but let it slide for a good story to be told. I don't remember the grades or even her helpful hints. I remember that she gave me an ability to pour out my soul and let it strengthen me. I remember that she pulled out of me, the gift that was waiting to be seen. I remember that I could forget time, place and everything for the joy of being a writer. It was a whole new world.

It was like opening the door to Disneyland, handing me the key and saying, *"Lock up when you've done."* Perhaps I do not remember this teacher in name or form or method simply because she did not draw attention to herself, but to your own gifting. She made you aware there were things inside you that needed to come out, be cherished, be used, and be shared.

From her, I learned that the greatest teachers in our lives, indeed the greatest people in our lives, are those who cause us to curiously look inside our very own beings to find treasures. For then, the lesson can truly begin.

"Therefore, encourage one another and build one another up, just as you are doing." (1 Thessalonians 5:11)

JUNE 15

"Every time you ride, you are either teaching or un-teaching your horse." – Gordon Wright

PARENTING IS HARD and a lot like...horse training. Horses learn quickly what the sound of a voice means. They know the fear or the love in such a short time. They learn things when no one is there to see the lesson.

Children do the same. They also recognize it when we say one thing and do another thing. They look at what we say only as a support system to what we have showed them by way of example. I found this to be slightly cranial terrorizing.

Me – an example? Well, this parenting was going to take a hit right there. It didn't take me too long down the trail to get that the more words you need, the less example you are setting.

Life is for learning. We are all teachers. Be a good one.

"Train up a child in the way he should go; even when he is old, he will not depart from him." (Proverbs 22:6)

*"God sends children for another purpose than merely to keep up the race.
They enlarge our hearts, make us unselfish and full of kind
affections, to give our souls higher aim."* – Mary Howitt

PERHAPS MORE THAN most, the Maori of New Zealand have a unique heritage –they believe that bringing a child up is a communal opportunity, that they are gifts from God.

Researchers found children were treated with loving care and often indulged. *"The father was devotedly fond of his children and they were his pride and delight,"* the report found. *"Children would entwine themselves around their father's neck for an entire day, asleep or awake, as a constant companion."* This instilled love, security, and confidence into Maori children. The whole warrior culture was balanced by the nurturing one.

Fathers, give your children three things which will make their life immeasurably profitable. Give them a heritage which roots them. Give them a love which sustains them. Give them a truth which transforms them.

You are so valuable.

*"Children are a gift from the Lord; they are a
reward from Him."* (Psalm 127:3)

JUNE 17

"The day is done, the sun has set, yet light still tints the sky;
My heart stands still in reverence. God is passing by." – Ruth Wager

I LOVE THIS PRECIOUS thought! We live with a spectacular view. It has come to mean more and more to us each day. We have tried to catch our sunsets on camera to no avail. The colors are never quite the same. The depth of the mountains, the height of the cornfields are all different on the still shot.

Nor can we capture the presence of God in the moment, or the awe of our knowing or the joy of being surrounded by beauty that has no words. There is a deep reverence in that. There is an uncontainable love in that. It is like having your Daddy stop by your room to say He loves you and to turn off your light as He slips by.

How often do we just stand still in a deep reverence for God's presence to be felt in our day? What a wonderful way to end the day. What a delight to know God is passing by. I hope you catch a glimpse.

"The heavens declare the glory of God, and the
sky proclaims the work of His hands." (Psalm 19:1)

JUNE 18

"It is better to have your head in the clouds, and know where you are…than to breathe the clearer atmosphere below them, and think that you are in paradise." – Henry David Thoreau

PEOPLE DON'T ALWAYS understand a positive, godly, purpose driven life. They ask questions. They tease. They tell me it can't be so all the time.

We, who live in hope and faith are not oblivious to pain and the plight of the earth. In fact, we often see it clearer.

You see, to embrace just the undone of life is often to exclude that which unveils the goodness. To know goodness, to choose joy, never means real life is not seen. Rather, we have seen the benefit of breathing deeper, going higher and letting go.

If life is sweet while living carelessly, you should feel what it's like to live beyond. Here's to all us Cloud Clear headed Lifers.

Fly well.

"Set your mind on things above, not on things on the earth." (Colossians 3:2)

JUNE 19

*"One of the most tragic things I know about human
nature is that all of us tend to put off
living. We are all dreaming of some magical rose
garden over the horizon; instead of
enjoying the roses that are blooming outside our
windows today."* – Dale Carnegie

I AM GUILTY OF this very thing. I am a visionary person. It is easy for me to dream and dream big. It also means I set myself up for great failures sometimes, and for unrealistic expectations. And it usually means that I focus more on what is to come, rather than what is here now.

Thankfully, God knew I would need a very present person as a husband who feels the moments as they are. He is also good at realizing what could go wrong. So, it works out well if we respect the other's perspectives. It has actually enlightened and strengthened both of us. I don't dream any less or any smaller, but I am trying to set more realistic paths. He is dreaming bigger than me some days and it's been one fun ride.

The magical rose garden is here. This is it. If this is it, what will you choose to do with it? Let it wither while you pine over what you are losing or not gaining, or will you cut a beautiful bunch for the kitchen table so that at least a few times a day, you might stop and value their presence?

Don't put off living. It's the goodness you seek.

*"This is the day the Lord has made.
We will rejoice and be glad in it."* (Psalm 118:24)

JUNE 20

"Be not angry that you cannot make others
as you wish them to be, since you
cannot make yourself as you wish to be." – Thomas A. Kempis

THIS MIGHT HAVE just been written for counselors, coaches, preachers and teachers, parents, missionaries, judges and doctors, but most of all marriage partners. Well, that covers most of us, doesn't it?

You don't even have to be in the helping industry to understand that when you are trying to help another, you become fully aware of your own shortcomings. While you are trying to inspire them, it may sound like you never faced such a thing in all your life. You want them to be this or that, but there's that one thing that keeps you from really glowing self- righteously.

That would be YOU: the other person who can't be perfect. Oops, it gets me every time. It takes a lot to dare to be honest. Parents are afraid to tell children things because they don't want to lose their authority in their child's life. But it is of great benefit to share our humanity.

Quit trying to change him. Change you.

Quit trying to change her. Change you.

May we always remember to be real, despite the flaws. In sharing our souls, we help each other grow into and out of each other's love. It can be very healing to be real.

"In your anger, do not sin. Do not let
the sun go down on your anger." (Ephesians 4:26)

JUNE 21

*"I am an optimist, unrepentant and a militant.
After all, in order not to be a fool,
an optimist must know how sad a place the world can be. It is only the
pessimist who finds this out anew every day."* – Peter Ustinov

I LOVE IT! TODAY is my birthday and I am turning up my optimism. I plan on being almost unbearable sunshine in your eyes. I have people ask me if have ever been through anything bad. Have I had a tough go of it? Do I know what it's like to...? I even get asked if I have ever had kids.

I get people who have left me on the basis that I make them feel it is all perfect. Of course, when I tell them my story, they think I am trying to show off my grief.

So, I have come to know this is my truth. I must keep on being me and being thankful and growing upward. I can't please a pessimist. Why try? I can get down anytime. But really, when I have my Creator Redeemer who chooses to give me Himself and so much more, how can I not live Joyful? When I have so much goodness and so much love, could I dare ask for anymore? I think not. It's a celebration every day!

Be militantly, unrepentantly optimistic.

"We know in all things God works for the good of those who love Him, who have been called according to His purpose." (Romans 8:28)

JUNE 22

"Never let a problem to be solved become more important than a person to be loved." – Barbara Johnson

WE OFTEN FIND ourselves trying to make everything okay for everyone. I have friends that I ache for because I want them to have a great marriage, or a terrific job, or a day without the pain of yesterday or the cringe of today.

I want to fix things.

We all have a tendency to want things to be good and right and wonderful. We also all have a tendency to want to fix the problem and forget the person.

News people say they do negative news because we, their viewers ask for it. Yes, the world can be a place of problems everywhere. While we may or may not be able to solve some of those problems, one thing is true and good and certain. We can always, always, always choose to love. We can love while we think, love while we do and love for the sake of the highest good.

Got a problem that needs fixing? What would love do?

"Let us love one another, for love comes from God." (1 John 4:7)

JUNE 23

"The richness of the human experience would lose something of rewarding joy if there were no limitations to overcome." – Helen Keller

S HE WAS A little girl with a mama who didn't like her much and a daddy who was killed before she was five. She was dirt poor. Her mama had a third grade education. She was hurt most by some of the people she trusted most.

But she came to know God one summer early in childhood. She fell in love. She was mesmerized by His Book. She determined to be different than what she knew.

She taught her mother to read. She got a job. She prayed to go to college. A childless couple adopted her expenses for school. She learned Greek and Hebrew. She married well, had six children who adore her and is known for her extraordinary teaching ability.

She has been a Registered Nurse, a Special Education Specialist, a Preacher's wife and a College Professor and an amputee. Her rich life has given her children marvelous opportunities to know limitations are simply things to overcome or things to embrace and use for the highest good.

I know because l am one of those children.

Live rich.

"Oh the depths of the riches both of the wisdom and the knowledge of God." (Romans 11:33)

JUNE 24

"My sorrow, when she's here with me, thinks these dark days of
autumn rain are beautiful as days can be; she loves the bare,
the withered tree; she walks the sodden pasture lane." – Robert Frost

I CAN SO RELATE to these beautiful words of barren times. There is such infusion of illumination in dark places where faith grows. There is something peculiar about the dense dark overcast of rain on wood and life past.

There is a beauty in our mourning that often we may miss but another may be blessed by. Sorrow seems to strip and simplify and mark itself with that withering in our soul. We trample through it, best we can, heavy in heart and foot and wishing for what is not. In the dark days of our deepest grief, there is a mark of beauty. It is the beauty of serendipity.

It is the kindness of our tears. It is the befriending of our sweetest memories. Trust that as time passes, and sorrow moves further away, that you will see the beauty and the blessing of the pain.

"He gave me beauty for ashes, the oil of joy for mourning, the garment of
praise for the spirit of heaviness, that they might be called trees of
righteousness, the planting of the Lord, that He
might be glorified." (Isaiah 61:3)

JUNE 25

"Not in the clamor of the crowded street, not
in the shouts and plaudits of the
throng, but in ourselves, are triumph and defeat." –
Henry Wadsworth Longfellow

YOU WANT ANSWERS. Someone gives them to you.
You think of more reasons not to follow good advice and you do what your own agenda seems hell bent on doing.

You get your way. God never created robotic humans. He lets you have your way. Then you face defeat. You are worn out from it, stumped by the cost of it; sworn to living inside the wall again.

Do not listen to the worldview of most of what you hear. You will find yourself thinking you deserve what they define for you. You will find you feel deprived and and must make that up.

Instead, look at spiritual laws that set your course. There is divine lighting in your path. You are not here just for you. You were created for greatness, power, divinity, joy, and usefulness.

When you are seeking self, you may find yourself more lost than ever before. Those made in the very image of God must seek to be like God to triumph. That is a choice from within that connects to the Creator Redeemer.

Live triumphantly in the image of God.

"In the image of God created he them." (Genesis 1:28)

JUNE 26

"Love rules the court, the camp, the grove, and men below, and saints above: for love is heaven, and heaven is love." – Walter Scott

THAT CRAZY THING called love.

In high school, I dated a County Tennis Champion for quite some time. I would go watch the games and hear the words, but it never quite made sense. Tennis scoring rests on the premise that sowing is advantageous over receiving, hence, it is only possible to win a set or match by breaking the opponent's service game at least once before a tiebreak is required.

I also traced it to the 17th-century expression *"play for love"* meaning to play without any wager, for nothing. It is this meaning of *"nothing"* that love takes on when used in tennis. The proper way to describe a score of zero to zero is to say love-all which is where you start.

Nothing to nothing is love! Well then! I'm inclined to believe Walter Scott's assessment is true. Love rules. Love is heavenly. Love is either all or nothing depending, I guess, on what game you are wagering.

"A new command I give you: Love one another
as I have loved you." (John 13:34)

JUNE 27

"Wisdom is in the ripples."

W E WERE AT the pool. Lightning struck and it began to rain. We were told to get out. As we sat, watching the ripples, Dylan found himself fascinated. Watching rain on water is one of my top ten favorite things, so I understand. He was excitedly telling me all about it.

Then he stopped. *"Can you see it the same way I can?"* he asked as he ran over to stand beside me. I could. He confirmed it. Then he went to his big brother, then his sister, asking the same.

I begin to ponder what might happen if we did that kind of processing with our spouse, our child, our boss, our co-worker, our parent, our sibling, our neighbors.

What if we just made sure we could see it from their angle. Think what we might understand!

Think if we just took that key moment to physically go to their side, stop and observe and see. It wouldn't change all our precious opinions, but it might just change the way we love.

Wisdom in the ripples, joy in the rain.

"For the Lord gives wisdom; from His mouth comes knowledge and understanding." (Proverbs 2:6)

JUNE 28

"No one would remember the Good Samaritan
if he had only had good intentions." – Margaret Thatcher

WE KNOW THE story of the Good Samaritan because it was written for a purpose we all need; the purpose of contribution with compassion. A man started on a journey. He was beaten, robbed and left to die. Several people passed him, but one stopped and helped him. One took him to be cared for and even offered to pay for it.

The significance was that the man who helped was like a KKK High Dragon taking care of a black man, or the Baptist deacon helping a homosexual, or a Tutsis helping a Hutus.

If that wasn't significant enough, God wanted us to know, it wasn't just the thinking good thoughts. It was the doing of something powerfully good. It was the power of doing something beyond the boundaries. Contrast that story to the way we often talk of these different groups of people born in the image of Gods Think what could happen if we took the power of love beyond the boundaries, the intentions, and the hate?

We could change the universe!

"Be very careful how you live, not as unwise, but as wise, making the most
of every opportunity, because the days are evil." (Ephesians 5:16-16)

"Relationships are never just about two people."

L OVE, IS A spiritual force at work.
If you have tapped into that wisdom before you meet a person, it will be empowering and sustaining. It is amazing when each of you comes with your own spiritual conduit and brings that to the relationship. This way, no one is empty upon arrival. No one comes in lonely and deprived, but energized and outpouring.

All relationships are divine gifts. Those resigned to logistical functioning are losing a great capacity for miracles. Love is the blessing of passion and a drive that draws your soul out into the open. This is deeper than just an attitude. This is the depth of the majesty of real love. This kind of love finds wonder in the being together, the ordinary days, the service and luminous connection intimacy.

Too many surface relationships have shipwrecked, because the energy shared is not life sustaining. Try a radical departure from the shelter of the status quo. Grow, heal, cultivate, and bloom.

Find your spiritual bearing wall. Bring something to the table when you meet the one you think you have been looking to find.

Everybody loves amazing.

"Wisdom from above is first of all pure, then peace loving, considerate with good fruit, impartial and sincere." (James 3:17)

JUNE 30

"If you want to lead learn to serve." – Jesus

LEADERSHIP IS A tough, hard call. Yes, it can be rewarding, but it is not an easy position. Lots of people seem to want to lead. They want to do big things. They want to be the American Idol. According to the Eternal Guidebook, a leader has three distinct qualifications:

They are an impeccable servant.

They are teachable followers.

They are confident and live with purpose and vision.

If we use other yardsticks for measuring leadership, we find the temporary walk is just a passing thing. True leaders invest in others who carry on after they are gone. They believe in multiplicity and exponential growth.

Want to lead? Learn to serve, follow and live purposely investing into others. Do more than just take a walk.

"How much better to get wisdom than gold,
to get insight rather than silver." (Proverbs 16:16)

JULY 1

"Sharing our stories makes a difference in all stories."

WHY DO WE share our times of growing, hurting, joy and journey? Because through those stories, another might just find a new song.

God recently delivered my husband from a very difficult place of work to a much better employment. That was a seven year old prayer! I have had people say it gave them hope to see God's goodness.

When our daughter died and we told the story, one friend said she knew her son might not live long and she would need my words. That has been true. We have been good to keep each other's song of hope alive. People tell me that seeing our love and faithfulness in our godly marriage has inspired them.

We share because we are inspired by each other. We share to strengthen another. We share because it makes us all wiser. You never know whose marriage stayed together, who got a new vision, who became their own star, whose child was blessed, who learned how to live or love, who found enough hope for another day all because you didn't conceal God's goodness and faithfulness and all because you didn't hide the way God brought you through alcoholism, abuse, grief or some other hard thing.

We are all part of a story, don't conceal your part. Somebody needs that piece.

"I have not hidden your deliverance...I have not concealed your steadfast love and your faithfulness." (Psalm 40:10)

JULY 2

"Failure is not an event, but rather a judgment about an event. Failure is not something that happens to us or a label we attach to things. It is a way we think about outcomes." – John Ortberg

S HE IS GROWING through 20 years of spousal emotional abuse. She recently told me how devastating it used to be when she made a mistake. She would berate herself and punish herself; almost celebrate in some weird way the event that she was just what her husband always said she was!

She had now learned that if she spelled a wrong word or was late, it was not a day ruined, let alone her life. It was just a *"little messed up, fix it, and go on"* moment. The more she practiced that, the more normal she felt, the less of a failure she became.

We often allow ourselves to become addicted to failure, creating life-long victimization where there is none. It's like climbing on a cloud. There's no substance. Wouldn't that look uncommon? Picture that next time you can't get past that last event you called failure for so long. If you messed up, you messed up. You aren't the first and you won't be the last.

Now, step up and turn it around. Whatever it cost to do that, you have within you, waiting to show you what a good piece of failure can do for you. I think you'll love the outcome.

"Be wise in the way you act toward outsiders; make the most of every opportunity. Let your conversation be always full of grace, seasoned with salt, so that you may know how to answer everyone." (Colossians 4:5-6)

JULY 3

"It's the flavor that holds the memory." – Chef

T HE CHEF WAS furious about the cook using canned olives and canned mushrooms in the dishes. "It's the flavor that holds the memory!" He hollered.

He couldn't be more right; it's easy to forget the "canned" things. It's not so easy to forget the succulent, freshest garden abundance. There's no comparison. I find we often give "canned" leftovers of just about everything. That's rather forgettable. I think that might also lend itself to our lessened degree of hearing. Or shall I say, listening. I think it has cheapened our love and potholed our lives. It's made churches predictable and politics tiresome.

There is so much out there, that is terribly forgettable. We need to consider what we say, how we love, why we live with the thought that we are leaving a memory somewhere.

We are going to be a smell, a snapshot, a burp of thought in someone's cerebral lineage. Just look at all those you keep! Maybe it's time to consider what we will leave long before it's our time. It's the flavor that holds the meory.

"Those who guard their lips preserve their lives." (Proverbs 13:3)

JULY 4

"God's blessing in America has something to do with me."

WHEN I STOOD in line to vote in 1980, I was 10 months pregnant with my daughter, Rachel. They let me go to the front since I looked like a giant bubble. I was voting for a leader I believed was bringing back the patriotic seam to the America dressage long past. He won the Presidency; and although in retrospect he made his fair share of mistakes, there were those hopeful moments in all of us.

Not long after Reagan was diagnosed with Alzheimer's, Nancy, his wife, found his fist clenched. She pried it apart to find a little plastic White House that has been in the fish tank. She asked him what he was doing with it. He replied, *"I don't know. I just know it has something to do with me."*

Every voting season, I cringe to see what happens in my nation. It feels like suddenly being surrounded by big, bad street gangs ready to rumble. I believe our unity and integrity wave in the balance during these days. But like Reagan, my joy holds to that place that has *"something to do with me."* God bless America. May He shed His grace on us.

"I thank and praise You, God, of my ancestors:
You have given me wisdom
and power, You have made known to me what we asked of You.
You have made known to us the dream of the King." (Daniel 2:23)

JULY 5

"E quini uscimmo a revider le stele. And so we came forth,
and once again beheld the stars." – Dante

EMOTIONAL WHOLENESS HAS many variations. Sorrow does not have to be depression. Some sorrow purifies and expands the soul. On the other hand, dark nights of the soul often embrace depression as a tactical way through the identity of grief.

Learning about light and dark is a human challenge.

But darkness often reveals the light to us. While we all may go through the language of the soul's conformation, there will come a time to, once again, see the stars. Seeing the Light in our deepest, darkest place gives us a whole new understanding of how the universe works, how God develops us in the darkroom.

Remember that neither grief nor darkness has limitations of time. All is a matter of individuality. All is a matter of priceless processing. Do not live constipated with fear. If you want to, you will see the stars again.

"You are not restricted by us, but by your own
affections." (2 Corinthians 6:11)

JULY 6

"Everything ever created contains unseen assignments."

A N OAK TREE is not born asking what it is to be. A lovely flower does not wonder why it landed in a child's hand. A tiny grape does not worry it will not be what it was created to be.

Whose pain angers you? Who do you want to protect? What makes you cry? These things are keys to your earthly assignment.

They are the things that will help you place yourself. Rather than always wondering if you are where God wants you or if you are doing some good thing or why you are in one circumstance or another...you can be like God's other creations.

You can enjoy Being and not insisting on doing what you want to do, because you will be doing it! Wherever you land, you will use it as a way of Being what brings awe to God. It will feel like stillness in your soul. Joy will be a part of its sweetness.

Everyone has an assignment. God is too economical to waste anything, but especially people.

You have a divine purpose.

"For this very purpose I raised you up, to
demonstrate My power in you, that
My name might be proclaimed throughout the earth." (Romans 9:17)

JULY 7

"Always take the challenge to be stronger."

IT WAS A debate.

Science. Creation versus Evolution.

The class was split into sides but that was the year we were all trying to think for ourselves. How it happened that I was the Creation Lone Ranger, I am not sure. I just know it was scary and I felt cast aside like an idea gone bad. I talked to my Science Teacher who insisted I would be fine in this Debate with no fair call.

I took on the challenge. I did my research.

I took my place at the lectern, my notes thick and studied. You remember that, all eyes on you, feeling. I began. I took on one person after another, sometimes more of a group. It was heated at times, curious at others and I learned I could stand for what I believed in even when I could not prove it all.

I won the debate. I also won the respect of my teacher and schoolmates.

Nobody went to church with me the next Sunday, but they did ask more questions. Everyday choices come that will require you make that choice alone. It won't always go well. It won't always mean respect or good come to you. What it means most is that you will be stronger because of it.

Always take the challenge to be stronger.

"The Lord of Hosts has planned, and who can frustrate it? And as for His outstretched hand, who can turn it back?" (Isaiah 14:27)

JULY 8

"The greatest thing a father can do to his
children is to love their mother." – Anjaneth Garcia Untalan

I HAVE ALWAYS LOVED this quote and believe it is true. Children enjoy hearing love stories. They like saying *"gross"* when they catch you kissing. They need to know there is a friendship of epic proportion right before their eyes.

That's how they are going to learn the most about relationships. They watch how you talk to their mother. Little girls let other men talk to them the way they see you talk to their mom. Little boys learn how to treat a woman by watching how you treat their mother.

Love is *"always a many splendored thing,"* but especially when it has a wise and loving father who knows his children are learning all about love from his example. Feel free to tell your children how awesome the woman you married is, any chance you get. Mamas, make the biggest deal you can make out of having a wonderful husband. Most children will soon be one or the other.

May they know how precious it is to have each other.

"Blessed is the man whose quiver is full of children." (Psalm 127:5)

JULY 9

"Listen well to judge well."

I HAD POURED MY heart and soul into the preparation of the presentation. My teacher was tough. I thought I was just as plucky. I knew she would love how I wrapped this concept here and concluded this there. I was certain I could impress her with content and emotion.

I was ready. I stood and presented. I was excited as she stared at me. Then I noticed, she was staring beyond me. She then turned and talked to someone, waving me to continue. I did, confused. I finished.

The class seemed impressed. The teacher dismissed us and there was not a word said to me. When grades came out, it was much less than I hoped for and though acceptable, I had to wonder. At the side, she had noted it was "Too emotional."

Is that why she had quit listening? Was that why she tuned me out? She really didn't hear me at all. I look back on that experience and promised myself to be a teacher who pays attention. If I didn't really hear it, I could not make a judgment call. I was hurt by her callousness and inattentiveness. That day, I learned the value of those who listen and those who judge fairly.

Judge well.

"Do not judge by appearances, but judge with right judgment." (John 7:24)

JULY 10

"I arise today through a mighty strength; God's power to guide me, God's might to uphold me, God's eyes to watch over me; God's ear to hear me, God's word to give me speech, God's hand to guard me, God's way before me, God's shield to shelter me, God's host to secure me." – Bridge of Gael

WHAT A CHALLENGING call to the soul! How often I have risen through the mighty strength, I cannot say. Indeed, it has been God who has been my Guide. I do not believe in spirit guides. I believe in a Holy Spirit. Oh, the difference in power this makes.

I trust the God who watches sparrows fall is more than sufficient in watching over me. I have noticed He picks up neither sparrow nor man, but strengthens us both to rise. I know He hears me. Even when a black night has covered His face to me, I hear His voice in the wind, His laughter in sprinkling rains.

He speaks, I tell you, and He speaks even in the still small voice. He is my guardian in the places I am fear filled and vulnerable. He shields me from things I am not even aware of knowing. And yes, the angels have held my hand in precarious times. It is barely enough that I thank Him for His goodness. To share it with you is sweetness to my soul and health to my spirit.

I arise.

"Having therefore these promises, dearly beloved, let us cleanse ourselves from all defilement of flesh and spirit, perfecting holiness in the respect of God." (2 Corinthians 7:1)

JULY 11

*"Biblical orthodoxy without compassion is surely
the ugliest thing in the world." – Francis A. Schaeffer*

WE DON'T LIKE to talk about it much, but people who claim to be Christians can be very nasty people. People who are of loving faiths can deeply grieve us by tongue or action. That is the sad truth.

A Bible may not make a person different any more than a finance book makes me rich or a diet read makes me thin. I have to decide to act upon the challenges given. If all you have is an order of service, you have no service. If you read the Bible all day every day but it does not change your heart, it has not been treated with honor. If we continue to build extravagant temples of worship but never feed the world with extravagant love, we are fooling ourselves.

Years ago, I remember a business meeting in an old southern church. The church was for sale. The black church wanted to buy it, but the whites were heated and yelling and must have surely broken God's heart, until a little old lady spoke. *"We can't very well send money to Africa and pretend we love people if we don't love the ones in front of us."* Everything got a bit quieter.

It's not what you believe it's how you live out what you believe.
*"Though I bestow all my goods to feed the poor, and give my body to
be burned and have not love, it profits nothing."* (1 Corinthians 13:3)

JULY 12

"For out of the abundance of the heart the mouth speaks." – Jesus

I F ANYTHING IS going to tell me what's in your heart, it's going to be your mouth. If you have an abundance of criticism in your heart, you are going to speak critical. If you have an abundance of anger, you are going to speak anger. If you have an abundance of dishonesty, you will speak dishonesty.

I am going to believe you are wise enough to have received that word without further illustrations. You cannot have a heart abundant in love and speak hate.

We are telling each other what is in our heart by the words we use in our lives each day. I find this profoundly fascinating. While I have loosely held to the thoughts of speaking positive, this deepened my growth much more. I had to admit, my heart had some abundance that was showing up negative. If l was going to say I had an abundance of joy in my heart, I was going to have to back that up by not speaking whining, selfish, complaining words. That's one powerful serendipity right there.

What was that you just said?

"A good man produces good out of the good storeroom in his heart.
An evil man produces evil out of the evil storeroom, for his mouth
speaks from the overflow of his heart." (Luke 6:45)

JULY 13

*"That it will never come again is what makes
life so sweet."* – Emily Dickinson

SOMETIMES, I JUST stop and actually breathe in the air. I survey that terrain of life around me. I breathe deeper. Life what a gift to be alive! In the year 2000, I was given two weeks to live. A blood infection had hidden in my heart, breaking a muscle. It did not look good.

There were and are no words to describe the pain. I wanted to die. I could not imagine feeling right and good and alive ever again. I have told how I came back to life elsewhere. I so vividly recall wanting to live again, wanting to jump out of bed and run. I remember standing in the hospital hallway like a racehorse at the gate. Alive! What an awesome awakening! It only comes once.

This is it. So, don't put off your dancing shoes. There's lots more where this came from and sweetness beyond measure, if you just catch your breath on the goodness.

Have a *"nonreturnable"* beautiful day.

*"Let the heavens rejoice, let the earth be glad,
let the sea resound and all that is in it."* (Psalm 96:11-12)

"Precious and priceless are different currencies."

THE WORLD IS seemingly run by people who have the currency we have deemed more than it is worth. Hold a hundred dollar bill in your hand. You will feel its worth, not because it is, but because you are told that it is valuable. Someone else gave it that value. In and of itself, it's just marked up piece of paper. What makes it different than a child's drawing on a piece of paper? The position of power we have given.

Try putting dimes through an IV and you will know, money is very limited in what it can give you. Try buying love. It will get you a warm body, but it won't get you love. Try purchasing peace. The more you try to buy it, the less you have of it. You can't buy admiration, respect, honor, righteousness, joy, kindness, gentleness, eternal life, character, worship, compassion, perfect health or so much else.

Try putting wisdom in your budget. (You can't buy it either.) But you can apply it to the currency of your life.

Real currency IS rarely money anyway. If you can live without it, it's probably easily bought. If it's harder to come by, it might have more worth than money knows. Precious and priceless have so little to do with true currency. Keep your books balanced. Adjust your life to the real currency.

"What does it benefit a man to gain
the whole world but lose his soul?" (Mark 8:36)

JULY 15

"A misty morning does not mean it will be a rainy day." – Stamp

I F YOU LIVE with chronic pain, you learn this quickly. I used to watch my mom do all she did and wonder where she put her pain. With six children, she didn't have much time to lounge in bed until she felt better.

She has more time for that now, but not enough patience for it. Smile. As I observed others who have learned to successfully share their life with pain, I have noted that many a morning is hard. It may be from a rough night. It may because the pain has gotten uncontrollable for a season. It may be just a weariness of having done too much the day before. Sometimes, it is a turn for the worse. Sometimes, it is just a fatigue in the spirit. Whatever it is, it is there and must be dealt with, for there is life to do.

Great and wondrous clays can come out of misty hard mornings. I mostly know that, because I have learned to live beyond the pain most of the time. While I oft have to learn it every morning, for as many know, it changes, I will not stay in the mist when I can clear the path. I may have to wait a bit, take some medicine, do some things that strengthen me; use things that will allow me to rise and shine.

That is okay. My life can still be rich and full and a place of great delight and power. I may not get the chance to choose the pain I will feel, but I can choose what I do with it.

"If you faint in the day of adversity, thy
strength is small." (Proverbs 24:10)

JULY 16

"Joyfully faithful, the best way to be thankful for something, is to enjoy it." - Ann Stewart Porter

THEY TOOK THE gift. They never opened it. They were polite to say thanks, but I got the feeling they would be re—gifting. I have not felt much like getting them gifts. They took the gift and chugged it in a bag for home. They didn't take it out and savor it. I got the feeling it was a bother. I don't want to bother them anymore.

Frankly, I prefer people like my grands who rip open the box, can't get it out fast enough, who squeal and huff and jump around until it's free of unnecessary wrap. Then they sit and enjoy. They stop periodically to show me what it does. They hug me and say it is what they wanted. They seem to be happy it is theirs.

How do you enjoy all the gifts God has given you? Do you whine about your loved one? They are a gift. Do you complain about your job? That is a gift. Do you at least say grace for your food? What a gift! Are you thankful for your body that works well? Health is a gift.

Treat your gifts as you would love someone to treat a gift you have given. Life is a Beautiful gift.

"Every good and perfect gift is from above, coming down from the Father of lights." (James 1:17)

JULY 17

"Do not teach your children never to be angry; teach them how to be angry." – Lyman Abbott

HOW YOUNG DO children feel anger? When do they recognize it or its power? Children feel anger before they are able to understand that emotion. The value of this emotion is the discovery of some of your child's deepest passions. It is also an important place to connect with your child, to give them priceless gifts of acceptance and understanding. When they are angry, it is of utmost benefit if you can stay calm. Many parents yell back, hit back; call them names and it ends with all feeling unsatisfied.

First, take time to hear what they are saying. Yes, it may be total nonsense to you, ***but if it meant something to them, rest assured it means something***. Be a good detective and find out what it is and use that knowledge to show them wonderful things about themselves.

Don't be too quick to just send them to their room to be alone. You don't want them to always feel alone or abandoned in their anger. You can give them time to think, but then go talk. Let them talk the most. This often dissolves anger before it becomes bitterness. It also gives you a chance to show them positive ways to use their anger. And to give a much needed hug.

Lastly, make sure the basics are not to fault. Are they tired? Are they hungry? Are they feeling something is unfair? Are they feeling neglected? Are they feeling ill? Did they have a sad thing happen or a trauma unnoticed? Don't let anger destroy your home. Use it to create positive, powerful people.

"Do not provoke your children to anger, but bring them up in the discipline and instruction of the Lord." (Ephesians 6:4)

JULY 18

"You can either go cry in the truck or cowboy up!" – Travis

THERE ARE A few cowboys around our parts. I do, after all, live in the wild, wild West. You can still see plenty of pick-up trucks, cowboy hats and boots just about anywhere you want to go. Cowboys like being boys, but they are, in every sense of the word, quite serious about being men. They tip their hat because mama taught them women ought to be treated well. So, the general cowboy population will treat a gal with some decorum. They wrestle cows and get up at dawn, / work past dusk and sleep hard.

One of our good cowboy friends only wears boots when it snows. Smile. You will see his feet bare most of the time. When he says he put a *"side of beef"* in your truck, he doesn't mean pretty little butcher chop wrapping paper. He means burlap and blood.

They seem to thrive on the dusty hard lands of life, lived mostly off the land. They don't much put up with nonsense. You better get in the arena or get out of their way. To stand around with your hands in your pocket better mean something.

They are here to live. It's a good lesson for all of us. No real cowboy sits in the truck. He's here to live deep and long in the grit of it. If he gets hurt, he gets up when he can. He's wrestling more than cows.

Don't live a peripheral life. Jump in with your heart and your boots on. Get ready to lasso your dreams and run till you are dry, work hard and stay for the long hauls. And don't forget to tip your hat and smile every once in awhile.

"Whatever you do, work at it with all your heart,
as working unto the Lord." (Colossians 3:23)

JULY 19

"Anxiety is love's greatest killer. It makes others feel as you might when a drowning man holds onto you. You want to save him, but you know he will strangle you with his panic." – Anais Nin

DEFINE ANXIETY.

Proverbs says anxiety causes depression. Webster says it's a feeling of being anxious about an outcome. In any case, anxiety appears to be a carrier of destruction. Do you find yourself anxious? If you are, what is the outcome you fear? Is it that they might leave you? Is it that you are not enough? Is it that others will disapprove? You fear one of you will cheat on the other?

To be so consumed with these fear based issues, you will lose the fullness of joy. You must learn to work through each fear or it will paralyze you in some way.

Write down these things that feel so troubling, especially if they are hiding in depression. Talk through them with the one you love. Then decide to save yourself from a dying love. Don't strangle your love with undercurrents of panic.

Live beyond the fear.

"Anxiety in the heart of man causes depression.
But a good word makes it glad." (Proverbs 12:25)

"The Apache don't have a word for love," he said. *"Know what they both say at the marriage?"* *"Tell me."* *"Varlebena. It means forever. That's all they say."* – *"Hondo"* by Louis L'Amour

S OME SAY THAT this isn't actually true and that L'Amour just made it up. I don't know. I just know I love it.

Faithfulness is a beautiful thing. To know that love has the capability of eternity is beyond any human comprehension. This we know, while we say it to each other, in hopes it will be so. Is it because deep down in our deepest springs, the divine knowledge is there, waiting for us to embrace the wholeness?

So much of love is not even for a decade. Can we think it would be so true as to be eternal? Still it's best to know, that among all that is not real, the real does not change. In amongst the lies, the truth is unchanged. And so forever it is.

Faithfulness becomes the joy of the promise, the song of forever.

"And I will betroth you to me forever. I will betroth you to me in righteousness and in justice, in steadfast love and mercy." (Hosea 2:19)

JULY 21

"What can you do to promote world peace? Go home and love your family." – Mother Teresa

WOW! THAT OUGHT to hit every single one of us right between the left and right ventricle. We are so pressed to create world peace the way we see it, that we have neglected the rooting of it in the first place.

Home is where our story begins. If we are not placed in a home, we find a family of some sort somewhere. This is becoming more of the rooting than we know as uprooting as that sounds.

Family can be hard to love. Siblings can be competitive. Marriages can hit potholes. People can create a continental divide. We have all seen it. But here's the deal. You either love or you don't.

You can disagree, but you can't QUIT love. Real love is not a quit thing. Just like peace isn't a buy thing. You can try changing the world, but if you haven't been home lately, you might want to reconsider.

What home do you need to go back to and love? A father who doesn't deserve forgiveness? A mother who gave up? A spouse who hurt you or walked away? A sibling who disliked you? An in-law who did you wrong? A God you abandoned?

Go home and love your family. Give peace a chance.

"Above all, love each other deeply, for love covers a multitude of sins." (1 Peter 4:8)

JULY 22

"Lose yourself, John. Lose yourself in your work of God, for then,
when you come home to me, I will know you are the version God
intended you to be and you will love me as that version."
- The Other Side of Heaven

WHERE DO YOU lose yourself? What takes your soul and wraps it around your heart? What seems to take you beyond time or space? If it's a life with purpose, this will involve a compassion making difference.

It will be an awakening of passion. It will be an intimate relationship with your Creator Redeemer. It will be a vision that enlarges your capacity to do the impossible. It will be a faith, fear cannot fathom. It will be a nether spring of joy, a spirit of overwhelming grace.

While it may be in the midst of untold angst, it is not overwhelmed. In it, you will find your best self, your most authentic being, and your divine imaging. You may find yourself having nothing to speak of, but possessing everything. You will find yourself on the other side heaven and there...nothing is lost.

Only found.

Find yourself in the lost.

"Whoever finds his life will lose it, and whoever
loses his life for My sake will find it." (Matthew 10:39)

JULY 23

"Who rescues who?"

I SAW A BUMPER sticker today that not only made me smile, but struck a chord in my heart. It was a simple paw print with the words: Who rescued who? If you have a rescued pet, you know exactly what I mean.

I went out not thinking I would ever get a dog. I didn't go to the shelter. I was entering a thrift shop when I saw her. She was tiny, frightened, looking at me with that look. She put her head on my shoulder and she was mine. Or I was hers. I thought my husband would surely send me back and bring me back to reality. Instead, he fell harder than I had fallen!

Why? Well, we think it is because we had a beautiful handicapped child for 25 years. We believe we needed somebody to fuss over, somebody small to hold and somebody we wouldn't have to explain everything to all the time.

We believe God knew we needed rescuing just as much as that little puppy. God knows our hearts and our deepest needs, ones we don't even know ourselves for a season. He knows what will excite us to live again, when pain has cost so much. He knows how we love. He knows our secret darkness.

So, don't be surprised if someday, you are out and about, minding your own business and get rescued!

"In Your righteousness deliver me and rescue me.
Incline Your ear to me and save me." (Psalm 71:2)

JULY 24

"Riding is a partnership. The horse lends you his strength, speed and grace, which are greater than yours. For your part you give him your guidance, intelligence and understanding, which are greater than his. Together you can achieve a richness that alone neither can."
- Author Unknown

A S THEY SAY, that unknown author person sure is smart. It has been a very long time since l rode a horse. But this sounds right to me. There is an exchange of gifts. There is a joining of companionship. There is an open field of grace and a touch of courage. What strength lies in one, the other finds comforting and accepting. If one tries to lord over the other, harmony is lost. If one wishes for the other's gifts, they will never honor their own.

What weaknesses lay in each other are never calculated as such. But rather, given over to the better choice of joining together for a cause greater than one. Together, respect and honor come with mutuality, common grounds and untold bliss.

While l know we speak of horses here, marriage stands on much the same ground. Achieve that richness in the freedom of being who you are with someone else whose being makes the ride fuller than you could have ever known.

"And the Word became flesh and dwelt among us and we have seen His glory, glory as the only Son of the Father, full of grace and truth." (John 1:14)

JULY 25

"Anger is a bad counselor." – Proverb

EVERYBODY GETS ANGRY. It's when you let anger steal your joy that you've crossed the line.

When you begin to let anger guide your life, you begin a domino effect in your world. You begin to isolate others from you. You begin growing into yourself. You begin to take in patterns of victimization. You fall easily. You damage anything in your way, mostly those closest to you. You hit hard when you fall. You are a selfish contender.

A life of unprofitable living doesn't usually come like a combustion fire. It's usually been festering for some time. It has been marinating in the desperate feelings of rejection, pain, borrowed or real sensitivities, clogged arteries that haven't seen an ounce of love. Once unleashed, it grabs you by the throat and slashes your life.

Anger is not all evil, but a life of anger is deeply unsatisfying and always damaging.

Watch for your anger. Keep it in its place. You are in control. Read the passion behind the anger and use it profitably. Don't let anger use you unprofitably. Its counsel may be hard to bear.

"Refrain from anger and forsake wrath.
Fret not yourself, it leads only to evil." (Psalm 37:8)

"Both in history and in life, it is a phenomenon, by no means rare, to meet with uncomparatively unlettered people, who seem to have struck profound spiritual depths…while there are many highly educated people of whom one feels that they are performing clever antics with their minds to cover a groping hollowness that lies within." – Herbert Butterfield

EVER MEET THAT simple person that seems covered in the most extraordinary spiritual wisdom? The speaker without all the gushing entertainment, but manages to mesmerize you for hours? The person without the trappings of wealth or educational pomp and yet, you have a knowing they are rich beyond this world's limitation?

Sometimes, because of their plainness or their simplicity of expression, you wonder, perplexed at their life. But always your anticipation of meeting them is filled with a tender, sweet knowing there will be great significance placed well into your soul. I have come to know, there are those among us who live in the realm that splashes eternity upon us.

Watch for these teachers in your life. They will carry no big name or entourage. They will change your life. I pray l will always be at least wise enough to take full advantage of their gift. I pray I will appreciate every drop that scatters throughout my life. The world is welcome to the performers. I seek the quiet, simple and profound spiritual significance of life, love and eternity.

"May the God of our Lord Jesus Christ, the Father of glory, give unto you the spirit of wisdom and revelation in the knowledge of Him." (Ephesians 1:17)

JULY 27

"Although our intellect always long for clarity and certainty, our nature often finds uncertainly fascinating." – Karl Von Clausewitz

WAITING ON THE things we want can be a test of faith, courage and visible lines of frustration. We surely think we will not produce the desired outcome and we often become addicted to our outcome.

We may call it our dream or our best or our fulfillment. We might dress it in gowns of clarity and shoes of right place, but the uncertainty remains, as though we needed it.

We do.

We need that part of us we can't tag and label. We need that whisper that makes no sense. We need the quiet night of wondering. Why? Because that is where we find out our truth, our underbelly of true desire, our moment of reckoning.

Do not fear uncertainty. It is here to welcome you into another place of BE-ing. Let not your heart be troubled. All is well.

"Wait on the Lord and be of good courage, and He shall strengthen your heart. Wait, I say, on the Lord." (Psalm 27:14)

"In a dark place, turn on some light."

THE SMITH'S CHECKED into a nice East Coast hotel. At 1:30 am, Mr. Smith got up to turn off the television. That's when he noticed the carpet was moving. Flipping on the light, they discovered the carpet moving was a ten-foot boa constrictor! Yikes!

That's how life goes isn't it? We are doing well, enjoying ourselves, finding the special times; hanging out. Then, there it is, the snake carpet.

Big surprise. Big nightmare moment. This is not what I wanted has come. Sometimes life slithers and changes in the dark. When it does, be prepared to assess, analyze, adjust and acquisition.

These days happen to everyone, so don't let yourself be isolated. This is just your turn. Once you have honestly assessed the situation... my spouse is dead, my child is in trouble or whatever it may be, you will feel a deep confusion at first. This will be the time to analyze how to act in the best way.

Most of us lose it for awhile, our sense of turning on the light in a dark place. As soon as we can, finding a workable solution will be good. Then set about to adjust your attitude, your thought patterns, your need to control, your relationships and your perspective.

Lastly, see what you can acquire from this time that will remain forever valuable. Nightmares pass. What we do with this time stays forever.

"You are a chosen generation, a royal priesthood, a holy nation, that you should show forth the praises of Him who has called you out of darkness into His marvelous light." (1 Peter 2:9)

JULY 29

"What do people mean when they say "I am not afraid of God because I know He is good?" Have they never been to the dentist?" C. S. Lewis

I LOVE OLE LEWIS. He just puts it right out there. He really had to learn how God could be good in those times when it isn't so good. His books about his wife's struggle before dying is worth a read. We can't always pretend well. But we always have a choice.

Harry had a friend who always sounded chipper and positive. He would say he was finer than frog's hair, or so happy he should be a twin or some other crazy thing. One day, Harry had a bad accident. His legs took a beating and he ended up in the wheelchair. A friend came in.

"How ya doing Harry?"

"I'm so happy, I should be twins wanna see my scars?"

Our very young music minister recently told of his car accident where he lost his best friend. As Kyle was put into the ambulance, he was singing the song "God is good all the time."

Neither one of these guys were in those "good" kind of life moments. But just because the circumstance doesn't merit the song, doesn't mean we don't have the choice to sing it. All of life is not good. (Aren't I profound?) But all of God is. Choose the blessing regardless the circumstance.

"The Lord is good to all. He has compassion on all He has made." (Psalm 145:9)

"What is your natural and spiritual nature? Many say they are changed by the power of god, but the truth is lived out as we allow God to turn the natural into the spiritual by sacrifice."
- Oswald Chambers

REMEMBER THE STORY of the fishermen who had fished all night and caught nothing? Jesus gave them new direction and they ended up with a boat that couldn't handle the giving! If we never surrender to the spiritual, we will live divorced. The natural life will mock the spiritual.

When we do not discipline our life, we ruin the whole of the personal spiritual life. God wants the relationship to be what brings us the most healing. He wants us to experience a relationship different from any other relation. The very things we may think we can't live without will become sweeter than we could know. We may not want to do something, but the sacrifice we make brings blessing.

A commitment to our spiritual being will produce transformations that are radically more loving than ever we produce naturally. Sacrifice is the discipline of the spiritual. If all we want is ourselves and the limitations of our being, we will remain unable to see the truth of all things.

Many settle for life as they want it, with all the limitations rather than sacrificing their unknowingness for opportunities beyond their greatest thought.

Break through the natural.

"You are my Rock and Fortress; for Your Name sake, You will lead me and guide me." (Psalm 31:3)

"He who binds to himself a joy does the winged life destroy;
but he who kisses the joy as it flies lives in
eternities house." – William Blake

BINDING MAY NOT sound like freedom, but it can be. I get done with a manuscript and it's a bunch of paper needing a binding. That is, if I want to get a message out of it. But the beautiful thing about binding yourself to joy is that it releases all things temporary.

Become intimate with joy and you open the divine in your life. You touch eternity. You live beyond the circumstance and go deeper into your soul for resilience and power.

With joy, you decide not the amount of money you have or don't have. Not the education you have, not the doctor's report, not the things people have told you, not your emotions, not if your car is running or your family is acting up you get to decide. Isn't that just awesome?

Live in the sunrise of eternity. Live joyfully.

"I drew them with cords of man, with cords of love." (Hosea 11:4)

AUGUST 1

"I, with a deeper instinct, choose a man who compels my strength,
who makes enormous demands on me, who does not doubt my
courage or my toughness, who does not believe me naive or innocent,
who has the courage to treat me like a woman." – Anais Nin

I'M SCOTTISH; STRONG, strong-willed, capable, independent and passionate. My husband claims I am caring, tenacious, spiritual and feisty. And he added with a grin that he likes feisty. I will add, with a grin, that he likes it until we do battle. Smile.

What I adore about my husband, among so many things, is that he respects the woman I am, challenges me to be all God wants me to be and inspires me to believe in what I am as a person.

In college, I had a list of three things that were absolutes for me in choosing a mate. The third one was that he love me as a woman. I knew exactly what I meant and if a man would know, it would be the right one for me.

He knew. He values women in a way that every woman would appreciate. His enjoyment of my strengths, his attitude toward my feminine power and his deep grace toward our journey together is such a gift of joy.

If you are looking for a man, find one with the courage to treat you like a woman. If you have one who already does, tell him thank you in as many ways as you can. It's a beautiful thing.

"Who can find a virtuous wife, for her worth is far above rubies.
The heart of her husband safely trusts her,
so she does him good all the days of his life." (Proverbs 31)

AUGUST 2

"What you grow in testing produces maturity in fruit."

DOUG WAS SO bitter from his dad leaving the family, he tried just about everything before he tried God. When he fell in love with Jesus, the whole of it changed. He had already been to several countries helping others when he was told he had colon cancer. He did radiation and it didn't look good. He had been watching the terror in Rwanda. He thought that he wanted to hold some of those dying children in his arms before he died. He told his doctor he was on his way to Rwanda. The doctor said he would be dead in three days or so.

But in Rwanda, a group of men who had been hired by the missionaries to carry people on stretchers had gone on strike. Doug, against all advice, stood, surrounded by 300 angry men. He told them he could never understand what they had been through, that all he had ever had was cancer.

Cancer in Rwanda was a death sentence. At first they quizzed them. Then they began to weep and feel foolish that they wanted more money when Doug was dying! They returned quietly to work.

And Doug? His doctor had no words to explain that his cancer has vanished. But Doug sure loves sharing the story as he heads for the garbage dumps of Manila or hugs the two Filipino children he adopted. Doug lacks nothing. Wonder what God wants to do with whatever He gives us?

"The testing of your faith produces patience. Let patience have its perfect work, that you may be perfect and complete, lacking nothing." (James 1:3-4)

AUGUST 3

"Go the extra mile...it's never crowded."

THIS HAS BEEN one of those things I was raised to do. Early on, if it wasn't Mama, it was Daddy.

Do more than is expected. Deliver more than you promise. Leave a little more than they think you will leave.

In a world where many want to be different, this is one sure way to leave your mark. Everything you do carries your touch. While you might think you need orange hair, a tat, a certain type clothing or a piercing to mark your territory, why not try going the extra mile.

There's lots less competition.

If you are asked to do one thing, do several. Too many are content to do just enough, just what is expected, just what passes inspection. Use the extra mile to arrive in beautiful places.

"If anyone asks you to go one mile, go with him two miles." (Matthew 5:41)

AUGUST 4

*"Never fear the hand of mercy, for it will
always lead you to the land of grace."*

D ID YOU EVER do something so awful, that you didn't
want anyone to know? Did you ever wish so desperately you
could turn back time and make another choice? Has there been a time
you truly felt unforgivable? Then you wondered if God would make
you pay for that awful thing. Or He would ask something of you that
was impossible. Or He would never trust you or bless you or use your
life again.

Chances are good you have been there. I have. I have been there
waiting for mercy, believing I had lost all my integrity and all my strength,
for a sin that cost too much. To someone else, it might have seemed trite.
To another person, it might have seemed like just another sin.

To me, it was my hand grabbing for life again. It was a heart begging
for that sweet forgiveness I needed to know was mine. Once I took
the hand of Mercy, I realized He had taken me to the land of grace. I
would now enjoy pleasures I thought would be forsaken. I was to find
that forgiveness brought peace and peace led to joy I could never have
imagined.

The land of grace is a beautiful place. I want to live here forever.

*"Surely goodness and mercy will follow me all
the days of my life."* (Psalm 23:6)

AUGUST 5

"If you find a thorn do you look for a rose?"

I HAVE A FRIEND who looks for roses anywhere she sees a thorn. She always makes me think twice, look at life with a unique perspective and strengthens the goodness in all I do. She is prone to a very loose interpretation of perfect. The kind that makes you smile to know how low she's set the standard. Of course, that is only so love can set it higher.

She never starts a sentence with a negative, and rarely lets you have that pitiful moment of self-unknown. She is exuberant and seems to include everyone into whatever festivity she is having.

The simplicity of seeing roses in thorns has carried her through great grief and past petty things that would have thrown the weaker off the path. For her, it's just well another day in paradise. Maybe that's the whole idea. Live in the Joy. Always look for the rose, when you feel the thorn.

"You make known to me the paths of life. You fill me with joy in Your presence, with eternal pleasures at your right hand." (Psalm 16:11)

AUGUST 6

*"I've learned that you shouldn't go through life
with a catcher's mitt on both hands;
you need to be able to throw something back."* – Maya Angelou

MY BEAUTIFUL DAUGHTER, Suzanne Nicole, was a teenager. We had moved in her junior year of high school after she asked us to return to Colorado. She had transitioned in several ways that year. We had a head on car collision.

We both survived. Our car did not.

The Columbine Massacre happened just down the road from us.

She had a profoundly retarded sister.

Life for her was always a different place of reckoning that it might be for others her age. She has always been very brave.

One day she sat on the countertop in the kitchen as I cooked. She said she wanted to "give back." She felt her life had been spared for a reason. She felt a bit guilty about that (which is normal). She said she couldn't imagine losing me in that wreck. So, the year she graduated high school while also managing two stores, she made a trip to Mexico. The children sat around her like she was Mother Teresa. She painted. She played. She gave back. Why? Because when you realize what life is really all about, you need to have something to throw back.

*"So that I may come to you with joy by God's will, and in
your company be refreshed."* (Romans 15:32)

AUGUST 7

"Is it well with your soul?"

I F YOU KNOW the old hymn, "It is Well with My Soul" written by Horatio Spafford, then you may have heard the story behind it. Spafford lost his only son at the young age of four, and then shortly thereafter lost his fortune in the great Chicago fire. It ruined him financially as he had been a successful lawyer. Then, in 1873, he had planned to travel to Europe with his wife and four daughters, but sent them ahead while he was delayed on business.

While crossing the Atlantic, the ship collided with another sea vessel and sank. All four of Spafford's daughters died. His wife Anna survived and sent him the famous telegram, *"Saved alone."*

While Spafford traveled to meet his grieving wife, he was inspired to write these words as his ship passed the spot where his daughters were lost. His friend, Philip Bliss, wrote the music and was shortly thereafter tragically killed in a train wreck.

The Spaffords later had three more children, a son that died as a baby and two daughters. They moved to Jerusalem and helped found a group called the "American Colony." Its mission was to serve the poor. The Colony later became the subject of the Nobel Prize winning "Jerusalem."

While we cannot imagine the unspeakable grief, we cannot deny this great man challenges all of us to ask: *"Is it well with my soul?"*

"For Christ's sake, I delight in weakness, insults,
hardships, in persecutions, in difficulties. For when I
am weak, He is strong." (2 Corinthians 12:10)

AUGUST 8

"You don't get harmony when everyone sings the same note." – Doug Floyd

I PLAY PIANO.

The other night I sang with our Pastor. As he started to sing the song I was playing, I couldn't help but harmonize. *It's what I do.* I'm a high tenor or a low alto and I love singing. I am especially drawn to harmony.

I don't mind singing solo and have done so many times. But what I really enjoy is finding that note that brings fullness to the piece.

There is a time for us to sing one note, one way, with one voice. There is also room for us to harmonize with points others make, and ways of thinking that challenge our own, or choices to try something we are not accustomed to for the sake of discovery.

Harmony is a brave thing to do. It's like a dare in the world of solicitations. I found out that marriage is rarely two people who think alike on any two subjects; but where there is great love, there is great harmony. If, as the old song goes, we are ever to *"Teach the World to Sing,"* we must lean into our part in harmony.

Harmony doesn't mean we lower our standard or treat another disrespectfully. Neither does it mean we wait for them to see it our way. Harmony comes from the Greek word meaning ***"joint."***

Let's keep our world from going too out of joint. Live in harmony.

"How good and how pleasant it is for brethren to dwell together in unity." (Psalm 133:1)

AUGUST 9

B Y OUR MOUTHS we are justified or condemned. Do you ever find yourself condemning yourself?

Words like how stupid you are, why you are such a failure, how blind could you be, when will you ever learn and other spliced up negatives play like a wall street ticker tape.

But what if you understood that every thought has an energy in your life?

What if you believed you had the power of life or death in your very words?

We have certainly talked about the worth of words. Once you begin to develop this process in your life, I can assure you, it will reveal so much to you.

Your greatest bother will be the length of time you generally wait to see the words become reality, but it's a small price to pay for justification. Think about it.

"Death and life are in the power of the tongue." (Proverbs 18:21)

AUGUST 10

"Praise is the beauty of holiness."

JEHOSHAPHAT WAS HAVING some issues in the kingdom. The battle looked ugly by any standard. So He got everybody together for a Singspiration! Anybody remember those from their growing up days? Churches would bring in quartets, trios and such, for a fairly rowdy night of inspirational singing. That sounds pretty risky for a king heading to battle, don't you think?

Scripture says he told them to "praise the beauty of holiness." The King had said sing, so sing against the enemy they did. We are told that when they began to PRAISE, God set ambushes against the enemy.

They never fought.

They just watched.

Then they took their trumpets and other instruments and went back to church! Because of this, there was a great fear on the other kingdoms. But it says *"Jehoshaphat's realm was quiet, for his God gave him rest round about."*

I enjoy this story because it has taught me how to act when I have a battle in my life. I have found it works. If I set myself, praise, get still, watch and fear not, I see victories won and peace come.

Is there quiet in your kingdom?

"You do not need to fight in this battle, set yourselves, stand you still and see the salvation of the Lord." (2 Chronicles 20:17)

AUGUST 11

"Losing doesn't make me want to quit.
It makes me want to fight that much harder." – Bear Bryant

IT WAS A big job. It was a big deal. It was at a place of high esteem. It paid well. It was a perfect position for me. And I wanted it like you want your mama's peach cobbler. Three times this happened to me. I can't tell you the endless interviews, paperwork and FBI checks I have smiled through only to find out at the end that it wasn't going to be me in that dream job.

"You were our first choice, but the politics…"

"You had the job, but we redefined and need more technological experience…"

"It seems like a perfect fit, but could you do it with your handicapped child?"

Oh, it stings. It defeats. It makes it hard to fight for another dream. Yes, I look back today, on all three jobs and know it is just fine that I am not in any of those places. I even look back and think they missed a swell opportunity. But I ultimately believe if God wants you somewhere, He can make that happen. And while it saps the fire out of you for a moment or two, a fighter stands up and learns how to do it all again. Never give up!

"Let us not grow weary in doing good, for in due season we will reap a harvest, if we do not give up." (Galatians 6:9)

AUGUST 12

"Pray that your loneliness may spur you into finding something to live for, great enough to die for." - Dag Hammarskjöld

LONELINESS AFFECTS MOST people sometime in their life. What do you do with it? First, recognize that you aren't usually just lonely. You are lonely FOR a specific person or group of people, which can make for other feelings as well, such as heartache and melancholy.

Are you lonely for companionship, touch, fun, creativity, mental connection of some kind? There are thousands of places in need of your personal gifting. Thousands!

A few years back, I was doing a practicum for my Nursing education. I began the morning at an elderly man's home, then a woman with cerebral palsy, then an AIDS patient. Next came an hour feeding at a Multiple Sclerosis Center, and to a Nursing Home. In every place, people were hungry for attention, desperate for a friend, hurting deeper than they could speak and so very lonely.

At each place, I thought of the thousands of people sitting alone somewhere – people who had told me they so missed their spouse who had left or their children now in college or that they wished for a hand to hold. Others who had no jobs wished for a place to feel useful, a song to sing, a mentally stimulating conversation, a good basketball game in the park.

Oh, if only we could think of another in our loneliness. Perhaps we could wipe it out with a mere day outside ourselves. Find somewhere to put your life.

> *"Therefore, welcome one another in Christ as He welcomed you for the glory of God."* (Romans 15:7)

AUGUST 13

"The portal of healing and creativity always takes us into the realm of the spirit." Angeles Arrien

WE LIKE TO think an aspirin cures us, when in fact, life is deeper than aspirins. We learn this as we grow older or struggle with our health. Maybe we discover it as a child of molestation. An aspirin doesn't make it all better.

Nothing really makes it all better for some of us. We are far too anxious to allow a creativity to hold our spirit.

Raina was such a girl. Brought to a rescuing place, she lacked the ability to feel, to love, to give. She was as hateful as the hate that brought her to this time. One morning, she wandered into the dawn and saw Sweet Betsy munching on grass. She just stared, the way you do, when you are mesmerized looking at such beauty and strength. She saw in Sweet Betsy the spirit of beauty, strength and power in wholeness. She began to imagine she was whole.

It took some doing, but she was willing to do. Mostly, that's all it takes. She became willing to enter the realm of her spirit.

The portal of healing always takes us through the realm of the spirit. Why? Because we are spirits having a human experience. We will always find our spiritual realm is our truest home. Everything is connected to our spiritual beingness. Everything.

"Heal me, O Lord, and I shall be healed. Save me and I shall be saved, for You are my praise." (Jeremiah 17:14)

AUGUST 14

"No matter what happens, there is always someone who knew it would."

ALWAYS! YOU BOUGHT something. They tell you it was on sale over there. You learned something. They tell you how long they have known it. You ask them a question they didn't know last week. After the fact they should have mentioned that, they say.

We humans are a snotty bunch of shenanigans some days. We have little quarrels of self-interest that jump like children in a school desk, wanting recognition, wanting to be seen.

This often takes the form of the obnoxious. We don't mean it that way. We don't always recognize it as such unless, of course, we see it in another. Sometimes, the edge of insanity gets paved down and we walk around in it. It's just humanity trying to find a warm place to breathe.

There's little way of rescuing yourself unless you simply love them. Love covers a multitude of sins and it works both in your sins and theirs. Today, when they start the process that feels right for them, but irks you silly, let them speak. Then hug them tight and thank them for thinking of you. Give them a genuine compliment in something they are not expecting. Then smile. It feels great.

"Many are the afflictions of the righteous;
but the Lord delivers them out of them all." (Psalm 34:19)

AUGUST 15

"The energy of the mind is the essence of life." – Aristotle

ENERGY HAS POWER. Simple acts of acknowledging healing energy can revolutionize your recovery. Be it physical or emotional, mental or spiritual, healing uses our energy. While the energy of our belief may hold the miracle of healing within, it is equally possible we do not know what is best, forfeiting our surety.

Trusting God means that we trust enough to use what has already been given to us. Energy deepens how we perceive ourselves and others. We use it all the time in reading another's actions and thoughts. When we respect our innermost expressions, we can notice patterns and observations others will not see. It will give you a resilience and stamina that carries a language of its own. Intuition will offer you the spirit and energy in emotional conundrums. Being aware of your energy and its worth brings fortitude.

When you can begin saying *"I can grow through this"* or *"I will survive and thrive"* or *"I can do all things through Christ who strengthens me,"* you are using your energy of trust to do amazing things. It is quite likely you will see it come to pass in due season. You are then in a stronger positioning of empowerment for all of your life, not just what brought you to this time.

Continue to speak death and tired words of hopelessness and the energy will follow as well. You will create and continue to create the life of a victim, a needy person without strength. Energy is a path of personal power. Let it bring healing.

"I can do all things through Christ Who strengthens me." (Philippians 4:13)

ANN STEWART-PORTER

"Never underestimate the positioning of a Loser."

SPARKY HATED HIS nickname. He hated school. He flunked out of 8th grade. He still holds the record for lowest physics marks in his school. Because of knowing he was a reject, he never asked a girl out. He made the school's golf team but one of his poor plays cost them the championship.

People made fun of his little *"drawings."* He drew some cartoons for the yearbook, but they turned it down. He even got up the nerve to apply for a job at Walt Disney. They rejected him. He admitted all he did just made him more of a loser. His life was one long cartoon strip.

As he thought about that, he just started drawing characters and putting his life into cartoons. It helped him grow as a person and eventually, he landed a job to use all his finely tuned "Loser" experiences.

You can read them every Sunday morning, in the newspaper cartoons you'll recognize him and Lucy and Linus and Beethoven and Snoopy. Sparky is known worldwide for his wonderful comic strip "Peanuts." He, of course is the Charlie Brown, the little boy whose kite never quite flies.

Never, ever, underestimate the power of a Loser.

"Blessed is the one who perseveres, having stood the test." (James 1:12)

AUGUST 17

"Do everything with so much love in your heart that you would never want to do it any other way." – Amrit Desai

WHAT A BEAUTIFUL thought. We talk of love in terms of relationships mostly, but love is good for all of our living. When we begin to live lovely, we see things we never see walking outside of love. We begin to develop wisdom that excites our spirit. Love is the fertility of life. It births depths of untold joys. It simplifies the complicated. It yields benefit, rewards and delights of soul delicious goodness.

Love is a refuge, a hope, a passion cut from the divine, like a kaleidoscope diamond. Precious and beautiful, priceless and incomparable, love changes us. We begin to notice things we did not know existed – hurting ones, sad ones, broken ones and those who are too fearful to even think of love as a way of life.

Your spirit is ignited to touch others, to serve another, to believe for greater things. And then, you find it does you more good than the finest fairy tale. The happier ever after is just getting started...when love unfolds in your life.

"Do nothing out of selfish ambition or vain conceit. Rather, in humility value others above yourself." (Philippians 2:3)

AUGUST 18

"Integrity speaks for itself."

S HE CAME TO me with a need for mediation. We were on the opposite sides of the issue. She knew exactly what I would say. She knew the questions I would ask. When it came down to it, she affirmed that she came to me because I would tell her the truth.

I agreed. I replied that she would not trust me if I did not tell her the truth. She agreed.

There is something powerful about being trusted with the truth. It speaks life into us even when we don't like it.

There is an excess of dishonesty in our world. It can be an overwhelming thing to address at times. Everyone seems bent on spewing out something less than truth. While the unvarnished truth is not always appreciated, it is still trusted for its value and is worth more than any lie.

As we love one another more, I believe we will find truth is the rule, not the exception. Truth makes way for a seat at any table. Be a Truth Speaker of the House, a representative of truth. Keep telling the truth and others will have no trouble trusting that you will. Integrity speaks for itself.

"As for me, You uphold me in my integrity.
You set me in Your presence." (Psalm 41:12)

"Don't let life change your name."

NAOMI WAS A happy woman. Her name meant Lovely. But she faced the death of her son and the loss of her husband... one thing after another. She actually changed her name to Mara, which means bitter.

Years ago, your name signified what you were or what you did. In our family, we still believe a name is very important. My name Ruth means *"Beautiful Friend."* Ann means *"Grace."* I have always been able to make friends and perhaps being named such helped that process. I continue to grow into grace. Smile.

But Naomi's name was drastic. She had endured so much pain, she couldn't do it anymore. Life changed her name. It wasn't until her daughter-in- law, Ruth, came in and truly became her friend, that she became Naomi again. God used Ruth (beautiful friend) to restore Naomi's spirit.

We can do that for each other.

We can change another's life by the very act of being. Don't let life change your name. Don't let bitterness change your heart. Don't let God's purpose go. Grief and disappointment may wrestle you to the ground. You still have the choice to rise again. Let others bless you. Let others love you, lift you up and challenge you. You are so very precious.

"Do not call me Naomi; call me Mara, for the Almighty has dealt bitterly with me." (Ruth 1:20)

AUGUST 20

"Hope rests in joy."

WHEN YOU CHOOSE where to rest, you are choosing what will affect your life in all areas.

We were traveling cross country and landed in New Mexico. It was way into dark thirty when we had finally had enough. We pulled into a park in pitch dark and laid our seats back to catch some sleep.

We were in that hard drive kind of sleep when the train horn scared every one of us out of any sleep at all.

It was louder than loud. It was early morning and dawn was outlining the tracks. We had parked right beside them!

Another time, we were at camp in the rainy season literally camping in several inches of water. We could actually wring out our thin little mattresses. Between the water, a snake, bugs, and sprained ankles, actually getting some rest was out of the question.

My stories are not unlike many who choose to camp right next to the drama, the overwhelming, the hits and runs and expect to rest. Others are always in such a small but defining crisis, they never really know what life is all about. Choose to rest in hope. Choose to let your tongue know gladness and your heart to know joy. Watch out where you choose to rest, to abide, to dwell, and to live your life.

"Therefore, did my heart rejoice, and my tongue was glad;
moreover also my flesh shall rest in hope." (Acts 2:26)

AUGUST 21

"Nothing in life happens to you. It happens for you." – Joel Osteen

J UST THE OTHER day, I told someone they were having a really hard time because they were in the middle of the story. Middles are hard places.

The yesterday doesn't make sense. The future looks scary. The now just seems frustrating. It takes a great deal of courage and strength to get through a middle.

But if you have ever had surgery, you know the middle of surgery is just part of the healing process. You can't heal without the surgery. It has to be part of the journey. It's for your own healing.

Life doesn't happen to you. It happens for you.

It's not always comfortable. It's not always understandable. But God does not do life without purpose. He conforms us to His will through life. How do you teach your children to do things that are best for them? You do it through aspects of their everyday life. You don't get them and wait till they go to school to learn how to eat with utensils or go potty or be nice or clean up their toys. You do it from day one, right there in their life.

It is to your advantage to thank God for whatever He is doing in your life. You don't have to understand it, to trust that it is the best for you, that God knows what's happening. Trust He is doing His goodness *for* you not *to* you.

"We know all things work together for the good of those who love Him,
who have been called according to His purpose." (Romans 8:28)

AUGUST 22

"Children are our greatest resource on earth."

HOW MANY BABIES do you think will arrive in the world today?

Would you believe the number is about 350,000? That's right, and another 350,000 will arrive tomorrow.

Will they be loved? Will they have enough to eat? The greatest resource we have today is the children God is allowing to enter our world. To be a good steward of our greatest resource, we have to teach our children that they are made in the image of God. The power of that alone will give them a sense of greatness.

When we teach them they were born with a purpose and that it will lead to serving others, they will feel the need to learn what they were built to do.

When we connect them to God they can speak and learn from Him on an everyday basis. It will become ordinary to be extraordinary. When we train them to care for themselves and others, to live a life of royalty in their soul, we give them immeasurable options for a fulfilling and joy filled life.

When we put them in places where they learn and grow and give back, we give them the very essence of truth and love in action. When we train them to walk with God, we teach them that their destiny has meaning and gives them a perfect place in the world. Whatever they face, they can walk through it in wisdom. If they follow God, mercy and grace will follow them and they will dwell in the house of the Lord forever.

May we pray for our 350,000 new gifts coming in today. May we be good stewards of them.

> "Children are a heritage from the Lord; offspring,
> a reward from Him." (Psalm 127:3)

ANN STEWART-PORTER

AUGUST 23

"Primum non nocere… First, do no harm."

A S YOU MAY or may not know, these are words your doctor has likely had to memorize. They are part of the Hippocratic Oath. Medical professionals are asked to take this oath as a promise to those who trust them to provide healing resources.

I think we should all have to raise our right hand, the other on a Bible and speak that oath of honor. We have become a nation, led by leadership, both godly and ungodly, to a throne of self-righteousness.

Before you go to wake up the stubborn child, first do no harm. Before you speak to your angry mate or unfair ex, first, do no harm. Before you reach your friend, first do no harm. Before you get to work, resolve to first, do no harm. Before you speak in church, first, do no harm. When you speak to an employee, first, do no harm.

Already, the very thought may alert your spirit to compassion and worth of honor. Oh, that we may choose health over wealth, peace over war, life over death, just by the attitude of a heart that promises *"To do no harm."*

"For I know the plans I have for you, declares the Lord, plans to prosper you and not to harm you." (Jeremiah 29:11)

AUGUST 24

"Often, God doesn't change your circumstance,
because He is busy…changing your heart."

WE ARE HUMANS. We take in our piece of data and we make a conclusion. We drop off our chart and we have to have answers. We get stuck in the here and now, forgetting there is a there and forever. We beg God to let us out of this place where, usually, we have put ourselves.

We often take on our role as victim, all the while squirming for the why of it. There is a huge lie that says God just wants you to be happy, healthy, wealthy and comfortable. He never said that. Any time God gets to choose between making you comfortable or conforming you to the image of Christ He sent for you, rest confidently you will be conformed first.

As a side note; I don't know if God even does *"comfort zones"* for us down here. He wants us to learn how to trust, manifest goodness, reveal His glory, express His joy, and know how to live as a warrior and a peacemaker.

His rocks and hard places are for growing. And growing in the Lord is conforming. If God hasn't changed that circumstance yet try to thank Him for changing your heart. Chances are good, that's exactly what's happening!

"I will give them a heart to know Me, for I am the Lord,
and they will be My people, and I will be their God,
for they will return to Me with their whole heart." (Jeremiah 24:7)

AUGUST 25

"Part of the joy of letting go is letting the Lord be your consolation."

MY GRANDSON LOVES to wrestle; he will wrestle with just about anyone who will wrestle with him. One thing I have learned about wrestling; there is little standing up.

What are you wrestling with today? Are you trying to find your balance? Are you trying to stand firm in your faith?

As long as we wrestle, there's no glorious victory. There's no standing faith. There's only the sweat and the grime and the falling, the twisting, and the ouch of trying to win.

You have to let go.

You have to surrender to letting go and that helps bring a balance to your positioning. A positioning you can't get if all you are doing is wrestling.

Today, choose to stand in truth.

"When the cares of my heart are many,
your consolations cheer my soul." (Proverbs 94:19)

AUGUST 26

"God chooses us in the fire; God chooses us, and God chooses the fire."

TEMPERED IS A term that means to be conditioned by passing through the fire over and over again, only to be pounded upon between passes. This conditioning produces a stronger and more useful utensil or vessel.

This is a perfect picture of the Christian life. God says in Isaiah 48:10: *"Behold, I have refined thee, but not with silver, I have chosen thee in the furnace of affliction."*

We are chosen in the fire! If you have ever seen a glassblower make the glass purer and purer in the fire, or watched a blacksmith fashion a horseshoe in his furnace, you know what this means. It takes heat to purify us, and it takes heat to fashion us into the servants that God intends for us to be.

Trust God through the flames, knowing that it is His work being done in you, that you may one day be able to stand in the full glory of God's presence, the place of absolute, pure, sweet Joy.

"That the trial of your faith, being much more precious than of gold that perisheth, though it be tried with fire, might be found unto praise and honor and glory at the appearing of Jesus Christ." (1 Peter 1:7)

AUGUST 27

"There are only two ways to live your life, one
is as though nothing is a miracle.
The other is as though everything is a miracle." – Albert Einstein

WHILE YOU ARE reading this, your heart is circulating five quarts of blood through 100,000 miles of veins, arteries, and capillaries. While all that is going on, you're on a planet that is traveling 67,000 miles per hour, while spinning at a speed of 1,000 miles per hour. It would boggle the mind to list the things happening in our brains at the same time.

Miracles? YOU are one!

Miracles? Everywhere. Every day. Every minute. All the time.

Every day, people are killing themselves because they don't see the miracle of who they are. People are hiding behind so much worthlessness, because they missed the memo. While I've only given you one small part of the human body's wonderfulness, just imagine picking any part of you to study. I guarantee you would see God in any part you looked. It's time to look at our children and say as if it were part of their name, *"You are a miracle!"*

It's time to thank our spouses and families and friends for the miracles they bring to our lives every day. It's time to see yourself in the vision of the image of God as a stunning miracle of divine design. After hundreds of years the human heart and body remain the miraculous mystery of all time.

So every morning, you can look in the mirror and thank God for the miracle of you!

"I praise You because I am fearfully and wonderfully made. Wonderful are Your works; my soul knows it well." (Psalm 139:14)

ANN STEWART-PORTER

AUGUST 28

"Joy is letting others have their space to grow."

THERE SHE IS, all dressed in her finest expectations. He has already fallen once, his shoes scuffed with insecurity. She rounds him out, with her invisible pen and checklist. He didn't see it coming. He went on about the business of wishing and hoping and grinding his teeth. He felt the crunch of the first egg shell and lifted his foot away. He learned to walk that peculiar way, because there was no other way to keep her tethered to him.

He had thought love was freer, more selfless inclined. He should have bought a ticket to a shrine. They would have appreciated him more. He didn't know how to make it different.

Worst of all, he really loved her. He does try to please her. He was not born to be cut down at every turn. He cannot breathe in critical air. He loses his ability to find himself without respect. His backbone becomes his wishbone.

If you are the person he is living with and you are bent keeping that critical spirit, you should know something right now. Eventually they leave. But at least, he can breathe again.

"Know the love of Christ, which passeth knowledge,
that you might be filled with all the fullness of God." (Ephesians 3:19)

AUGUST 29

"Words don't make dreams. God with effort creates His best in us."

H E WAS EXPECTING a little boy. He was expecting a football player. He pictured himself on the field, yelling and pacing and giving those Dad cheers.

Then the doctor came in to say his son was "different."

They had to buy a wheelchair.

But his boy loved music. He seemed to be special in his ability to play the piano and the trumpet. He made the marching band!

One night the marching band was in the middle of the field, putting on their show. There Dad stood, thinking how he would have taught his son to play ball and proud of him he would be. Yet, here they were, on the same field of his dreams, and the true teacher was his son.

He stood there almost unbearably proud of his son, watching as he played the trumpet in the night.

Can we ever take for granted a God with a dream for us bigger than ours could ever be?

He can twist your dream till you hardly recognize it as you had first seen it. Place your dreams in the hand of God and trust Him to do as He wishes. You will find yourself almost unbearably full of Joy just to be a part of it.

"For the dream comes through much effort and the voice of a fool through many words." (Ecclesiastes 5:3)

AUGUST 30

"God does not call us to success. He calls us to faithfulness." – Mother Teresa

WHAT A POWERFUL clarity comes into our being when we grasp this truth! What unmistakable transformations come into our lives when we allow the truth of our assignment here on this earth to penetrate the layers of lives we are fed.

Living in faithfulness removes so much of the cerebral coronaries of our illusions. Giving up the venue of performance and trading up to real value takes a strong creature of less habit. It takes a truth you embrace in the wholeness of your entire being. It can never be just an annual event or a get to it someday sort of thing.

Faith and faithfulness are pieces of the heart with eternity in view.

Faithfulness is a flow…and good and natural spilling of true success that has been grounded in the beauty of being all you were intended to be.

Do not miss your calling to be faithful to know the Joy of obedience over all else.

"Let us hold fast the confession of our hope without wavering, for He who promised is faithful." (Hebrews 10:23)

AUGUST 31

"Truth changes everything."

I T WAS THE dark of the night when I went to Mama insisting I was late to school. She said it wasn't even morning, but I would have none of the reasons it wasn't time for school. I was fully convinced in my 7-year old mind, that it was time. The dark argument wasn't convincing. It was usually dark when I got up. Why wasn't Mama able to understand this? I argued.

Finally, she put me in the car and we drove by my school. It was dark there, too. The doors were locked. No one was there. No one was standing on the stairs or playing on the playground. There was the truth right before my eyes. I went home and went to bed and waited for morning to come.

What a spiritual lesson! Sometimes, in the dark, we can get very disorientated. We can believe something because we want to believe. We can feel frustrated that others can't see what's going on. When we are shown the truth, it makes us capable of finding out what wasn't true. **Truth requires facing the reality, not changing the reality.** And that changes everything.

"For their sakes, I sanctify myself, that they also might be sanctified through the truth." (John 17:19)

SEPTEMBER 1

"There are two basic groups of people; those who toss
coins in the fountain and those who fish them out."

WHICH ONE ARE you? Is tossing in the coin and dreaming big just part of who you are? Would you rather stick to the doing the work and getting something done? I mean, why waste time dreaming when there's work to be done. Funny thing is these two different kinds of people usually get married! That can really be quite advantageous if...one of you thinks the other one has amazing dreams and they want to help you accomplish the very best in your life...or if one of you thinks the other is such a great practical asset to your home.

Of course, many people just fight over why the dreamer dreams or why the worker bee has no vision. Or why the dreamer can't pull their weight in the work of life. Or why the boring one lives for tedious mundane things. It's so much perspective! Dreamers need doers. Doers need dreamers. Really, if you can find a way to lock in on the goodness of the others' gift, you might just enjoy dancing in the moonlight in the fountain!

Share your life.

"Having gifts differing according to the grace
that is given us, let us use them." (Romans 12:6-8)

SEPTEMBER 2

"When you are most discouraged; encourage."

T HE HUGE BODY of a quarterback stood bigger than usual. With broken ribs and a broken hand, bundled like a mummy, he was poised for play. When asked why he felt he had to play, he said he would rather play in pain than sit on the sidelines in pain.

While I can't vouch for the intelligence of that decision, the message is worth the keep. Whenever you are in pain, there is a tendency to step out of life. There is a grief you want everyone to share. You feel like you won't be able to get past this hurt. But there is healing in resting, getting help and staying in the game.

Even if you have to play in pain, stay in the game. Reach out to others at places you most hurt yourself. When you are most discouraged, try your best to pen a note to a person you know is discouraged. Or drop some homemade muffins by to a friend who is hurting.

Resist the temptation to lather yourself in pity and deserving cuddling. Yes, take your time to rest, to process, to bandage up, to take your medicine and talk it through to acceptance. But remember that you cannot just make a life out of what was or is at any given moment.

Be willing to try and play, even in your pain. It will help change your focus, give you good distractions and give you a different perspective. Never give up too soon.

"Let us think of ways to motivate one another
to acts of love and good works." (Hebrews 10:24)

SEPTEMBER 3

"None are so empty as those who are full of themselves."

I OFTEN HEAR PEOPLE say they feel empty. This generally follows a conversation of total self-absorption. They had an affair because their spouse wasn't enough. Their children have been taken from them because of some poor choice. They have realized how damaging their lifestyle *"that didn't hurt nobody"* actually hurt more than they thought. They are quitting to find themselves, only they never found themselves at all.

One mother wants me to help a son get off the drugs she supplies him. Another wants me to keep them from choosing the life she chose. Oh, we are so full of ourselves! Wise living is just a choice away. Yet, the selfish pursuits we have never weaned have become lives that are empty and trying.

Today, let us begin to consider a life of fullness, goodness, giving, changing the world, encouraging, strengthening.

I guarantee if you spend your life with eternity in view, you will fill it up with the richest of living. You will be "emptied out" and you will have no call to choose lesser living. You can be full of purpose or empty of goodness. Live rich.

"The pride of man will be humbled and the loftiness of men will be abased; the Lord alone will be exalted." (Isaiah 2:17)

SEPTEMBER 4

"To reach God, you only need to humble yourself and call Him."

HAVE YOU EVER wondered why churches have steeples? Some of them are so high, you would think they were trying to reach the heavens.

They were!

The pervading opinion was that the higher the steeple, the closer to God. Oh my, we can certainly find ways to invent our own religiosity. Nowadays it isn't just steeples; it's a hoard of enlightenments. So we can't laugh too hard or too loud at the misguided.

If you ask me how to get close to me I will tell you to spend time with me. Ask me things. Listen to me.

A steeple won't get you closer to God anymore than it would get me closer to you. A church can be a wonderful place to learn about God but you are responsible for the amount of time you spend with Him. He is *always* available.

He says to call on Him and he will answer. So go ahead, call on Him.

"The Lord is near to all who call upon Him,
to all who call on Him in truth." (Psalm 145:18)

SEPTEMBER 5

"God is still in the details."

I HAD BEEN ARGUING with God the better part of two weeks when I finally surrendered. I wasn't all that sure of what that would mean. I just knew it was time. I did a five-mile walk through the countryside each morning. I used this time to chat with God.

I had decided I wanted something that was not in God's will for me at that time. I squawked about it like the proverbial old wet hen. Everything seemed a little quiet on the God side until I finally gave it up. I had insisted God show me He had heard me. He remained quiet. I reiterated my trust that whatever He wanted, I wanted too.

No, I didn't *"feel"* better. That's not what faith is about.

I got back home and went to hear a debate a local pastor was giving near the University. He was proficient and powerful in debate; great fun to hear. It was a big crowd and a big building. The first words out of his mouth were exactly what I had been praying just a few hours earlier. Exactly. Like word for word, you must have been right behind me, exactly. I shivered. I got it. God had heard me. He knew my heart. He understood. Oh, it was sweet!

To know Him is to love Him. Several years later, I got exactly what I wanted. I appreciated it all the more because God was in the details. He's in yours, too.

"The steps of a good man are established by the Lord,
and He delights in His ways." (Psalm 37:23)

SEPTEMBER 6

"You were made perfectly to be loved; and surely I have loved you,
the idea of you, my whole life long." – Elizabeth Barrett Browning

WHEN YOU START looking for someone you want to love in hopes of being loved back, there is an idea floating around in your head. It goes something like I want them to have a sense of humor like my Dad, I want them to cook like my Mama, I hope they have green eyes, and I hope they can sing. And there's pieces of your idea of love that has come from the time you were first feeling love.

Inside all of us is that place of creating love from what we know. If you have not experienced love in terms of family or circumstances or such, you may well face an error in your view of love. You may mistake something for love that isn't true, maybe even dangerous; your hunger for love may keep you from getting what you really want.

I suggest to clients to think about this before they start looking. Doesn't matter if it's your first time looking or your third time's the charm ideal. This will take time. Get to know yourself is a process. But you are worth it. Once you feel ready, practice and see. Take your Top Ten list and read it every day and by all means be open to anything not on your list, but don't be so open minded that your brains fall out and you fall in. Wait perfectly for you were meant to be perfectly loved in the whole of all imperfections.

"Wait for the Lord, be strong, and take heart,
and He will strengthen your heart." (Psalm 27:14)

"Use your pain as fuel."

KNOWING HOW TO use your energy in battle is a challenge all of us face. The kind of battle doesn't matter nor the strength of your attire and weapons, nor your experience.

It's always about *this* time, *this* struggle, *this* growth, *this* trust, and *this* sweet surrender to God. There is no rising up in strength without first lying down before Him. The battle is never about you. The battle is about what God is working in you.

Too often as Christians we go running headlong into a battle without even inquiring if it's the battle God wants us to fight. When we choose our own battles, there is no lesson learned, and no growth. Don't worry, God has plenty of battles lined up for you; just make sure they are the battles He has planned for you, and not battles in which you find yourself using your own strength and fight for things you want for yourself, instead of the stronger person He is planning on making you.

We will all face battles. Learn to surrender to God, and the victory and the Joy will always be yours.

"Fight the good fight of the faith. Take hold
of the eternal life to which you
were called when you made your good confession." (1 Timothy 6:12)

SEPTEMBER 8

"Don't die in the valley, with the mountain in clear view."

I BELIEVE THE BIGGEST disappointment in life is a disappointment in our-self. There can be any number of reasons for being disappointed with ourselves. Sometimes our expectations have been set too high. Sometimes we have made bad, damaging choices.

These days of such disappointments are hard days of contemplation. It can be a deep, agonizing time in our life. Some people find themselves there and they stay there; whining and complaining and forever seeking helpers and healers and anyone who will give them the attention they crave. This is not wisdom.

Wisdom is taking time to make an honest evaluation of the disappointment and then using it to grow, clarify, and make the necessary changes, and then use the experience to help others.

We must not give up in the valley with a clear view of the mountain. A healthy trust in God always moves past disappointments and reaches for the Joy laid before us.

"Therefore encourage one another
and build each other up." (1 Thessalonians 5:11)

SEPTEMBER 9

"The more you lose yourself in something bigger than yourself, the more energy you will have." – Norman Vincent Peale

IT WAS NOT uncommon for me to be tired in the morning when I was teaching school. With the two o'clock feedings of a medically fragile daughter and the health issues I tackled, morning wasn't good some days. Still, I remember getting up and getting to school. Before l knew it, the kids had energized me.

I remember we would drive 15 hours into Mexico and l would wonder how we would build a house the next several days. But it was so energizing to be caught up in the glory of giving.

I think of mamas rising to feed babies, soldiers rising to the call, people all over the world who will be giving out of that great place inside themselves. It was and is true of anyone who feels they are doing something bigger than themselves. It is true that love and passion are energizing.

It is a wonder to stretch out on the table of life and give yourself beyond yourself. Until you get there, l don't know if you can really say you have given. To give something of yourself is to lose something of yourself in the sweetest way. It is an incandescent light of divine pleasure. Energize yourself and give!

"Whoever seeks to keep his life will lose it and whoever loses his life will preserve it." (Luke 17:33)

SEPTEMBER 10

"A trained conscience gives you a higher power."

DO YOU WANT to know if something you are doing is wrong for you? Look at what you have to justify in order to get it. Listen to what you say to yourself in order to convince yourself it is right. Listen to the sound of your thoughts trying to sift through all the reasons you should not, hoping to find a supportive purpose.

If it's right, you won't need to figure out how to make that feel good. If it's right in your heart, you don't have to work so hard to make it work. You may ask me how I am so very wise on this subject. Smile. Because, I have been at this place more than I will ever admit.

There's always work, but if you are so busy figuring out how to make it work, you have fallen into the trap of manipulation. You are losing the benefit of all the goodness you could be experiencing.

You are trading peace of mind for pieces of a mind.

I have also seen a great many folks like me who did a great job convincing themselves something they wanted is right. One of my favorites is that whatever is in question is a *"gray area."* I ask them if they realize gray is still a color too. Sometimes, it's just faded black!

Hold yourself to a higher calling, a higher honor, a higher expectation than you do anyone else. You don't have to live with my conscience, but you sure do have to live with yours.

"Solid spiritual food is for the mature, who because of practice have their senses trained to discern good and evil." (Hebrews 5:14)

SEPTEMBER 11

"Spiritual shielding begins with spiritual affirmation."

LIVING A SPIRITUAL affirming life begins with the need to *"settle up"* with your Creator Redeemer. You need no spirit guides. He gives you a Holy Spirit. Any other spirit guide is not a figure of the True. They are unnecessary and crowd your life. God is simplicity in power.

That is also why there are not more gods and goddesses, as in other religions. You do not need more. You need less. Once established, you will want to abide in the flow of peace and good, right and joy.

You grow on the basis of your Creator's design. He says focus on Him is the key to peace.

The Holy Spirit convicts, guides, and comforts. This is intimacy with Christ. This means you will regard certain things as off limits for your spirit, just as many athletes do for performance sake. You will be in a mode of consistent conversation with your Creator. You will be mindful of toxic thoughts, invaders, emotions, choices and people.

The more you shield, the more vulnerable you will become. Jesus describes it as dying to self. The ego prevents us from growth and goodness. This is no different. You are now responsible for your own joy. Choose to live a spiritually affirming life.

"The Lord gives strength to His people and
blesses them with peace." (Psalm 29:11)

SEPTEMBER 12

"How is one to live a moral and compassionate
existence when one finds darkness
not only in one's culture but within oneself?
There are simply no answers to some
of the great pressing questions. You continue to live them out, making your
life a worthy expression of leaning into the light." – Barry Lopez

I F SOMEONE LOOKED at your light, up close and personal,
would it be enough to light their path?

We have a great deal less heroes than ever before. We have lies that
surface from the most unexpected places. We are in direct need of light.
It is getting darker out there. We can't answer all the reasons why the
dark has come often and the light seems dim at times. We can only
know that living a life that expresses our leaning in to the light, will
open more roads for courage and faith to take a stand.

Love and light have always overcome the darkness, even though
time feels like it's running out. The questions will not go away, but you
won't feel the need to have them all. Live by lightly leaning into the
light. It's how the Joy gets in.

"I am the Light of the world; he who follows Me will not walk
in the darkness, but will have the light of life." (John 8:12)

SEPTEMBER 13

"In every moment, something sacred is at stake." – Rabbi Heschel

WE ARE, AS a collective group, not as aware as we might believe ourselves to be. If we were truly aware and honoring the sacred, all hungry children would be fed, abortion and abuse shelters would be closed down, peace treaties would stand for peace rather than manipulation, war would be without casualties, the outcast would know only the beauty of love, the elderly would be messages for the youth, churches would not be in buildings, hospitals would be more preventive experiences and perhaps marriages would be 90/100 divorce rate.

Isn't it fascinating just to imagine what could be if we actually put the sacred to the test? Fear would hold no one hostage. Joy would be like a waterfall all through humanity. Generosity would be so extravagant; there would be no reason for taxes or social security.

Are you thinking with me yet? Or are you willing to grasp the quality of life the sacred can give us? In the context of the everyday, in very practical ways, we seem to tell our sacred to find another place to shine. But it has to be ordinary to be extraordinary! That was the plan from the time that Christ was born not in the kingdom, but in a nasty, smelly, not so sacred manager. An animal feeding bowl! Well, that does seem odd. Embrace the sacred in your life today.

"Don't give dogs what is sacred, don't throw pearls to pigs. If you do, they may trample you underfoot and attack you." (Matthew 7:6)

"Pray that your loneliness may spur you into finding something to live for, that is great enough to die for." – Dag Hammarskjöld

I OFTEN HEAR PEOPLE say they are lonely or bored or both. So many of us are so busy and accustomed to being entertained when we are not busy that that we have lost the ability to find the gifts inside ourselves and to use them.

One day someone mentioned to me how lonely it was to be divorced, but I knew her long before her divorce and I reminded her she was lonely in her marriage as well.

Another gal, who literally owns just about anything and everything money can buy, but very little that it can't, asked me if she would always be unhappy because that was simply her nature.

I have always attributed my delight in being alone to being the oldest of six kids. The truth is that I value it because I have always had someone to love. I have not been lonely in the traditional sense. I do miss people and am lonely for them, but there is no feeling of being withdrawn and without because I have so much to live for. There is always something to do.

I have always been this way and I have come to realize how much of a blessing it is to always be reaching out; to love, to give, and to enjoy life by choosing to continually fill it with meaning and purpose.

I agree with Dag; find a whole lot of living to fill your whole life!

"Teach us to number our days that we may get
a heart of wisdom." (Psalm 90:12)

SEPTEMBER 15

"Make the most of your regrets; never smother your sorrow,
but tend and cherish it till it comes to have
a separate and integral interest.
To regret deeply is to live afresh." – Henry David Thoreau

YOU KNOW THE latest thinking is to NOT regret anything you do. Some of the big media persons have said it has made them who they are, so they don't regret anything. I understand that but I think Henry David has it in perspective.

While regrets are inevitable, so is the sorrow from choices that grieve our spirit. To not honor their place in our lives is to be arrogant and selfish. It should be a place of growth and learning and letting it be the ground that moves around us, allowing us to walk more free in the joys of that which we do not regret.

Regrets play an integral part in our growth as human beings. They may carry more weight than is real or less attention than is needful, but regret is part of our lives and loves. If you have ever had a deep dire regret, you know that to meet mercy is to live anew; more alive, more aware of goodness.

Naturally, the way we get the most out of our regrets is to learn every possible thing we can from them. And to go on Joyfully. Cherish all that you are.

"I do not consider that I have made it on my own. But one
thing I do: Forgetting what lies behind and striving forward
to what lies ahead. I press toward the goal for the prize of the
upward call of God in Christ Jesus." (Philippians 3:13)

SEPTEMBER 16

"Are you being led by your spirit or by your wounds?"

S HE DIDN'T STEAL because she was hungry. She didn't steal because she was poor, though money was sometimes an issue. She stole because deep down inside she had been wounded. She felt betrayed, abandoned, invisible, and cheated on for so long.

Sure, big business is often a form of legalized thievery, but sometimes when you see a shoplifter on the news, there is a reason beyond the obvious. They want others to see and to hurt for them. They want to know they are not alone.

There are many people out there who do bad things because they are hurting and need attention. They don't even know why they are stealing or doing other bad things and they can't explain it. They attempt to justify their behavior and come up short.

If you find yourself trying to justify your wrong, it might be a sign you need to listen to your true self and ask what's wrong.

If you are struggling with emotional pain, betrayal, loss, or something worse, work those feelings into submission. Bring them before the Lord and put them on the altar of submission to Him. Stop making those little adjustments in your thinking to justify sin.

Never let your pain ruin your future. Go to God and let Him cleanse you white as snow, and begin again to pursue the Joy.

"The Lord is close to the brokenhearted and saves those who are crushed in spirit." (Psalms 34:18)

SEPTEMBER 17

"Love that touches in a healthy way speaks to the soul." - Ann Stewart Porter

HAVING A CHILD that could not hear or see or speak words taught is a lot. One of the things we learned to do was to speak into our daughter Rachel's cheek. She never learned but a few words, but she always tried to imitate the way we said something.

With our lips pressed to her little cheek we would slowly speak words or sing a song. She was highly attentive even though she mostly didn't understand. What she did understand was that she was deeply loved, that we were there for her, and that she was in our heart.

Healthy touching teaches many things and expresses even more.

Today, speak into the cheeks of your children and into the lives of your loved ones. Make sure they know what the words and touch of love feel like. And when you are done with that today, do it again tomorrow.

Love that touches is a wonderful way to speak. It's a reminder of the great way our Heavenly Father loves us!

"The Lord your God is with you, He is mighty to save.
He will take great delight in you, He will quiet you with His love,
He will rejoice over you with singing." (Zephaniah 3:17)

"If our children were to grow up truthful, they must be taught by those who had a regard for the truth; and not just a casual regard, but a delicate regard. On this point we are adamant."
- Amy Carmichael (Gold Cord)

AMY RAN AN orphanage. It was hard and demanding and lovely work. When interviewing for workers, she would ask them if they minded hard things. She also asked if they could be lonely. She always questioned their faith and integrity. She had long come to know that for a child to understand truth, they must see it lived out before them.

I recall a recent conversation with a father who had disciplined his son for dishonesty. In a very short conversation with me, I counted four lies! He had a casual regard for the truth. I found it frustrating. I am sure his son is confused. I also know this parental behavior is in no way unusual today. Most teenagers who ever come my way are pretty open about the fact that their parents say one thing, but do another.

Have a *"delicate regard"* toward integrity today. Don't frustrate your children by being untruthful in your parenting. None of us appreciate two-faced people.

Hold yourself to a higher standard. You've got great responsibilities! You are sharing with the next generation what the world should be. Don't think too lowly of yourself.

"I obtain understanding from Your precepts;
therefore, I have every false way." (Psalm 119:104)

SEPTEMBER 19

*"The beginning of love is to let those we love be perfectly
themselves, and not to twist them to fit our own image. Otherwise
we love only the reflection of ourselves we find in them."*
- Thomas Merton

MANY HAVE A great tendency to fall in love, blindly assessing what they see in another as so much like themselves, the love makes sense. But once they have settled in, they find the *"right one"* seems sort of wrong. Without realizing it, they have begun to make another person themselves!

We vehemently deem that not true, but it is so pervasive, we hardly see its sprouts. You think she should drive like you. He should pick up like you. She should be nicer to your mother. He should discipline the kids your way. She should speak her mind like you do. If you want to experience joy in a relationship, you will need to love them as they were created.

Your expectation may be very wrong. It just seems right to you. Or your ideas of happy may be unattainable until you give up some unrealistic perfection. Let your love grow in the beauty and wholeness of each self-represented. The real thing is always better than the reflection anyway.

*"Let the words of my mouth and the meditation
of my heart be acceptable in
Your sight, O Lord, my Rock and my Redeemer."* (Psalm 19:14)

SEPTEMBER 20

*"The misguided opinions of others will not breach
the borders of my self-worth."* – Dodinsky

S O, WHAT DID you hear that could have hurt your self-esteem?
You weren't as pretty as your sister.

You can't play ball like your brother.

You don't know how to handle money.

You couldn't possibly think you could be a doctor.

You have a speech impediment.

You have never done that before.

What makes you think you could do that now?

Who picks out your clothes? Why is your hair always in your face?
Do you ever think?

I bet you have a list an hour long. It can be tough to hear. Take some time to readjust your spirit when your borders have been attacked. Be responsible for what you receive.

You determine what is really true about you.

Misguided views can come from anywhere. They sting, but only you can let them damage you, keeping you chained to someone's opinion rather than knowing yourself. Today, determine you will be free to notice the beautiful thing in you, the delight of your own wisdom, the discoveries that make for loving yourself. Misguided opinions need not apply.

*"All that the Father gives Me will come to Me and the one who
comes to Me I will certainly not cast out."* (John 6:37)

*"Should you chance to meet an adversary in your day,
overcome them with love for it is the best way."*

THIS SOUNDS SO sweet and simple. It even sounds grand and glorious. But the minute you put it in working gloves at the barb wire of life, look for its striking pose. It will cock its head at you, daring you to do what you think you cannot do. It will sputter and spit, like it's hardly ready to let go of that thing it cannot. To live a life of love and joy, peace and blessing, you will have to learn to overcome all things with love. You cannot know how much you will win if you do. It must be done to know. A pretty poem, a vision to see, is not at all like wrestling in the mud and the mire of pain.

But there, in that grime and grunt of life, is where you win the sweetest fruits of love. Anyone can live the loveable. Go ahead. Your adversary is expecting you to fight.

*"Above all, keep loving one another earnestly
since love covers a multitude of sins."* (1 Peter 4:8)

SEPTEMBER 22

"God is good, and God is good at being God." – Lysa Terkeurst

IN YET ANOTHER grief, we bear the burden of speaking enough hope into our children, to keep them from bitter retreat. We must be mindful that while fear is real and evil is too near, our children must know God has not stepped away from us. He is in these times with us. He is allowing these days for a purpose we may not understand now, but He has proven He can be trusted.

They will listen to our talk. They will hear our anger. They will read our faces, sense our emotions, try to find a place they feel safe.

We must indeed build a shelter where we talk and listen, where we can bear their burdens and lift them away as best we can.

We can teach them to pray, to meditate on the beautiful words of Scripture, to sing and praise in the night, to believe people are many times better than we appreciate. We can remind them of God's goodness.

This is a good time to teach compassion. These times show us that we must become soldiers of goodness. We are responsible for the energy we bring to the world. The fears we give to them are often the ones given to us. These become generational curses.

Today, bend your ear to their heart. End your day with Joy and with truth. We prevail when we trust God. We win when we love.

"Teach me to do Your will, for You are my God;
let Your good Spirit lead me on level ground." (Psalm 143:10)

SEPTEMBER 23

"The colors of the reflection depend on what
you planted." – Ann Stewart Porter

I HAVE HAD SOME beautiful backyards. Some came with ponds and little bridges, pergola covered in roses, swings in trees, views to cherish, apple trees and lilac bushes big and tall. Some were tremendous work. So, when we moved into a fresh house with grass, a fence and a view, we kind of liked the *"less is more"* idea. We haven't planted much. We haven't built any bridges or waterfalls or ponds or pergolas.

Maybe someday.

Maybe not.

What I do know, is that if we don't consciously go buy plants or trees or wood for the bridges or rocks for the waterfall, it is not going to just happen. Or if I plant a rose bush, I will not be getting carrots to eat. We won't wake up some morning and look out back and marvel at how a pond grew overnight. We would be silly to sit around and think that would happen that way.

But many people live their life just like that! They don't invest in good planting or good design or good at all. Everything is just a careless plot where any old weed can come in, any bug can eat, and storm can uproot. Their colors aren't true. They say one thing and do another.

They aren't intentional. They are maintaining. Yet, they are surprised things get in such a mess. They act like they didn't know their choices affected their life. Be mindful of what you plant today. Live intentionally.

"Be steadfast, unmovable, always abounding in the work of the Lord, for you know your labor is not in vain in the Lord." (1 Corinthians 15:58)

"We can't be afraid of change. You may feel very
secure in the pond that you are in;
but if you never venture out of it, you will
never know that there is such a thing
as an ocean; a sea. Holding onto something
that is good for you now may be
the very reason why you don't have something better." – C. JoyBell

CLARICE WAS STUCK in the middle. She had married a very strong personality. She worked for a power hungry man. She was stuck in her pond where she knew all her colors, the residents of her place and the things she could see in her safe, good world. She convinced herself for more than 20 years that this was just the life she had to live.

It just was. It gave her fear, cancer, anxiety, loneliness and insecurity, but she held on because she was afraid to change. The pond then became a trap. Until…she learned she could be brave and strong.

She had once come from an ocean, but it had been a long time since she swam in it. She had never swum well. Now, she's beaten cancer. She left that place that kept her in her place. She's got a new job with a boss who thinks she hung the moon.

She's changing like autumn in New England.

I have a feeling she would never have gotten anywhere she wanted to go until she let go of where she was. Give change a chance to do something amazing in your life.

"Seek ye first the Kingdom of God and His righteousness,
and all these things shall be added unto you." (Matthew 6:33)

"We need a witness to our lives. There's a billion people on the planet."

I MEAN, WHAT DOES any one person's life really mean? But when you marry, you're promising to care about everything; the good things, the bad things, the terrible things, and the mundane things; all of it, all of the time, every day. You're saying, *"Your life will not go unnoticed because I will notice it. Your life will not go unwitnessed because I will be your witness."* (From Shall We Dance?) How true.

Marriage may often keep us in the guardianship of another. When the world forgets the mate, we will have been there noticing the value of their life and their story; noting their journey. I believe out of the many things love does for us, witnessing the value of our existence is one of the greater. It happens from the time our eyes first meet that person and it becomes all too real that we have been blessed. Everything seems more real! Us, them, the air we breathe. No longer will we die unnoticed, unloved or without the beauty of our being seen, touched and felt.

Never take the witness of your life for granted. It is true of any marriage and anyone who comes to love us. They are our witnesses. They make our life true. We are witnesses for each other that our life mattered. We give us the promise of never letting the world forget there was an incredible, fantastical you. Be a witness for someone today.

"Therefore, since we are surrounded by such a great cloud of witnesses, let us throw off everything that hinders and sin that entangles." (Hebrews 12:1)

SEPTEMBER 26

"Extraordinary just means God is involved."

I T WAS JUST a bush; straggly and squatty sitting in the middle of a desert-like place. There was no significance to it, no award winning color or showy fragrance. We wouldn't even know a thing about it, nor think anything of it, except for the day its Creator came by. God had a message his servant Moses needed to hear.

God often uses things and people we don't expect Him to use. You might remember the story in Genesis. God spoke out of a burning bush. God told Moses to *"Take off his shoes."*

If you were going to hear from God, you might think it would be something bigger you heard, right? I think God actually waited before saying the other part. He waited for Moses to see, hear and do first. That kind of faith marks a man.

Maybe you feel unnoticed and of little value in the great desert of life today. Be prepared. You might be the next *"burning bush"* God chooses to use. God may need your limbs and your place to give a message to another person He wants to use and bless. God uses the ordinary for the extraordinary. He always has. He always will.

"Take off your sandals, for the place where
you are standing is holy ground." (Acts 7:33)

SEPTEMBER 27

"What's the big joy about a Savior?"

I BELIEVE IN GOD. I believe in Jesus. I believe Jesus is my Savior. I know not everyone believes this, but I do. I have heard that this is an issue for many. While I don't believe Jesus is "still on the cross," I do believe He rose from the dead. But it's a question I think might need some contemplation. Want to know the big deal about us needing a Savior? Because a lot of people don't think they need a Savior.

There is a great deal of "enlightened" thought that says things like:

"There is no sin."

"Therefore there is no need of a Savior."

"We are our own savior."

"We are god."

"There is no hell."

What a suave little lie. I just noticed these same sweet liars have a new course on how to get rid of your guilt and shame. To which I ask, *"Why would you have guilt or shame if there is no sin?"*

I would also like to know how to define the rape and slaughter of children and other unspeakables because *"mistake"* doesn't cover that for me.

Until there is no more war, murder, anger, fear, evil, pain, abuse, self-consumption, materialistic greed, religious dogma and dishonesty in humanity, we will need a Savior. Even if there was no hell, we would need a Savior.

Even if heaven was not real, we would need a Savior. I can't imagine any other way we would know these things, if not for a God who was made flesh. And that's the big deal about a Savior.

"The light shined in the darkness and
the darkness did not comprehend it." (John 1:5)

ANN STEWART-PORTER

"Fill up your child's capacity to care by surrounding them with those they feel responsible to bless." – Ann Stewart Porter

THERE'S A FUN show that teaches good lessons. This one features a grandson and his new girlfriend. The Grandson brings his date to pick up the fishing poles and Grandpa becomes their chaperone! He takes them out on his fishing boat. Grandpa talks about not having sex or getting venereal diseases.

They end up having the girlfriend for dinner. Grandpa prays for them to stay pure and have a great life as part of the dinner prayer. He says if more Grandpas did this sort of thing, there would not be so much... well, you get the picture. At least, I hope you do.

If you want to raise kids, one of your best bets is in the number of people watching out for them. Sure, that can be annoying from time to time, but it can also be very helpful. If you are a kid who knows they will have to answer to ten people when they mess up, they are going to think about it a lot harder than the kids who have nobody that cares what they do.

In the end, my thought as the show closed out was not how lucky they were to be wealthy, but how rich to be surrounded with such love and care. Every child should be so blessed.

"When someone has been given much, much will be required in return." (Luke 12:48)

SEPTEMBER 29

"The secret joy of quality time is being there."

I WAS WRITING AN article on quality time. I was trying to explain it to my grandson, Dylan. He finally nodded his head and said, *"Oh, I get it. Just be there."*

Yep, he got it. Wherever you are, just be THERE. Quit being somewhere and thinking about yesterday. Quit sitting there and thinking about what you need to do tomorrow instead of being in the moment.

As they say let your presence be your present.

There is a great deal to be said for those who can live without baggage or a baggage claim. It's hard to be "there" when there's so much to be done and so much you want to do. But to embrace the moment just as it is, is to give yourself an extra special treat.

I struggle with this concept because I am always planning or catching up. To stop and grab the moment as it is given often feels more like an interruption. I know interruptions can often be divine appointments. So, I want to learn how to JUST BE THERE wherever I find myself. I'll meet you there.

"Love the Lord your God with all your heart, soul and strength; repeat them to your children. Talk to them when you're at home or away, when you lie down or get up." (Deuteronomy 6:5-8)

SEPTEMBER 30

"Joy is learning to be real."

S HE COULDN'T SAY it out loud. Everyone would know. Everyone would look deeper and find that she was real. Then they would think she was just like them. She couldn't bear that thought. She had worked too hard and too long to be sitting on the wall above others. It was a facade she worshipped with paints and fixings the carnival brought to town. If she felt herself slipping, she asked for another prescription. She could not bear the light. It made her feel not right.

She's been this way since she first tried on the mask and found it worked. It blocked out most of the light. The rest she could diffuse. So, she literally began to shrivel up into this tiny form. At first, it was just to keep her wanted among the unwantables. She needed them to like her, but she did not need their touch. That's what she said to herself.

What became of her was the worst of all perfections yearned. She got what she wanted only to find she hated it. But she was stuck there. She felt condemned to die there. As far as l know, she's still there. Soon, she will be little more than the worm at the bottle end. She will be dying in plain sight. I wish she had wanted to live harder. I wish she had wanted the Joy of the truth.

"I have no greater joy than to hear that
my children are walking in truth." (3 John 1:4)

OCTOBER 1

"Tell your stories. They matter."

I T'S A STORY of mercy, grace, goodness, and God's healing of
my life.

"So Grandma, you were really unconscious?" Dylan asked.

"Yes, but Grandma is good. I am all fine now."

"Well, thank God for that!" Dylan replied as he smiled.

"Yes indeed; thank God indeed."

Stories we tell our children and our children's children are pieces of
their heritage, both physical and spiritual; they are their generational
gold. They are the treasures of yesterday. Some people are stingy with
their gold. Some of us don't have the delight of remembering those
stories.

I am a lover of stories. I wrote our life story to leave a heritage. These
stories build value in what a person comes to be. They speak through
us. They speak of God's faithfulness; of bravery to embrace. I hope
we will cherish the honor of our stories. I hope we will create generous
gifts to our tomorrow, for it builds a sweet security. Tell your stories;
they matter.

"Tell it to your children, and let them tell it to their children." (Joel 1:3)

OCTOBER 2

"For faith to count, we must trust."

IN DEEP STRESS, short term memory is often lost. For a time, remembering will be difficult. Panic attacks lure us to the overwhelming of our fears. We are deep sea diving and can't get our breath. All we want is air! We don't care where or how we get it; we just know we have to get it now. Thinking to and thinking through events before we got here are almost lost in our despair. We are operating on the deepest instincts we have received at birth or learned in order to survive. This is where we retreat when we feel part of us has disconnected.

Much of what we do in a great stress is robotic and confusing. We do because we know at some level we must do, but our level of functioning is hindered by our inability to think clearly. Sometimes, it can be very frustrating and agitating to us and those around us. People don't appreciate this kind of thing. They like us all put together already.

This is why it is valuable to train yourself to think outside the box, to operate in the field of faith as opposed to feeling or sight. That is why God continues to put us in places that stretch and grow our instincts in faith. It is a way of life which changes everything.

Let your faith become instinctual. You were born to live it!

"Whenever I am afraid, I will trust in Thee." (Psalm 56:3)

OCTOBER 3

"It's not a fight if you don't fight."

YESTERDAY, I WAS with the grands in a store. We were looking at the books and CD's in a narrow aisle. A couple with a big stroller asked if they could squeeze by. We moved our buggy and three bodies out to the center aisles. They stepped through and saw a friend. They just stopped and chatted, showing off the baby, talking about jobs. We waited, trying to get back to looking. I admit my first thought was less than kind. It was kind of a "really?" sort of aggravation.

That's what most of my life is like. I have had my share of big things, but it's the little ones I ponder most. I was reading that when a grain of sand penetrates an oyster's shell, it is a small irritation that makes the oyster uncomfortable. The oyster relieves the pain by coating the sand with a warm, soothing liquid. When it hardens, it is the precious pearl we cherish and admire.

This made me consider if I had been as kind as I could be. There were certainly a few things I could have done. I was thankful to have been patient. It didn't hurt me. I learned the man had just lost his job. He didn't need me to be ugly. He needed warmth and kindness.

I'd love to say I am always a pearl, but the truth is I am quite normal. Little things irritate me just like you. Still, I know the choice is mine. So, I am learning to be a pearl.

"Don't have anything to do with foolish and stupid arguments, knowing they generate strife." (2 Timothy 2:23)

OCTOBER 4

"The transformation is an inside job."

WHERE DOES YOUR spirituality take you; inward, outward, upside down and inside out? The greatest mystery of truly knowing God is to know the intimacy of the Infinite. What an experience! You will never be the same when you experience the Infinite and the Eternal, Creator. The adventure is incomparable.

This experience with this mystery is a clue to all the vast riches we have yet to know. If you have ever watched someone die, you will see this in a new way. There they are, breathing, alive, whole; and then they are gone. It doesn't take us much to know the pain of separation, but to know that it is temporary gives us a hope and peace far beyond our understanding.

We see the empty shell of a being, but we have seen the shell full and able. We know, now more than ever that the utterly intimate is the vastly infinite. We feel the heavy breath upon us as we touch the eternal so up close and personal.

Be open to truth and spirituality. Let it transform you. Let it become an intimate meeting place of power and strength.

"Therefore, if any man be in Christ, he is a new creation; old things are passed away, behold, all things are new." (2 Corinthians 5:17)

OCTOBER 5

"Trust ways not your own. If God takes you through, rise higher."

WHAT HAPPENED TO you as a child when you felt the disapproval of your parents? Were you left to cry or put in a place that felt as though they quit loving you?

Babies and children, who did not receive comfort during the displeasures of their youth, often find they need to feel unhappy in order to feel comfortable in their world.

All parents get angry or irritable, so that is not a concern here. If, however, the overall consistency of their behavior toward you was uncomfortable, you will feel drawn to that which will position you to become addicted to unhappiness.

As children, we don't understand the outside filters which affect parenting. But when Dad is usually angry and pushes you away when you want a hug, this will mean you have to find a place for that. If your Mom's constant critical spirit disapproved of you in many ways, those feelings they created in you will not be disposed of in adulthood without due diligence.

Arrive in your own joy through the door of trusting God. Let go of yesterday.

"My thoughts are not your thoughts, neither My ways your ways,
says the Lord. As the heavens are higher than the earth,
so are My ways higher than your ways."(Isaiah 55:9)

OCTOBER 6

"It is only when men begin to worship that they begin to grow." - Calvin Coolidge

WORSHIP MEANS TO adore, to embrace deeply, and to celebrate in spirit and truth. It is not a group of people who sing at church together, or people who pray together. It is not a preacher calling for a quiet time of reflection or a study in Scripture with many or few.

Unless you in your own deep heart and entire being are not adoring, embracing and celebrating your Creator...then you are just there in a ceremonial religious pursuit. It might make you look good, but it isn't going to transform your spirit. Worship is the powerful seed of our deepest growth. That happens in the intimacy of true worship. That happens when you have stepped into a relationship, fallen madly in love and breathe in that joy. That happens when you can't stand not being in that mercy, that overwhelming grace and eternal truth.

Few of us will know the abandonment of worship and fewer still, its strength and power in our lives. But for those who do, nothing else compares. In Him we live and breathe and have our Being. He is an all- consuming fire. I wish you the incomparable.

"God is a Spirit, and they that worship Him must worship Him in spirit and in truth." (John 4:24)

OCTOBER 7

"Some wish to live within the sound of church and chapel bell...I want to run a rescue shop within a yard of hell." – C.T. Stud

C T WAS THE kind of guy who liked to make people think. He didn't much care what they thought of him. He was that rough around the edges kind of man some of the refined and sleepy avoid. They feared his passion and yet, knew his truth was sure and real. CT was known for being the son of a wealthy English family.

While he excelled at cricket, an odd thing happened to him on his way to greatness. He discovered God and in God, found himself. He soon left his comfort zone for what he called *"masculine holiness."* As intimacy with God turns the heart toward service, he left for China, Africa and India. CT married Priscilla and they had five children. The three girls lived but their two sons died.

This did not stop the call God had placed on their lives.

CT could be quite offensive to the wealthy class he had once known. He never went back to the privileged lie because he was privileged to be called to a greater good. He has been gone for quite some time now, but like all eternal voices of service, his words leave a rowdy space for grabbing the reins and making a world of difference.

His question would still most likely be: Where do you want to live?

"To each one is given the manifestation
of the Spirit to profit all." (1 Corinthians 12:7)

OCTOBER 8

"Learn to let others learn on their own."

GINGER WANTED TO protect Annie from any of the things she had faced in high school. She always had free advice. She wanted her to experience more, but to have less anxiety.

Finally, Annie looked at her Mom and said, *"You know, Mom, if I don't learn some of these things on my own, I won't have any stories for my kids!"* and she was right.

We do want to give good advice and protect our kids, but it is important that they learn too.

Sometimes, we can do more harm rescuing them instead of letting them experience life for themselves. Once we have brought them to a good understanding, we need to trust them to make good choices or to learn from their own mistakes.

Parenting is hard. We don't need to make it any harder. Chill out. Let them grow strong in their own right. Likely, they will make you proud. God willing, you will make them proud too.

"The Spirit of Truth will guide you into all truth." (John 16:13)

OCTOBER 9

"Darkness creates opportunity for light."

GRIEF OFTEN FEELS like everything has gone dark. It is a cold and deep place to fathom at times. In the extreme grief, just as in a wintery dark night, something comes in grief we cannot see in bright sunlight of summer. Once it is dark enough our perspective changes. We see entire pieces of life we missed before. Many people speak of having experienced a deep grief that changed their life. This is not uncommon.

When our arms are touched with emptiness, we value life more and things less. When things are taken from us, we appreciate the gifts of God's generosity more. When we have known loss in any form, we may also see that life is clearer after a season.

If ancient navigators gauged their living on the stars, perhaps there's something we can learn from them. For you cannot see the stars as bright and influential until the dark and cold hold them up for you to see. There they are more beautiful than ever you remember. Their value holds more weight in the whole of things.

The experience of grief will clarify your life in a way nothing else can do. If you will look to the Maker of the stars, He will guide you just as He always has done for those who looked for direction in the vastness of the shaded areas of life. Look for stars in the darkest night.

"Be joyful in hope, patient in affliction, faithful
in prayer." (Romans 12:12)

OCTOBER 10

"Be what they are when they need you to love."

SOMETIMES PEOPLE GET upset that they aren't changing fast enough. They think they are being disappointments. The connect being a disappointment to how others love them. We have often set it up just that way to get good behavior. It is difficult for them to believe everyone isn't grading everything to see if they are lovable enough.

I once had a student in school who vowed she was stupid and that is why people hated her. I told her I would prove to her that wasn't true. I told her that whatever grade she made in my class would not affect how I felt about her. I would love her no matter what. She didn't believe me. She tested me. She flunked out. I still loved her. I never changed a thing about how I treated her.

What a great day it was when I was able to gain her respect and she honored us both by becoming the beautiful intelligent student I knew she could be. It takes us all time to work through the best in our lives. Love given when we are disappointed in someone is like putting love into our own reserves because often our greatest disappointments are with ourselves.

Keep on believing love can make a difference and it won't stop making a difference...in yourself and in others.

"Rejoice with those who rejoice, mourn with those who mourn." (Romans 12:15)

OCTOBER 11

"Love is not the reproduction of our humanness."

I OFTEN GET ASKED what a healthy marriage looks like. It looks kind of like an apple pie where all the pieces still fit after you cut the slices. Apple pie is made out of flour, sugar, salt, apples, and a few other things.

These things, by themselves have value and purpose. Once mixed in proper place, they take on the smell, texture and taste of each other. Once baked, they are pieces of a whole in their wholeness of pieces.

Marriage is made out of love, trust, integrity, communication, intimacy and a few other things. These things by themselves each have value and purpose, but mixed together they make a marriage whole.

Every piece of apple pie that you cut will have the same basic ingredients. Maybe Jasper likes ice cream on his and Taylor likes chocolate syrup on hers, but that does not change the makeup of a basic apple pie. The integration of the valuable and the useful have remained even through the changes in taste and additions.

Do not withhold from each other the wholeness of your ingredients and enjoy the love that creates goodness.

"Be completely humble and gentle; be patient, bearing with one another in love." (Ephesians 4:2)

OCTOBER 12

"One forgives to the degree that one loves." – Rochefoucald

THIS IS TRUE because love and forgiveness are tethered together. You may forgive a person and not be their best friend, but it will still require love to bring forgiveness to the table. We do not forgive in the natural. We give...for.

Forgiveness is an act of the divine within us, as is love. These are attributes of a character outlined by truth. These are gifts of those who have made footsteps into the eternal of their here and now. These are blended families where hope and goodness follow. We may forgive someone and walk away, because we were responsible for our heart's need being met.

True forgiveness is a duty of the heart.

Love cannot grow in the sensibility of unforgiveness. So, whether it is received well or ridiculed is never the point. We give for we love bigger than our pain. We give for our own spirit begins to die without a love strong enough to conquer pain. We give for the desire of the best of life. We forgive because we were forgiven. We forgive because the energy of love embraces life with grace. We forgive because we love.

We forgive to make room for Joy.

"For unto whomsoever much is given, of him
much is required, to whom men
have committed much; of him they will ask more." (Luke 12:48)

OCTOBER 13

"Your usefulness doesn't always depend on you."

I T WAS YEARS ago. I was down for the count. I had been given two weeks to live and a pic-line to my heart. Of course, there were other issues. Dan's boss didn't think he could give one hundred percent at work with a sick wife and a retarded child, so he politely fired him the week of Thanksgiving.

There we were about as down as down gets.

But we made it.

We made it through and we made it up and we got to thinking we might could help somebody else. Then a lady came to tell us we were too broken to be of help to anybody else. She said that we had just been through so much, that we needed to just concentrate on us. We couldn't give what we didn't have. We thought she was right.

It sounded right.

But it was a lie. She meant well. She just didn't know God well enough to know that even if we were perfect, we wouldn't just want to give what we have to give. That doesn't depend on how we feel or look or where we came from or who we think we are not or who we think we might be. God uses who God wants to use. Who am I to tell Him I am of no value? He'd just smile because He knows better.

You are worth everything. Feel free to be useful. You were designed to make a difference.

"Give, and it shall be given unto you, good measure,
pressed down, shaken together, and running over, will be poured
into your lap. For with the measure given, it is given you." (Luke 6:38)

OCTOBER 14

"What do you pay attention to?"

TRISTAN HEADED OFF to college and was soon disgusted by the pursuits of all he saw around him. He began to pray that God would show him what broke God's heart. It wasn't too long after that, he was asked to help in an AIDS mission in Africa. As he stood, trying to fathom the understanding of where he was, he felt an immense pull in his heart. He felt God saying to him: *"You wanted to know what breaks MY heart, well, this breaks my heart."* Tristan began to weep with a changed focus on his life. He stayed and loved and made a difference.

Olivia wanted to do something for God. She wanted it bad. Not because she was so talented or smart, but because she was so thankful. She began to pray for God to show her where she could serve other people. She prayed: *"Show me what you love God and I will serve there."* She went about life and ended up sitting at a playground one day. That is where she says she heard God say: *"You want to know what I love? I love children!"* and her work with children began.

Years later, she's still in love with what she enjoys every day. I don't know what your prayer might be. I know God has us all here for a reason and there are many needs around us. What we pay attention to tells us who we are and leads us in what we do. Like all common sense, we sometimes miss it in the whole of our being.

Today, be aware of where your attention wanders. There's a secret in that awareness.

"For if the willingness is there, the gift is acceptable according to what one has, not according to what one does not have." (2 Corinthians 5:12)

OCTOBER 15

"Insecurities cause selfishness."

INSECURITIES COME FROM many things. One of the most powerful strongholds of insecurity is the inability to develop true integrity. This comes from knowing that there IS no security here on this earth. Anything we think might make us feel more secure, can easily be discounted. It is also important to know that security is an illusion as well as a place to build our own kingdoms. Insecurities are things which make us feel we are inadequate. We will not keep up. We have been irresponsible.

Integrity gives us security.

If your life has contained enough feeling of unworthiness or disapproval, you may have unknowingly turned to external sources to produce well being. If you have lived in a state of constant disappointment, you may have learned how to live just on the events of a day or circumstance. When all you have received has been something like an on and off button tied to your actions, then that is all the security you retain.

It only lasts as long as you are able to feel you are worth it....because of something you did or did not do.

It takes practice to embrace the wonder of our Creator's love which secures us through any circumstance or emotion.

We can become people of eternal security and release the feeling and need to be insecure. We would be wise to reflect on our being in our Creator's hands, as opposed to the many varied opinions of those who only know us in the external and temporary. You can be sure His love, even in judgment is filled with grace and mercy. What a secure and joyful feeling that can be! What a truth to hold and live out of in our everyday walks.

"The integrity of the upright guides them, but the unfaithful are destroyed by their duplicity." (Proverbs 11:3)

OCTOBER 16

"Defeat can be harder than victory."

DO YOU SABOTAGE your own victory? What is it that makes us work so long and hard for something and then create an adverse situation to our success? Maybe it was a careless act or an intentional act or a bound to happen in due season act, but it has reversed the victory to defeat.

We got that wife, but we gave her up for that secretary. We got that place on the team but we didn't keep out grades up. We made a lot of money but forgot to pay our taxes. We got the dream job and embezzled money.

Oh, it isn't always chocolate chip cookies that make us lose our best footing. It's even more difficult when the defeat seems unrelated. At first glance, it may appear so. Watch those things that you don't pay attention to in the whole of it. Keep an eye on the risky behaviors that you take. I am so guilty of knowing and not doing. I know many of us are prone to think it just happens.

People who undermine themselves in ways that cause them discomfort do so because it fits with the principles and values they gained in childhood. It feels to them like they deserve to have defeat more than victory. But defeat comes with penalties.

The cost may be immense and life altering, or it may well be we can keep on renewing our spirit and giving ourselves the chance to know victory.

"Thanks be to God who gives us the victory
through the Lord Jesus Christ." (1 Corinthians 15:57)

OCTOBER 17

"Where God cooks yams is exactly where the devil roasts his fish." – Ghanaian

WHEREVER GOD IS at work, the devil will arrive without invitation. My Mama used to say that the devil always got to church first and sat on the front pew. I always stayed away from the front pew. Smile. Truth is, if God is busy doing amazing things in your life, then don't be one bit surprised if negative comes slipping through the back door.

Don't be shocked if your greatest sin is at a time of your greatest growing. Don't be dismayed if every time you try to do the best and rightest thing; the stupid seems to engulf you.

I have been meditating in the Bible, reading about Joshua, the greatest general of all time. Over and over and over, in the very first chapter, it says: *"Be strong and of good courage!"* I love that.

Am I strong and of good courage? That has to be the life of an Overcomer.

I have long warned friends that to be my friend means they will encounter just about as many demons as angels. My life is such that I know there is great spiritual connection. But I continue to know that just as God told Joshua not to be afraid or surprised, to be a person strong and of good courage, I also take those words for my life. And while I rather enjoy my yams with brown sugar, butter and marshmallow, I will keep an eye out for the negative. But I will always be strong and of good courage because God is a great cook. Great cooks know how to keep kitchen fires under control. Keep strong. Be of Good Courage.

> *"Be strong and of good courage. Be not afraid,*
> *nor surprised for the Lord thy God goes before you."* (Joshua 1:9)

ANN STEWART-PORTER

OCTOBER 18

"Do not throw away an empty net for you do not know what God will do next." – Nigerian Proverb

I'M JUST ENOUGH Scottish to believe this is most surely true. That, and I have seen God do some phenomenal things with empty nets. I was recently talking to a long-time friend. They have been in a work in another country and loved it. But it has closed to them due to violence. So, they began another work of love, but it doesn't feel enough. It feels empty.

I know that feeling. Maybe you do too. That in between and wait and see time where the hands on the clock seem to mock you. Limbo and not knowing aren't all that comfortable. They seem too much like something is going on, and you are on the outside wanting in.

But this is a particularly valuable time. You are learning a host of things about a host of things.

I like the story of Jesus and the disciples who fished all night and caught nothing. Jesus didn't say to them, *"Sorry guys, that's just the way it goes."* No, He sent them back out and gave them some specific insight.

He wanted them to go somewhere new and somewhere deeper. That hasn't changed.

Keep your net ready – you ain't seen nothin yet!

"Throw your net on the right side of the boat and you will find some." (Luke 5:4)

OCTOBER 19

"Life is an investment."

T HE FLOWER BUSINESS is a billion dollar phenomenon all for a mostly non-practical material. It would boggle our minds to know how much money has been made and lost on the humble, beautiful flower.

I have heard one in three flowers pass through Holland. From the first cutting, the flower begins to die. But since no one likes the dead flowers quite as much as the freshest...it's a race to get them out and to the buyer.

When I consider the history and stories of flowers for sale, I stand intrigued. I have always said that if I were wealthy, I would have fresh flowers in every room of home. I love them but I am not a not a person who truly knows the cost and value of seeding, waiting and harvesting. I feel no rush to water them (which my hub refers to as my torturing them), and I don't make money from them.

Something tells me my perspective would be quite different if my livelihood depended on such a fragile thing. Something tells me what you put into it will always be what you want out of it. But like life, that may be more difficult when the investments may appear to be more than the returns. At that point, I am sure you have to look to the love of the fragile things. For when you love, the cost is of no consequence. The joy is in the love.

May love and joy bless every fragile moment today.

"Teach us to number our days that we
may gain a heart of wisdom." (Psalm 90:12)

"I am here to be a good pointer to Jesus." – Joseph Prince

IN JOHN CHAPTER Twelve, there is a wonderful, rarely shared story of a conversation between God the Father and His Son, Jesus. Jesus is preparing the disciples for His death, but not only His death, He is trying to prepare them for His resurrection as well.

It's as though He is saying, *"Do you think I am worried about this, that I want to change My mind about the cross? Well, think again! This is why I came! This is My time to glorify My Father!"*

It was at that time a *"BATKOL"* was heard from heaven. (This is a unique Hebrew expression meaning a voice that is not a direct voice, sometimes meaning a divine voice.) The Bible tells us that some of the people present heard the voice thought it was thunder. Others thought it was the voice of an angel. Jesus told them it was not a message for Him, but for them.

It was time.

He was ready.

Whatever it took, He was there to be obedient; knowing it would mean His own crucifixion and death, and ultimately, His resurrection.

That was where the Joy remained.

> *"He that loveth his life shall lose it, and he that hateth his life shall keep it unto eternal life."* (John 12:25)

OCTOBER 21

"This too shall pass."

I T'S AFTERNOON. THE days have been full of stink and stunk. We are all nearing that exhaustion of numb and numbing. We have held fast to our faith. The rooms surrounding my Mama are full of people from all over the place. My night in the salmon Naugahyde chair has not been restful. But I don't care. I am where I need to be. We are a large, gregarious, and strong Scottish family who has been through more than we could have thought we could endure. All of us have our stories.

After a week in ICU and the amputating of a leg, Mama is turning around from night to day. There is celebrating in the hall. We feel like winners of the war. Victory is ours and it is sweet.

Mama is told she will do almost a year of rehabilitation.

She does eight months.

She goes home. She teaches. She travels to Korea and India. She came to see me. She will tell you that's how God does things. She will tell you she is still in love with Him. She still finds joy in the miracles.

God has healed and He still can. We must always remember this. It gives us one more time to say thank you.

"The Lord is slow to fulfill His promise as some count slowness,
but is patient toward you." (2 Peter 3:9)

OCTOBER 22

"I am confident that the Spirit generated by the Truth is stronger than the force of any circumstance." – Albert Schweitzer

I LOVE ALBERT! I love where his confidence lies. I love that he believes in the strength of the Truth, the truth that is Spirit generated.

Over and over, I have seen the truth penetrate and transform. All around me I see the spirit thriving and loving and living through all kinds of circumstance. Truth has been so attacked today. It's been raped of its truest identity. It's been used and abused and some days we wonder if some people would recognize it at all. I also believe there is a constant ache and yearning for integrity.

There is an ever increasing desperation to live true, to love without deception before God and everybody.

If Joy is ever to be ours, we obtain it by walking in the truth. Never settle for less.

"I have no greater joy than to hear that my children are walking in the truth." (3 John 1:4)

OCTOBER 23

*"In faith there is enough light for those who want to believe
and enough shadows to blind those who don't."* – Blaise Pascal

FAITH IS STILL a *want to* thing. If you don't want it, that's really a choice you make. I can't make you take it and I can't explain it so you would understand. I can't shine it in your eyes and expect your heart to respond. You have to decide faith is what you want in your life. You have to choose to live a life that is marked by faith or not.

Way too many people like the idea of faith, but have not yet learned the walking in it. Faith can challenge the strongest Believer and surprise the weakest non-Believer. Faith is not something one can manipulate.

So, it will always come to that point of choice. Faith, like most of life is an act of the will and that, in and of itself, is enough to keep the debate going for a hundred years. I will keep the light on.

*"He is the radiance of the glory of God and
the exact imprint of His nature,
and He upholds the universe by the Word of His power."* (Hebrews 1:3)

"Keep close to Nature's heart, and break clear
away, once in a while, and climb a
mountain or spend a week in the woods. Wash
your spirit clean." – Artist John Muir

NATURE IS FULL of wonderful and vibrant lessons for each of us. It can teach us ways of movement, replenishing, gentleness and more. The fruit of the spirit is found in nature.

Long suffering? Watch the waiting of time as growth comes and changes go.

Gentleness? Watch the way a leaf falls.

Peace? Look at the stream winding around the biggest boulder.

Love? What about warm sunshine on the river's edge.

Self-control? Aww, the tides so sure.

One of the main reasons we chose to live in Colorado was because we discovered we needed the mountains. They fed our spirit. Some people need good shopping or medical services or whatever. We needed the aesthetics of the beauty we found in this place.

It changes us to spend time within the confines of wildness and openness. It keeps us tethered to our Creator like nothing we have ever known. I have been busy in the city this week and I am eager for a mountain drive.

Spend as much time as you can in amongst the nature of the Creator, for inside are little secrets for life. It can refresh you and wash your spirit clean.

"Let the fields be jubilant and everything in them,
let all the trees sing for joy." (Psalm 96:12)

OCTOBER 25

"You must lose a fly to catch a trout."

THERE'S ALWAYS A trade off, isn't there? Always a give when you take. We can choose whatever we wish but wisdom weighs the trade.

My husband is a horse trader. He loves a bargain and lives to trade. He had stopped at a garage sale and thought a dollar was too high for his item. As usual, he asked the gal if she would take less. Quick as lightning, she smiled and said 99 cents. He gave her a dollar and said she deserved it because she was a good trader.

They say when you are trying to break a bad habit; you have to replace it with a good habit. If you just say you aren't going to do something, you will likely fail if there is nothing to take its place. This makes sense to me. To have a loving attitude, you have to trade in your hateful one. To stay in the joy, you will need to trade in worry. To be strong, you must give up being weak. To be faithful, you will need to give up fear.

May all your trades be profitable.

"Can the Ethiopian change his skin or the leopard his spots?
Then you also can do good who are accustomed
to doing evil." (Jeremiah 13:23)

"More marriages might survive if the partners realized that sometimes the better comes after the worse." – Doug Larson

MOST MARRIAGES START off all stars and milky way. We love a good love story. We get married thinking we will get more time to be together. We get married thinking their eye will never miss our gaze. They will be all we need them to be and all we will ever want will be in them.

Things seem to escalate if you decided to have a baby. Having children often takes away from intimacy. Not all of us get to be independently wealthy, so the price of groceries will make for good fighting almost anytime. We get more insecure than we were and then again, we might have married a shy version of Don Juan.

Things can get out of hand so much quicker than anybody planned. The sweet romance has turned into sweat pants and the candlelight smells of truck oil.

Sweet nothing's have become swear something's. People get scared.

The wise know that all of life is a process. You have to take some time to settle up what you really want out of this holy union. It can be the divine experience of a lifetime.

Make your *ever after* a happy one.

"Therefore, what God has joined together, let no one separate." (Mark 10:9)

*"Thank You, God, for this good life and forgive us if
we do not love it enough."* – Garrison Keillor

I AM SO GUILTY of needing God's forgiveness in my ungratefulness. My life is a story of more blessing than I could write in a thousand page book. Every morning I wake up with eyes I open to many things to be thankful for right from the get-go. I don't have to take a step outside my home just to know I am abundantly blessed, but when I do, there is another million and one things.

I would dare anyone, anywhere, to begin listing one thing after another in the gifts of goodness. See if your list doesn't get longer and longer. Yes, you can do that with negative things too. There is always more good; but if you aren't looking for good, you will be bound to miss them.

To be held captive by an ungrateful spirit will break you down. It will hold you down. It will bruise your life and you can choke to death on the phlegm of ungratefulness. So, if you are finding yourself in need of God's forgiveness for not being thankful for your good life, get settled up and live in the richness of joy and goodness. Love it enough to say thank you.

*"Praise the Lord, O my soul, and forget not
all His benefits."* (Psalm 103:2)

OCTOBER 28

"Foundations support faith."

I WAS WATCHING A documentary and the woman asked a young man: *"What are your principles?"* and my first thought was what a great question! My next thought was that in sixty years, I have not been asked about my principles.

I suppose it is kind of like the time a board was deciding on some work with gangs we were to do. They were concerned about us having a retarded child. Maybe we would be ridiculed and not strong enough to handle it. But one man spoke up and said he thought they would be very open to us with our child Rachel. Why? Because he said when we told them we loved them, they would believe us simply because, they would say, that if we could love Rachel, we might be able to love them too. Our principles were in clear view.

A principle is the foundation of our practiced belief system. One of the principles that guides my life is love. I believe in God's principles for my life. However, I think it might be like asking what our life mission might be. Until I was asked, I don't know if I had settled it quite as firmly.

Do yourself a favor, and know your life mission and the principles that guide your practice. It will make a difference.

"If you lack wisdom, let him ask of God, Who gives to all generously." (James 1:5)

OCTOBER 29

"What if your words are lamplights?"

I AM OFTEN CALLED an inspirational writer. Inspiration as defined: "Inspiring by a divine power; ecstasy; hence, a divine possession and revelation, or of being directly subject to some divine impulse..." as the dictionary defines it.

It also says it is "A state of impassioned emotion; transport; elevation of fancy; exaltation of soul; as, the poetry of enthusiasm...or the kindling fervor of soul; strong excitement of feeling on behalf of a cause or a subject; ardent and imaginative zeal or interest."

But my favorite would be *the lively manifestation of joy or zeal.* Bottom line? That is real inspiration. It touches down deep in the joy of the soul.

The word "inspire" comes from the original tongue to mean *"Divinely breathed."* Lf, as a writer or a person of any worth at all, it seems to me that to be one of divine breathing would be most delightful of all. I may not be the type of writer who has much of a call in a culture impassioned by stuff and statue. But I gladly delight to be inspired by divine breath.

"Your Word is a lamp to my feet; a light to my path." (Psalm 119:105)

OCTOBER 30

"Humanity is never so beautiful as when praying for forgiveness, or else forgiving one another." – Jean Paul

WHEN WE ARE in need of forgiveness, we are more humble. We are less flagrant in our demise. We are more able to clarify what we want and even what we need. We are able to release our pretense and our pride. We are coming into a place of true thankfulness. We are receiving the joy of giving.

When we forgive another, we have had to step outside of what is unnatural to us. We have to grasp the hand of divinity to give a gift that we, in and of ourselves, might struggle greatly to do so. We are open to the experience of learning from the pain. We are given a strength we would not receive in our unforgiveness.

Receiving an apology can be as difficult as giving one. The Enemy sees to it that we feel awkward. But to forgive as Christ forgave us will refine us and give us greater joy in all we do. Give and receive as Christ gave and received. Grasp the hand of divinity.

"If you forgive others, your Father will also forgive you." (Matthew 6:14)

OCTOBER 31

"Search thine own heart. What painted thee in others, in thyself may be. All dust is trail. All flesh is weak. Be thou the true man thou dost seek." – John Wittier

THERE IS A Bible verse that reads: *"Where thou judgest another, thou condemnest thyself for thou that judgest do-est the same thing."* (Since I have started with all the thees and thous, I think I could possibly put in a post, I thinkest thee mightiest not graspeth this most valuable truth.)

Whenever I judge you, I tell on myself. Whenever I condemn you, I condemn myself. Whatever I judge...I do! Yikes.

I have noticed it feels better to me if I judge you. I don't like it as much when I am judged. But what I know to be true is that often the very thing I have said about you is found in me! Maybe it is because we are all of human composition. We like to think it's normal to criticize and tear down others.

There are at least a hundred shows that tell us its okay to weigh everybody on our scales. And if you want to live that way, just be prepared. The person who can stop talking about another is a person struggling to love themselves.

Quit telling on yourself. And live that other Bible verse: *"Love thy neighbor as thyself."*

"Search me, O God, and know my heart." (Psalm 159:23)

NOVEMBER 1

"When you have really exhausted an experience,
you always reverence and love it."
- Albert Camus

THIS IS SO true! I know this is why we have these times where the lines are drawn and we are unable to move ahead, until we stop and find that inner reverence. That is really the essence of resilience. We go through many an experience that passes with hardly a glance. We might miss even more if it wasn't for the places where we can't climb out so easily. Then we have to process and sometimes in triplicate.

It seems when we come to the end of our self, to that hard but beautiful place where we know the power at work is so beyond our human capacity, we can finally embrace the loving of what we are learning. We never forget what it cost to get there nor what we were given there. It is most precious. He fills us with Joy even in the pain of it.

Exhaust your experiences with God. Reverence your growth.

"Whoever is patient has great understanding." (Proverbs 14:29)

NOVEMBER 2

*"I have not lost faith in God. I have moments of anger and protest.
Sometimes I've been closer to Him for that reason."* – Eiie Wiesel

I F YOU HAVE ever read any of Eli's work, you know he
understands moments of terror and anger. His life in the Nazi
prison camp was filled with places of deepest darkness. I can't even
imagine some of the protests to God I would have been making.

But I have had my asking ground. I have had my moments of horror
at the grief I was asked to bear. Like Eli, these are often just part of the
reason I trust and love God. He's big enough to take whatever I can dish
out. He doesn't feel obligated to tell me anymore at that time of anger
than He does anywhere else. He is a God who knows our fragility. He
loves us in it, but also through it; for to rise up in great pain and walk
toward God is courageous.

To live in trust is brave. To be faithful is to see God's reward in
due season. To honor and respect God in any circumstance is wisdom.

"The fear of the Lord is the beginning of wisdom." (Proverbs 9:10)

NOVEMBER 3

"You want me to hide? No, I just don't want
anyone to see you." – Burnt Notice

THIS REMINDS ME of how some people do life. They don't mean to hide, but they just don't want you to see them. Some won't lie, except by omission. Like that makes it okay.

Somewhere in the hiding, you trip over the very things you thought were so out of sight. They also get larger than life the harder you try to keep them hidden.

No, we don't have to live with all our insides hanging out to dry, but there's no sense in living life in a closet either. No matter how nice you have built a closet, it's always better for storage than living life. Stay hungry to live real. Stay thirsty for truth.

Stay determined to be transparent so that God can use you; so that God can clearly be seen.

Stay out of hiding in plain sight. Be a light on a hill; truthful and shining bright.

"Sanctify them in the truth; Your Word is truth." (John 17:17)

NOVEMBER 4

"I argue not against Heaven's hand or will, of heart or hope;
but still bear up and steer right onward." – John Milton

WHAT DOES REGRETTING really do for you? I'm thinking, not much. You did it. It's done. You can't change it. You can learn from it, but only if you let go of the regretting it alone. We only show what we learned from that moment when we turn rightward and stay with joy, in the moment of grace. Eventually we need to quit going to therapy and confession, and quit talking with girlfriends or buddies about what we did.

Sooner or later, you have to ask: *"What am I doing now?"*

Don't live addicted to regret and unable to rise to your divine position. A friend once asked me, after a grueling grief, where was my joy? I never forgot that divine question. Whatever regrets we have, let us lay aside those weights and give ourselves to the Joy of today!

"Lead me in Your truth and teach me, for You are the God
of salvation; for You I wait all day long." (Psalm 25:5)

"When you pray, move your feet." – African Proverb

THERE ARE A lot of things about prayer that are supposed to be true. If we pray, God will hear. If we pray, God will answer. We may or may not be able to see God at work, but our faith should be such that what He is doing is of less concern than what we are doing. In due season, we will see His work.

It might help us more to see faith as a dance. God invites us to dance with Him. If we sit watching, we will not feel all His movements. The dance means more to us when we are engaged in intimacy with God. Faith is resting in the activeness of God. When He leads, we feel almost free in our own movement as though gliding in response. No wringing your hands in a dance where you are holding onto Him; just a sweet communion of trust and peace. Faith is the ultimate dance. God is a magnificent Dancer.

"Teach me Your way O Lord, that I may walk in Your truth;
unite my heart to fear Your name." (Psalm 86:11)

NOVEMBER 6

"We continue the celebration every time we worship."

IT'S A QUIET hush of a day. The hustle and bustle of a dark day of death is over, but don't mistake the quiet and thoughtful stillness for silence from heaven. Oh No! Heaven is bustling like a crown on the Eve of Christmas. Everything Jesus came to do is being done.

All is on task. Jesus is busy taking keys and taking names. He's not just laying there waiting for the sun to rise. He's not thinking about yesterday because He knows about tomorrow. The stone could not hold Jesus captive.

Make no mistake; there was a purpose to everything that transpired, right down to that ear that Peter cut off, after spending hours in prayer. The stories and rumor mill are working overtime today. The earth has shaken. The temple veil has been torn. Then the darkness seemed to overcome.

Do you feel like that at times? Just keep waiting in faith. See how you feel tomorrow. Heaven is planning a party like earth has never seen. The Guest of Honor will be arriving at any time.

Don't ever mistake the silence for defeat.

"Rejoice in the Lord and again I say, rejoice." (Philippians 4:4)

NOVEMBER 7

"Let joy kidnap you."

J OY IS THE captivating of the soul, in whose freedom even others enjoy. Give a child a balloon and you can catch a glimpse of joy. For a small while, they will chase it, expecting it to entertain them. At some point, they release it to find if they don't grab it back, it will soon be lost. But the more they enjoy it, others find it hard to resist.

Joy is contagious. Joy is unbridled and still. Joy is lifting up and letting out, embracing and releasing. Joy is worship. Joy is celebrating eternity in the midst of the earthly. Joy is basking in forgiveness and giving it at will. Joy is beyond circumstance and human ability. It is the divine design of a Creator in love with the beauty of His greatest wonder. Let joy consume you! Play in its wonder.

"When anxiety was great within me,
your consolation brought me joy." (Psalm 94:19)

NOVEMBER 8

"Give what you get."

I JUST SAW THE car commercial where the grandson is taking his Grandma to see where she grew up. It's great to be so blatant about the idea of caring for someone else, of caring for the older, of caring about family connection, of caring about past heritage and a connection to yesterday in a positive way.

Yes, I know they are selling cars. Still, I applaud any commercial that can tell a story and sell something and touch your heart to do something positive.

We are a people who need connection.

Lately though, we are putting away our elderly at an alarming rate. We are losing family heritage pride as people are changing views of family. As all research shows, young people who have connection with grandparents who are close to them, and have pride in their family heritage, are most able to go onward to make positive contributions to their world.

"Home is where your story begins." Homes with connection, empathy, love and giving make a difference in the world.

Here's to all you amazing people who tuck kids in, spend time with Grandma and those who had to save up money to buy that first car. There's no telling what you'll do tomorrow.

"Each of you should give what you have decided in
your heart to give, not reluctantly or under compulsion,
for God loves a cheerful giver." (2 Corinthians 9:7)

NOVEMBER 9

"Godliness is joy."

DALTON GAVIN JONES was the child of famous and wealthy people. He lived a life that those outside of his life would have envied. He has letters and pictures from movie stars and presidents. But his parents are as gone today as they were when he was growing up. He began collecting their things in his small apartment, until he had to use the fire escape to get in. If he saw an empty hole of a space, he filled it. He wandered the streets at odd times looking for things to, fill his holes.

To get into his apartment, you were required to slither through a self-made tunnel of stuff. That is how he lived until the landlord saw it. Then the next battle began. Why did he do this? What was wrong with him? How could he get out of this mess of a life he had created in hopes of finding love?

You see, there was a hole in his heart. Like many people he tried to fill it up, to make it close up around him and love him and protect him. When his parents were out busy playing and making their way in the world, he was slowly dying in their mixed up values.

When one loses love, they may never find their way home. Love one another. Let your love feed another's hungry soul. You may be just what they have needed all along.

"Command those rich in this present world not to be arrogant not put their hope in wealth, but to put their hope in God who richly provides everything for us to enjoy." (1 Timothy 6:17)

NOVEMBER 10

*"He is best who wins the most splendid victories
by the retrieval of mistakes."* – Fredrick Robertson

FORGET THE MISTAKE.

Trade it for victory. There's always a trade.

You stay in the past? You will live in that mistake and not pass through its lesson. Use your mistakes as great learning material and you will be teaching the class someday!

Life is a series of mistakes for all of us. Some have more severe consequences, but we all make mistakes. So it's never if you make a mistake, it's when…and when you will be strong enough to trade it for victory and comfort for another. The right tool is never complaining and mumbling about victimizations. Nothing is changed unless you take the challenge. Forget the mistake and grab hold of your victories.

*"Your statutes are my heritage forever, the joy
of my heart."* (Psalm 119:111)

NOVEMBER 11

"People living deeply have no fear of death."

P EOPLE WHO HAVE had near death experiences learn that death is more transitional than positional. It is a form of bodily changes to be sure, but it is no more about a casket than money is a sign of true worth. If you have ever had the words spoken to you, *"You are dying"* or something like that, you consider a great many things as though you were heading out the back door and mentally checking off things to make sure are done before you leave.

It isn't a big deal if the basics are taken care of beforehand. But, if your house is on fire and you are trying to stop the fire before you leave, this could be an issue. Or if you don't know where you are going and someone asks you on the way out, it might stop you in your tracks. It might bother you if you felt you were leaving way too soon...or way too late.

Suppose you know where you are going, are well prepared for the trip and okay with leaving things back at the earthly house, then you are apt to find (as I once did) that life and death live together. They process through a lot of the others thinking. Life worries about death and death wonders about life. In fact, they are intertwined as one usually comes with another. So, there is no real need to fear death unless you are afraid of the things you don't know in life.

"Sow with a view to righteousness. Reap in accordance with kindness. Break up the fallow ground. It is time to seek the Lord until He comes to rain righteousness on you." (Hosea 10:12)

NOVEMBER 12

"The greatest good you can do for another is not just to share your riches but to reveal to him his own." – Benjamin Disraeli

PEOPLE TELL ME they could never do what I do. They ask me if it's hard to be helping someone and watch them fail miserably. It is. But I fail. I expect that failing comes with a lesson and I hope they receive it. I am asked why I listen to people's problems and if I really think I do any good.

My answer may depend on the day, for sometimes even I have wondered if this is what I really want to do. Still, in my heart of hearts, I live to love people because I see them as our greatest resource. People save whales and trees and other great resources. I like to think I get to save a marriage or a wrong path from regret. I have seen some very sad things. But I also have the pleasure of knowing I have made a difference.

It's not because I am so good at my work. It's that I get to be there when someone finally sees their worth or purpose or answer. It's that I get to cheer them on and challenge them to dream. It's that there is a certain quiet hush that rushes in when they realize their own riches. Then I smile all the way down to my soul. Live in the truest wealth.

"Let each of you look not only to his own interests, but also to the interests of others." (Philippians 2:4)

NOVEMBER 13

"For nothing worth proving can be proven, not yet disproven;
wherefore thou be wise, cleave ever to the
sunnier side of doubt." – Tennyson

I HAD AN AWESOME friend who died of cancer a few years back. She had been *"Teacher of the Year."* She was always a person who made you feel terribly important. I loved her dearly. I miss her greatly.

One of the greatest things she ever taught me was a simple rule of thumb for life. *"Always err on the side of mercy."* She had a lively daughter, who tended to gather opinions; sometimes criticism for her parenting. She would often confide in me that maybe she wasn't strict enough, but that she preferred to err on the side of mercy.

Today, you may encounter that child who will get on your last nerve or the spouse who just made our life harder or a relative we are sure is evil. I don't know what you will face today. But I have found Judith's rule to be precious, right, and good. Think first how you can show mercy. It has worked wonders in my life. That very daughter now cares for her disabled father in a loving way. So, while mercy may not get a big neon sign, it's still the most wonderful thing.

Err on the side of mercy. Stay on the sunnier side of doubt.

"Because of His great love for us, God, rich in mercy,
made us alive with Christ even when we were dead in our sin;
it is by grace you have been saved." (Ephesians 2:4-5)

"My times are in Thy hand." – Psalm 31:15

THERE IS NO question of what God will do. Many times He tells us that He will finish whatever He starts. It is us who must choose to be guided. We are usually in such a hurry to fix it, that we choose out of our anxiety. This often puts us in more situations where we must learn what is ours to do and what is not.

God says that every purpose of His will be performed. We can overestimate our ability to fix a situation, but never God. His timing may not be ours. His way might not be our way. His how may well change us as much as the situation. Our times are a constant work of God at work. We can embrace with trust and love in knowing He is doing what He says He will do. Or we can call him a liar by choosing to do it our way.

We are here on a journey by divine destiny. Let us embrace the joy of trusting our God as He goes about His work in us, about us and most surely, through us.

"He has saved us and called us to a holy life; not because of anything
I have done, but because of His own purpose
and grace. This grace was given
us in Christ Jesus before the beginning of time." (2 Timothy 1:9)

"Evil is real. God still wins."

I KNOW YOU SAY your mother-in-law is evil. But what does that mean? A truly evil person has four distinguishing characteristics.

First, an evil person engages in acts that cause harm in a grievous, sorrow filled harmful way.

Second, an evil person commits harmful acts that are consistently conscious and repeated intentionally. Evil is deliberate action.

Third, evil people have a warped and depraved mind so they can always justify hurting the other person. Evil does not have the ability to look inside its own evil. It makes perfect sense to them.

Fourth, evil people have no concept of remorse. Normal human response to hurting another is guilt. Evil does not operate on that premise.

If you encounter evil, you cannot hope that they will see the error of their way. You can only get away from them and the sooner, the better. You should avoid them in the future.

Remember, that you don't overcome evil with evil. You overcome evil...with good. But it can be very emotionally and spiritually draining, so be prudent.

"Do not enter the path of the wicked and do
not proceed in the way of evil men." (Proverbs 4:14)

NOVEMBER 16

"It is easier to forgive an enemy than to forgive a friend." – William Blake

WE HAD KNOWN each other for over ten years. We had shared some life. I had stopped by her home and we chatted. Later, I began hearing what *"She said."* I lost clients who were sure it was true. I though they agreed there was no proof. She had even lied to them before. But this time, she won. I lost financially but was even more hurt by the falsehoods of a friend. A friend who had said she loved me more than once. A friend whose family I had cared for physically, spiritually and emotionally.

It hit hard.

I agonized over it for months. I recalled anything I could think of that might have been taken wrong. I also realized that for me to release her, I would need to forgive her and move forward. I don't have many enemies, so forgiving strangers here and there hasn't been much of an issue. It's the family and friends program that gets me most of the time.

I did forgive her. Then God was gracious to move her away from me. He doesn't always do that. But I do know that friends and family need forgiveness too...and l can do that. God gives me forgiveness but holds me accountable. That's what I try to do too. It helps in loving me enough to guard my own spirit. It helps me live free and Joyfully.

"Get rid of all bitterness, rage, and anger,
brawling and slander, along with
every form of malice. Be kind and compassionate to one another, forgiving
each other even as God in Christ forgave you." (Ephesians 4:31-32)

NOVEMBER 17

"Rest is holy too."

THIS SOUNDS SO lovely. We say it. We even say we believe it. But it's about the last thing we do! Ever watch a child who is hurt and clings to a parent? The child knows instinctively no one else, but that intimate relationship will do. They run to them, bury their head in their bosom and know it will be alright. They know the parent can't take away the pain. But they know their pain can rest. They feel the security of the strength beyond their own.

Should it surprise us that God uses these words to assure us He has our best interest at heart? He is able to hold us. This is like we do our own children. We see them burdened; hurting, falling down and we say *"Come here."* If we truly believe God could give us rest, then we would come when He says *"Come."*

Have you fallen down? Have you been feeling overwhelmed? Are you burdened by the latest news? Come. The simple act of coming to God shows we are intimately trusting Him. He's just waiting to hold us, and everybody needs holding sometimes.

"Come unto Me, all ye that labor and are heavy laden,
and I will give you rest." (Matthew 11:28)

NOVEMBER 18

"Parenting is the most humbling job in the world."

A HEALTHY CHILD WILL be taught how to be a strong and productive adult. That means they will need an adult who can show them how to live a life of joy and giving. They will watch everything you do much more than they will ever listen to your voice. But if your voice is in harmony with your example, it will produce some remarkable children. The greatest issue I have consistently seen to be detrimental in children is an inconsistent parent.

When a child argues with an adult, they have seen that. They needed to see talking it out productively. When a child uses inappropriate language, they have heard it at home. I can't count how many times a child has been spanked or punished for what they see in a parent.

The other issue I think is huge is when we only discipline and don't praise. Wherever your attention goes to, is the place that will grow. That includes praise and positive words. Often we fail in this area almost as much as in being an example. We must discipline and praise more if we are to have children who are strong healthy adults.

When we teach them, there are consequences for their behavior, positive as well as negative; we enable them to be self-reliant and productive. Love your children enough to be as good a parent as you can possibly be.

"Behold, children are a heritage from the Lord,
the fruit of the womb a reward." (Psalm 127:3)

NOVEMBER 19

"Life is an adventure in forgiveness." – Norman Cousins

. . . **H**OW VERY TRUE. If my past few weeks were put into a Manila folder, it would be stamped *"Forgive and Go On."* People often think that people who are in the life work of caring for people can take just about anything. In a way, it's true. We know when we come into the life of a hurting person, we risk the chance of getting caught in a cross fire, that has little to do with us. But we still have this weird little thing called feelings. They still allow us the beauty of seeing our own fragility, therefore keeping us ever humbled and in need of training wheels.

Just when you think you are seeing some exciting breakthroughs, you feel the sting of the right hook of judgment. You are caught a little off balance and that black eye on your pride will need some care, but otherwise you know you will just cry it out and stand up tomorrow. I am sure you have experiences just like mine. If it isn't one thing, it's your mother...isn't that the way the song goes? Life is full of the need to forgive and if it isn't somebody you know well, it will be that driver in front of you. If it isn't a stranger, it will be you. So, let's all just keep on forgiving and keep on loving and keep on letting our light shine.

*"For we are His workmanship, created in Christ Jesus
for good works, which God prepared beforehand, that
we should walk in them."* (Ephesians 2:10)

"A two year old is kind of like a blender, but you don't have a top for it." – Jerry Seinfeld

THAT'S THE WAY two year olds come most of the time. We all expect it. We plan for it. We understand their tantrums will pass much as we understand this is a critical time for them to value authority in their life. If you have not properly doctored the two's in your child's life, you may find that age can be quite the introduction to tantrums. And I know a bunch of people who start trying to corral the wild horse too late. A lot can get broken in that process. Then we claim we don't know what's gotten into them.

I recently saw the stupid video of a dad shooting his teenager's computer because of what they put on Facebook. All I can say is that apple isn't falling too far from the tree. The son had a tantrum and then the Dad responded by having a tantrum. Well, I wonder what the son learned from that! When something gets heated, destroy property.

I already had an issue with the language, but that's just me. I think parents of teenagers need to learn about teenagers...just like they learn about two year olds. Things can go remarkably well. I've seen it in my own family as well as a few others. In fact, as my child neared those years, I heard all the stories. I just never got them at my house. I remember asking my dad what was his favorite age. With six kids, I did not expect him to say our teenage years!

"Discipline your child and they will give you a rest;
He will give delight to your heart." (Proverbs 29:17)

NOVEMBER 21

"The groves were God's first temples." – Will Bryant

I ADMIT I'M A little jealous of Adam and Eve in their perfect garden. There they are, just walking through the fruit groves, the vineyards, and the evergreens, with the smell of fresh peaches filling their nostrils. To meet God in that place must have been extraordinary.

There is a church a few hours from us who have property that overlooks a flowing stream. They have a small waterfall in the backdrop of tall pines, aspens and greens of all color. It's over 8,000 feet up in the sky; the air is crisp and clear. Talk about worship.

There are no words. The church is a small log church. It doesn't compete with the creation around it. Instead, it grabs the hand of the Creator and the whole of Heaven seems to open.

I just don't believe God is a big, fancy church building kind of God. His idea of a building program looks different than most I see. My own taste is much akin to the small tiny white steepled churches. I get lost in the big, showy, smoking stage churches. I have always been drawn to gentle, quiet, simple and awesome places of worship. I don't need a fancy program or a place to impress my friends. I just need a place to meet God face to face. Walk the groves. I am certain God will meet you there.

"Ascribe to the Lord the glory due His name, bring an offering and come before Him. Worship the Lord in the splendor of His holiness." (1 Chronicles 16:29)

NOVEMBER 22

"This too shall pass."

THERE ARE PLENTY of days where we wonder if this will ever pass. "This" covers a lot of things, but knowing that it will pass enables us to shine our shoes one more day, pack those lunches, go to that job, change that diaper, write that paper, go to therapy, and find our joy, one more time.

Some days that's all you get. So go ahead and ask those significant questions:

Am I getting out of this time what I am supposed to be getting?

Am I using this time to be more profitable as a person or am I just whining?

Am I able to trust God with how my now fits in to tomorrow?

Am I able to keep dreaming?

Those are the things to value when it's been too long and things have become congested in your spirit.

Hum a joyful sort of song. Pass the word along.

This too shall pass, but squeeze out all the goodness while you can, for that too shall pass.

"For our light affliction, which is but for a moment, worketh for us a far more exceeding and eternal weight of glory." (2 Corinthians 4:17)

NOVEMBER 23

"This is the hour of lead – remembered, if
outlived, as freezing persons, recollect
the snow, first, chill, then stupor, then letting go." – Emily Dickinson

OH, HOW L feel the weight of this grief! It might have happened the night she left you or the day you caught him cheating. It might have been the day the doctor said there was nothing else he could do. It might have been when they buried your child from a drug overdose. Or like me, when your baby dies. And another is dying. That is the hour of lead. That is the hour of freezing cold.

I remember walking into my son, Matthew's hospital room. He had died an hour before we arrived. The room was like a freezer locker. We shuddered as we entered it. I will not forget that chilling stupor. What an apt description for a horrific moment. As our daughter Rachel, left for heaven and prayers and songs had been done, I had to finally tear myself from her limp body and let go...almost running from the room.

Many of you know this feeling all too well. Grief is heavy. Grief is suffocating and difficult to release. And yet, we are required to live beyond the lead days; to find the comfort and embrace the Joy. But know that the feeling of lead can arise anytime. And then you must let go....again, and hold to the unshakeable Kingdom.

"Therefore, since we are receiving a Kingdom that cannot be shaken,
let us be thankful and so worship God acceptably
with reverence and awe." (Hebrews 12:28)

"God's will is what I would choose if I had all the facts."

T HAT SAYING HAS been a magnet on my Parents fridge for as long as l can remember. I learned it way before l left home... the words, that is, but not the value it brings to my principle of trust. The fact is no one human can possibly know all the facts. We can see only in a short time, a small window, a perspective that includes little in comparison to God's infinite wisdom and omniscience. Therefore, it seems that God has set a standard and we must rise to that standard, if we are to know the worth of our faith as God has given. We must then choose to live out this principle, not just address it conceptually.

We either believe it or we do not. We do not have to be an atheist to NOT believe in God. Our choices reflect our belief system, regardless of what we say. Perhaps it's time to keep our mouth shut and our trust open. Then time will tell, and our doubts, fears, and questions will be where they should be: in the safekeeping of the Eternal One who does know all the facts. Live in the truth.

"Rejoice always, pray without ceasing. Give thanks in all circumstances, for this is the will of God in Christ Jesus in you." (1 Thessalonians 5:16-18)

NOVEMBER 25

"There is joy in service."

TRY SOMETHING FUN today. Define the details. Instead of working, you are caring, sharing, loving and opening. Instead of picking up the kids from school, you are serving, loving, and giving. Instead of eating, you are energizing or fueling. Instead of visiting, you are expressing, enjoying, or listening. If you are exercising, you are lifting, kicking, rejuvenating or discovering the idea!

We so often use words that hardly tell anything about anything, like the proverbial *"How are you? I am fine."* We kind of round up the words and let it ever so often define the details in a positive way. This helps you clarify that your life is definable and that what you are doing is affecting your being.

If you have never *"done"* inspiring or awakening or encouraging or grace or worship or soaring or embracing or caring or...whatever, then maybe it's time to find their sweetness in recognition. And now, I'm off to think, taste, prepare and wonder. Maybe l will incite an encore of delight. Smile. Wonder what you will do in your being?

"The Kingdom of God is not a matter of eating and drinking, but righteousness and peace and joy in the Holy Spirit." (Romans 14:17)

"Attention is the rarest and purest form of generosity." – Simone Weil

A LITTLE BOY WAS tugging on his Mama's leg and she, busy making dinner, gave him a quick *"What?"* and kept cooking. But he said: *"No, Mama, listen to me with your eyes."* How many times do you look the person who is speaking to you in the eye? You probably do that more often with people you don't love, compared to those you do. For example, you will look at your boss eye to eye, but not your child.

Time is an extravagant gift. When it is given to one, it should always be counted generous. When someone looks us in the eye and listens to us, as though we are the only thing important to them, we will relish those moments. They are generally rare and this makes them even kinder. It seems as though this would be one of the easiest things to do, but it is not.

We live in a distracted world. People are crying out to receive attention. We all desire to be seen and heard, from the youngest to the oldest of us. Today, listen with your eyes. Let your heart speak through them. Be generous with your attention.

"Be quick to listen, slow to speak and slow to anger." (James 1:19)

NOVEMBER 27

"March to the beat of that different drum."

S HARE YOUR LOVE, your joy, your time, your food, your material goods, your patience and goodness with anyone who comes near your life. You do not know what they need, but God does. He sends them to you just as surely as He sends you to another for the balm of the soul.

Weary not yourself in faithless pursuit. Let the courage which holds you steadfast become a bridge for others whose feet are torn. Live, letting your purpose be simple and good. The humble heart sees ever further and places roses in the empty places. This is your day to mold into eternal wealth and spiritual gifts. While others are minding the world's store or insisting we watch them walk in self-glory, dare to be that one whose footsteps are different.

When they come calling, and they will, give them everything, for you will miss nothing that Joy and Love cannot bring back to you a thousand times more. Live precious.

"Blessed are those who hear the Word of God and obey it." (Luke 11:28)

NOVEMBER 28

"Just because it's not here yet, doesn't mean it's not coming."

I HAVE THIS LITTLE sign on my fridge. It helps remind me that faith is often just a waiting game. Just because something isn't in my hands at the moment, it doesn't mean that it isn't coming. It just means it might not be here at the moment. Often, that's because it isn't needful at the moment. At other times, it's because my heart needs time to change, my spirit needs to respond, or my mind needs time to embrace it.

Sometimes we don't know the when or the how of God's will, His timing or His purpose, so we may be tempted to listen to those doubts and fears.

"You will never get well."

"You will always struggle with those finances."

"You will never be a good Dad."

"You will never find a mate."

You have heard these rumors of war before. It is a war waged against yourself. Those wars have little value and worse, they keep you from experiencing what God really wants you to experience, and from what God really wants you to receive.

I am finding there is a great deal of comfort and peace in the choice to say, *"Thy will be done on earth as in heaven."* It's the way Jesus taught us to pray. It's His way of telling us things are going to get done whether we are with the team or not. So why not choose to believe all is well, that everything is on schedule, and that earth is simply being adjusted to receive heaven's miracles?

I am excited to know that just because it's not here, doesn't mean it's not coming. All it means is that His will is being done on earth as it is in heaven. That's a glorious thing to know.

"Thy Kingdom come, Thy will be done,
on earth, as it is in heaven." (Matthew 6:10)

NOVEMBER 29

"You do not have to be what you were given."

TAD WAS A man with seven children and twins on the way. Someone had seen the way he handled his children. He was always yelling, always pushing and shoving, intimidating and beating them down. If not with words or a slap, he had a belt they all knew well. He had recently lost his job and the fear of that made him worse than usual. Finally, someone asked him what his Dad was like. He said he didn't have one. At least, not one he had seen since he was three. His only real memory of his Dad was when he was that three year old. He was trying to help his Mama with the milk. He dropped the jug and his Dad had beaten him for it.

A three year old.

And he never forgot it.

He thought he would be different. He wasn't.

He claimed it was what he was and all he had known. But he was wiser than most. His family was in chaos. He needed help. He asked for it. Someone had the opportunity to teach him wonderful parenting skills. He was a fast learner. His little girl said she was so happy Daddy wouldn't hit her anymore. His sons now have a figure of fatherhood that will change the next generation. Every day, he's growing and nobody is as proud of him as he is of himself.

Never let what was keeping you down keep you from what you can be! You hold the power in your own hands.

"Whoever gives heed to instruction prospers, and blessed is the one who trusts in the Lord." (1 Psalm 16:20)

NOVEMBER 30

"The question is laid out for each of us to ask whether
to hold on or to drop the mask." – Boesing

HAVE YOU EVER dressed up for Halloween and put on a mask? They are generally ill-fitting and uncomfortable. Children think we can't tell who they are, and sometimes we could trick them. Imagine if we lived that way all the time, unable to take off our real face.

All kinds of people do just that. They hide behind the most common things, believing themselves to be seen as what they are not...believing we are all buying their lies.

It is not uncommon for me to listen to a client lie to me. In my line of work, that is just the way it is. I will often listen for quite some time before I ever challenge what they tell me. Sometimes, after I do confront them, they will hold out their lie without excuse, so convinced it must be true.

Now, I am not self-deceived. All of us are prone to this masking business. I have heard it is rampant on social and dating sites...which frankly I find well, stupid. If you aren't who you say you are or at least believe who you think you are, what is this point of deception? Give it up. It is useless. Drop the mask and become genuine. In the end, you aren't fooling anyone but yourself. And that just makes you look like a fool. Be true to yourself.

"You shall not give false testimony." (Exodus 20:16)

DECEMBER 1

"Life often requires death."

BROCK'S FIANCÉ HAD dumped him. While he knew it was probably a good thing, something inside died. He sat at the ocean, screaming at God. *"I'm dead inside God! If you are there, how will you get me through this pain? What can you possibly give me?"* Suddenly everything stopped, even the sound of the ocean, the wind and even his anger. Into his mind, clear and instantly focused, came one word; "You."

This began Brock's serendipity after his grief. He began to find himself again. It had been lost in the exchange of being what someone else wanted. He began to discover the beat of his heart again. Time with his son became more precious and more of a priority than ever before.

Dreams that had been placed on hold were now brought to the forefront. He was able to explore again, to listen to the still small whisper. He discovered that there, in the midst of a great loss, he had indeed found himself. Sometimes, the magic within has to suffer a release to open it up to even greater things. Discover you.

"When He opens doors, no one will be able to close them; when He closes doors, no one will be able to open them." (Isaiah 22:22)

DECEMBER 2

*"Give what you don't need because someone will
need what you give." –* Ann Stewart Porter

BERTIE HAD BOUGHT a new laptop. She put the old one aside, planning to sell it. The young man arrived to show her how to get the most out of her new computer. He had tricks and cheat sheets and was patient above all. He spotted the old laptop and asked if she was going to sell it.

It was then she remembered thirty years before in a first apartment. She needed a stove. One of the doctors she worked with heard she needed a stove and brought one over. She asked him why he wasn't selling it. He smiled and with a twinkle in his eye said, *"Why sell it when you can give it away?"* So, Bertie handed the young computer tech a present for his wife, who was an aspiring writer.

Is there something you are done with and have attached it to a someday sell? For several years, I had accumulated too many dishes. So, when company came, I served them with a beautiful table. If they loved the dishes, I'd put a bow around them and have them ready when they would leave. That was so fun!

Go ahead. Find something you don't need any more and then find somebody who needs it! Believe me when I say...the pleasure will all be yours.

"...the Lord opened a door of opportunity for me." (2 Corinthians 2:12)

DECEMBER 3

"Look hard for things of Joy!"

I F YOU ARE addicted to unhappiness, the world will always live up to your expectation. It is a little bit of a journey to find out, that for some reason or another, you are addicted to unhappiness, but it happens. Even when there is a good reason to be happy about something, you find yourself looking for the negative.

If the sun is shining, you are already expecting the rains. If you have stopped to smell the roses, you got a thorn stuck in your paw and your back is keeping you from getting up.

See? It's easy to find your way to unhappy. The everyday notions of life don't generally help. There are usually specific reasons why you have the addiction to unhappiness. Perhaps you have been given too much and are spoiled too excessively. Perhaps you have suffered a lifetime trauma.

Unhappiness is common among the human race. It is also quite contagious. It keeps you entangled in the unprofitable

Stay in the Joy. Let someone else be unhappy. You've got things to do, places to go, and people to love. It's a beautiful life.

"The Lord your God is with you, the Mighty Warrior who saves. He will take great delight in you. In His love He will quiet you and sing over you with joy." (Zephaniah 3:17)

DECEMBER 4

"We are living monuments of God's good grace." – Oswald Chambers

W E WERE IN Washington, DC. It was a town of circles and monuments. We had to visit the New Zealand Embassy for paperwork and then, we wanted to see the Smithsonian. Things at the Embassy put us way behind schedule, so we made it to the Smithsonian just as they were closing.

Our hotel door had bullet holes in it. We were told this wasn't the safest place in our country. So, when we got back to our truck and spotted the tailgate down and the window up, we panicked. Most of our life was packed in that truck as we did ministry around the country. Believe it or not nothing had been touched – must have been the angels who traveled with us. Smile.

We decided to take what time we had left and take in the trail of monuments. There's FDR and his dog, Fala. There's Abraham Lincoln with knobby knees and long legs. There's the George Washington obelisk and the bronzed Thomas Jefferson. There's Andrew Jackson and Ulysses S. Grant all chiseled in stones that tell a story of value and richness.

But all around us are people who are living monuments of God's grace. They have histories of magnificent stories which give us a reason to hope and a story to tell our children. May we be the generation that exalts God.

"This is the generation of those who seek Him,
who seek Your face..." (Psalm 24:6)

"Fresh rains come through God's Word."

HAVE YOU QUIT pressing on to know? Did you get tired of walking the jungle and feeling the fear? Did you give up on finding out? It is a terribly empty feeling.

Deafening Silence.

Creepy accusations from that pit.

One step forward feels like two steps back. Your perspiration is sticky and your assumptions aggravating. Everything is itchy, weighty, and full of itself. Others swing by you like they are going to wondrous places. You are grabbing at the Vine constantly, because you constantly feel like you are falling.

Yeah, me too.

Sometimes I have walked miles in my spirit and gotten absolutely no where. Sometimes waiting on the Lord can be disconcerting. It feels like you are so thirsty, no amount of water will satisfy. But I know He will come.

I stand waiting.

He has promised to come and He always keeps His promises.

It may not be my timing, but when I wait on Him, He comes to me, and there is joy again. I am satisfied in Jesus.

"My teaching will fall like drops of rain and my Word
settle like dew, like gentle rain on new grass and showers
on tender plants." (Deuteronomy 32:2)

DECEMBER 6

"Marriage is like a phone call in the night: first
the ring and then you wake up."

I CAN HEAR YOU saying it while you are laughing: *"Yep!"* What was your big surprise? Where did you *"wake up?"* After nearly forty years of a very good marriage, maybe even exceptional, I still have moments were I cock my head and ask, *"Really?"* I've had plenty a young married gal asked me if what he did yesterday was normal. Most of the time I get to laugh and assure her he is the same man she married, and yes, all that is normal. And he might be a little peculiar, too.

Many young men are a wee frightened by the whole of having to please a woman. It's not that they don't want to because they do, but women are so deep and scary. Smile. I am not too concerned over these negotiators, for if they have bothered to ask the questions, they most likely will think it through a little more than the *"whatever happens in Vegas never stays in Vegas"* people. Those are the scary ones. Wherever we got the free-to-be-stupid me, I don't know. I do know I am really weary of children being born to marital invalids. One man told me everybody has mental illness and so it just doesn't matter anymore. Huh?

Look, there are enough surprises in marriages without being thoughtless. When you get your ring and you wake up, I hope it is to laugh and enjoy the next fifty years. It's a hard time when you wake up and want out and when what you have done affects innocent people. Choose wisdom. Choose Joy and let God build your home.

"Unless the Lord builds the house, they labor in
vain that build it." (Psalm 127:1)

DECEMBER 7

"Be a timeless millionaire."

Twenty Ways to Live Like a True Millionaire

1. Give a million hugs away
2. Visit a million beautiful places
3. Share a million encouragements
4. Be generous a million times
5. Breathe a million days thankfully
6. Let a million wrongs go by
7. Embrace a million songs
8. Listen to a million voices
9. Whisper a million I love yous
10. Take a million naps
11. Give away a million things
12. Smile a million smiles
13. Let go of a million negatives
14. Sail past a million needless things
15. Praise a million people
16. Change a million moments
17. Grasp a million joys
18. Say a million thank yous
19. Reach out to a million opportunities
20. Sleep in peace a million nights

This does not take into account the fact that based on our time of 365 days,

One Million days = 273,730,926 years.

But then, real millionaire living is ***timeless.***

"Whoever hears these words of Mine and puts them into practice is like a wise man who built his house on a rock." (Matthew 7:24)

DECEMBER 8

*"There will come a time when you believe everything
is finished. That will be the beginning."*
– Louis L'Amour

KIDD HAD GONE to Africa on a trip to rid himself of a broken heart. He had been in the bush with the great bull buffalo that had frightened him into an anxiety attack. He was now on his second trip in and fearful it would happen again. It had been awhile since he had felt God speak to him, not that he had been listening. On this day, he stood fifty yards from a bull looking straight at him and stomping the ground. He threw up a prayer of *"God, please be with me."* Then he felt his spirit grow calm. All at once he knew why he has come here. It wasn't for the adventure, the bulls or even his healing past a hurt. He spoke out loud: *"God, my strength is in you."* It was then he heard the whisper in his heart. *"I am always here."*

Kidd has forgotten he had open access to God. He had forgotten God could still respond. He had neglected a relationship of intimacy and eternal understanding. While it had felt all was finished, he was able to see that the beginning was really that place where he surrendered all his agendas. Maybe it's time for a new beginning...right in the middle of the end.

*"I love the Lord for He heard my voice; He heard my
cry for mercy. Because He turned His ear to me, I will
call on Him as long as I live."* (Psalm 116:1-2)

DECEMBER 9

"All the way to heaven, is heaven."

WE OFTEN LIVE in the alternatives of heaven. We bask in our problems, our issues and our mundane. We look at our fragility and keep it as a bauble for show. We feel the dark threads of fear and we cringe in the ocean of everyday. We wait for heaven as though it is so awful here on earth, we only have heaven to look forward to...as though we could never have heaven here and there.

The Bible tells us the story of Enoch...a man who walked with God, which may not impress you, until you realize he walked so closely to God that Scripture says he was the only man to just walk into heaven. He walked so in step with God, he just transcended earth and stepped into heaven! Can you imagine?

While we wait and live down here, may we see the glory of the muddy roads. May we seek to not live bogged down in our moments of earthiness, but also be so bound for heaven, the door seems to swing both ways. On your way to heaven, enjoy your heaven here.

"By faith, Enoch was taken away so he didn't experience death, his testimony pleased God." (Hebrews 11:5)

DECEMBER 10

"Blessed are those who can give without
remembering and take without forgetting."
- Elizabeth Bibesco

I WAS LISTENING TO an elderly lady telling her life story one day. Every chapter of her life was a compelling story of what had not gone right for her. Each time, she asked us to think about what that felt like for her. She had given substantially. She felt she had never been given much in return. The life we knew and the life she knew seemed somewhat like a canyon. We stood on the sides looking in, one by what we saw and one by what she felt. She recounted what all she had done. She detailed the measures taken to do each hard thing.

She did not recall that which had been given, only that which was taken away. She cried every time she told another story of some despair. We left almost depressed. Certainly feeling like there had to be more. It's easy to forget, we say. This is true. But it is also easy to remember those terrible things and cling to them long after the day.

How blessed to be happy you have had the privilege of giving! How blessed to think of all that has been given you and to recount it in glorious detail...rather than in terms of what you did not get. Are you prone to want to be paid back for all you give out? Do you take blessing after blessing without a moment of gratitude? Start today by gathering your memories and remembering with thanksgiving.

"Go out with joy and be led forth in peace." (Isaiah 55:12)

DECEMBER 11

"God wants to delight in you the way you delight in Him."

G OD DELIGHTING IN me? I was reading this verse in my quiet time and it stopped me in my tracks. The last sentence was...can you let that in? Whoa. This ancient path enfolds me in a wisdom so rare today. I pondered if I have ever allowed God to delight in me.

I am reminded of when I had my babies. Oh, the delight in watching them discover their tiny hands, stumble trying to walk, giggling as they grabbed a nose. It did not matter that I changed a dozen diapers just that day alone. It did not matter that their words were in no way close to conversing with me. It did not matter that I provided everything for them, that without me, they would be helpless. It didn't even matter that they didn't like the food I fed them, and might burp up a mess any minute. All that mattered to me...was that I had given birth to them, and they were mine.

They were precious to me. They were my life. I would die for them. I would do anything for them. I loved them beyond measure. And that is just how your Father feels about you...Can you let that in?

"He brought me out into an open place; He rescued me
because He delighted in me." (Psalm 18:19)

"Don't hesitate to be a hero."

J AN'S HOME WAS a sick place...literally. The cat feces were so hot and smelly. The toilet was stacked with human feces. The city threw her out of her own home in order to save her own life. She had experienced a series of bad events; her parents died and her husband left. Her shame had consumed her. She tried the anti-depressants and counseling for a few months. And then she went home to die in the squalor.

Jan is not the only person to take this exit. Along the way, people tried and gave up and walked away. But in the end, there needs to be a bad guy to say, "Enough!"

Often, nothing happens. People who begin to punish themselves will continue to believe they deserve it. The behavior will become more and more bizarre and anxious. People die this way all the time. **People often tell you who they are, and what is going on inside their heart, by how they choose to keep their body and personal environment.**

The stories we tell each other are ways of reaching past words. If God has put them in your path, decide to be their hero. Maybe sometimes you even have to be your own hero. Start with a song and a prayer.

"Is any among you suffering? Let him pray.
Is anyone cheerful?
Let him sing praise." (James 5:13)

DECEMBER 13

"Fathers can nurture too."

HEY DAD! YES, you, the one who keeps saying your kids didn't come with an instruction book. Yes, they did. And frankly, this sounds like Somebody knew what they were talking about. Dads like to make their kids strong. No man wants to introduce his son as the wimpy little sissy. So, Dads are especially prone to *"provoke their children to wrath."* Wrath is anger.

Ever watch any Dads you know pick on or pester or tease or even wrestle or box a child until you can see the pain on their face? Or they are crying in frustration? Or trying to get away from their predator? See...God knew. Men are especially designed for manhood which may often include that wild and rugged we adore.

But in parenting, it can be dangerous. Just picture God sternly saying to you men: **"Quit making your children angry!"** We have way too many angry kids today. Dads are often the reason. Instead, Dads are to NURTURE their children. Does that surprise you? And that word *"admonition"* is simply an example of authoritative counsel. Are you a Dad your children can trust in this area? Now that you have the instructions, it may just prove quite helpful.

"Fathers, provoke not your children to wrath; but bring them up in the nurture and admonition of the Lord." (Ephesians 6:4)

DECEMBER 14

"Sometimes what you want to do has to fail;
so you won't. – Margaruit Bro

YOU ARE GOING to fail. This is what we should teach our children. It is more valuable to them than telling them they can be anything they want to be, (Which is not true). Natalie can't be the cat she wanted to be when she was four. I can't be the Vogue model because I am four inches under the height and a few pounds over the weight. I might be able to lose weight, but I can only be stretched so far. Good thing I hate modeling, right? I would, however, like to pilot a plane. My eyesight disqualifies me.

Limitations may look like failures, but we need our children to know they are often guidelines for being our best in another purpose of life. We need them to know it is part of growing to fail. We need to let them see our failures and talk through them in a positive way.

Yes, I believe in the pursuit of excellence in everything. But I am wise enough to know humans fail. They make wrong choices, terrible decisions, and choose stupid, arrogant and damaging behavior. To live like those don't exist causes needless pain.

Failures teach us a great deal about who we are and what is really best for us. We may fail in one area so that we are siphoned into our divine calling. We may fail in one relationship so that we are able to embrace true love. The list is sure for all of us. Let us be brave souls who help each other cross over the ravines to our best life. Let us not fear failure, but let it be our teacher.

"You know if a man falls down, he will get up again. If a man goes the wrong way, he turns around and comes back." (Jeremiah 8:4)

"Love isn't just a noun."

FOUR FRIENDS HAD a buddy who was paralyzed. A great Healer had come to their town. He was well known for his amazing miracles. The four friends decided they would take their buddy to be healed – after all, what could it hurt? They believed so much that they made him a mat; a mat with ropes. You see, the Healer was in a large crowd, in a house. The four friends had devised a plan that involved the crazy stunt of cutting a hole in the roof. Then they would lower their friend down, right smack dab in front of the Healer. This way, their friend would get the first place for being healed. We don't know, but we can speculate a man being pretty embarrassed by the attention, the plan and busting through a roof! But that's how it went down.

Four friends had a heart. They had love that made them act. They had a creative plan to make a dream come true. It was going to cost them something, but they were up to it. Crazy and loving as it sounds, it worked. They saw their friend walk that day. In fact, the Healer suggested that it was because of their faith, working with their paralyzed friend's faith that brought about healing. This makes me wonder what the conversation looked like the next day. Five men walking and talking and knowing their faith had made a difference for all of them. What's your faith doing for your friends?

"Love is patient, love is kind." (1 Corinthians 13:4)

"Courage inspires courage."

YOU HAVE TO be brave with your life, so that others will be brave in theirs. Contrary to some popular beliefs, we are not just here for our journey, our dream, our learning, our whatever. We are affecting other people every day. Even if you are deaf, dumb and blind, your presence will be affecting someone else in some way.

We draw on one another for spiritual, emotional, physical and even mental support. We all have gifting and skills and talents to use. But if we are always concerned about our depression or our issues or our past or our grief, when do we benefit another who needs us? Sure, we all have feelings of fear, low self-esteem, grief, and being of no value. But we cannot live in that feeling.

We are powerful Beings. We can change someone's life. We can give hope. We can show the light. We can give strength. We can make it okay for a passing moment. We can give courage. And we must! Even when we start like the little engine who could...just the very thought of doing it will begin to excite our spirit to aliveness and joy! Start your day by saying *"I can!"*

End your day by saying *"I did!"* It's a fantastic day to be brave!
"Do not fear or be dismayed! Be strong and courageous,
for the Lord takes care of your fight." (Joshua 10:25)

DECEMBER 17

"Life is short and we have never too much time for gladdening hearts of those who are traveling the dark journey with us." – Henri Frédéric Amiel

IN ALL MY borne days, I have never heard anyone say, *"Hurry up and be kind!"* I just love the way Henri thinks! Life is too short for all the drama, all the silly, all the headache and out of control spiraling. Let's get a grip. Let us hurry up and love. Let us wake up eager to be kind!

Imagine what rush hour traffic would be like if we just remembered to be kind. We should get some neon signs on the highway. Smile. Quit thinking of reasons NOT to love somebody and get to where you can show them love through kindness.

Kindness is the quality of consideration and generosity. We don't know how far we get to go on this journey. But we do know we need an encouraging word, a touch of joy, a little grace and an ounce of inspiration. The most incredible thing about that is it really cost us very little to do the highest good.

To share a smile.

To give a word of praise.

To consider another.

To be generous.

If we are being those things, it's just a matter being; and doing comes out of our being. Be swift to love and hasten to be kind.

"You do not know what your life will be like tomorrow. You are just a vapor that vanishes away." (James 4:14)

DECEMBER 18

"Divine design is the gift of God."

AT THE DNA level, we are all 99.9 percent identical! That applies, regardless of nation, color or otherwise. This scientific fact truly makes us part of one family. It will always be hard to fathom the unbelievably low level of genetic diversity within our species. Francis Collins, the foremost geneticist among us points to this mapping as our first glimpse of God's instruction book. As a rigorous Scientist, he contends that a belief in God does not require a descent into irrationality.

There is no real compromise of logic. Science proves God and God sustains Science. Just because our knowledge is limited, does not mean that door is closed. Opening up oneself to the spiritual through science can be enriching and a glimpse of the Creator's wonder.

Collins says that of all worldviews, atheism is by far, the least rational. The more dots science connects, the fuller we can invite the spiritual in without fear it will be ridiculed. As family, we ought to begin to process the radical view that there is a part of us in all of us. 99.9 percent which doesn't leave a lot of area for uniqueness. Does it? And yet, we are, so alike and so different. If this is possible, who are we to imagine anything else is impossible!

"For You created my inmost being, You knitted me together in my mother's womb." (Psalm 139:13)

"The state of mind we call meekness is characterized in a high degree by inward harmony. There is not a jarring thought contending thought. Not a conscience asserting rights which it could not maintain." – Thomas Upham

I ADORE THIS THOUGHT! How it challenges me to keep in balance, to produce a residual residence within trusted principle. The smallest discontent can rage a war on our harmony. A moment of wrong can sear the conscience for years. Small irritabilities often clobber big and heavy pain.

Meekness is a fruit of the spirit. It is a marking of the divine in our lives. It is a call to unity and harmony, that we might bring that to others in due seasons. When we have few secret stings and live in joy from a holy spring in the depths of our soul, we maintain the form of gracious and powerful presence. There is a clearing for the light to break through and the warmth to penetrate.

What a high calling! Live in harmony within and without.

"Have unity of mind, sympathy, brotherly love, a tender heart and humble mind." (1 Peter 3:8)

DECEMBER 20

*"It's not how long one can wait, but how one
behaves while they are waiting."*

I AM NOT SO good with patience, how about you? I especially don't like it, when it lasts too long. I prefer my patience short and sweet. It rarely is. We wouldn't make good trees. It takes years for them to be tall enough to even be called a tree. Still, patience remains a virtue.

It is what you do with the waiting that does make a difference. If we can remember there are valuable lessons hidden in the waiting room, we can go about finding those, instead of looking for the door. We would likely find we are growing during this time, even when we don't feel we are doing much of anything.

But it's hard not to worry, to assume, to imagine, and to begin to mess with the process. Patience really is best seen in the little caterpillar's cocoon. After they are all wrapped up in the mess, if we punch a tiny hole for them to get out, they could die. All we can do is wait till it is time. Not our time. Not their time. The Creator's time. And then...just like He said, He has made everything beautiful in His time.

*"I wait for the Lord, my soul waits and in
His Word I hope!"* (Psalm 130:5)

"There is joy in the hard things too."

A FRIEND, WHOSE HUSBAND was struggling with cancer, hugs long and hard. She thanked me for the little ways I try to connect. She says little things make a big difference when you are in these times. I know that is true.

She worked the farm and told me it felt so good to do heavy labor. It's funny, but sometimes that is exactly what you need. Hard things have their own blessings; their own way of feeding your soul.

It's like cutting down your own Christmas tree. Lots of people quit doing that a long way back but I think if I could, I'd find a way to take a truck into the back country. I'd chop and wrestle and drag that tree. I would feel the accomplishment and go to bed tired and happy. For in certain seasons, our heart is called upon to smile, while we do the hard thing, because there is Joy in that too.

"Consider it pure joy, my brothers and sisters,
whenever you face trials of many kinds." (James 1:2)

DECEMBER 22

"Rest you heart in His."

A S A PERSON of chronic pain and heavy doses of no rest, I can tell you that sometimes you can get so weary that you can't pray, you can't sing, and you can't even help someone else.

You can just stay still.

The Lion of Judah has saved me and I rest my heart there because He knows it better than anyone. He knows how badly it aches and why. He knows what broke it and what binds it. I don't have to fill out any paperwork for the Great Physician.

He knows how I think. He knows His peace can keep my mind more occupied than worry. I rest my spirit on Him because I don't have to tell Him how downcast I am. He knows how my spirit flails and flounders in my anxiety. He knows these powerful changes require guidance and comfort.

He sings over me with His love.

I rest my soul upon Him for He holds it secure.

The battle is His and not mine.

I am His, and not my own.

All is rest.

"The Lord your God in the midst of thee is mighty; He will save,
He will rejoice over thee with joy, He will quiet you with His
love and rejoice over you with singing." (Zephaniah 3:17)
December 23
"Sometimes, your greatest enemy is your "to do list."

Have some fun today!

Some of you are so uptight you can't let loose! You have so much to do you don't even know what you're doing. It's okay to stop all your madness. It's okay to sit in the sun, to read an old book, or visit an old friend and let yourself have a belly laugh.

I'm one who had to train myself to just peel off that layer of self importance and let my clock stop.

Take a day where you don't have a clue what time it is. Wake up when you want to, play, work, pray, walk, and read the Bible like you want to read it, not because you think you have to read it on schedule.

Get your feet dirty or wet and sandy and get your giggling down pat. Quit thinking about your hair and your clothes and your to do list.

You will be amazed at how your eyes sparkle when you play.

"This is the day that the Lord has made. Let's rejoice and be glad in it!"
(Psalm 118:24)

DECEMBER 24

"Petty complaining reveals a great weakness. If you have the whine in you, kick it out ruthlessly. It is a positive crime to be weak in God's strength." – Oswald Chambers

THE CHRISTMAS SEASON is the season for whining; everywhere, someone is whining. When I first read these words, I said out loud: *"Ouch! I have days of unrelenting whine."*

Oswald talks about the beauty of someone we might think has nothing but joy. If we lift the veil, we see the truth; the fact that peace and light and joy are there...is proof the burden is there too! This is a powerful revelation for me.

The only way to know the strength of God in our lives is to live alongside Him in our pain! Oswald says so beautifully: "God squeezes the grape and out comes the wine; most of us only see the wine." He's right. You never get wine without a crushing to the grape. The grape, in all its radiance, was made as God created. But if it is to be even more useful, it must be crushed in due season. Got the wine or the whine in you?

"Do all things without complaining or disputing, that you may become blameless and harmless children of God." (Philippians 2:4)

DECEMBER 25

"How is one to live a moral and compassionate
existence when one finds darkness
not only in one's culture but within oneself?
There are simply no answers to
some of the great pressing questions. You
continue to live them out, making
your life a worthy expression of leaning into the light." – Barry Lopez

CHRISTMAS DAY IS the eternal lighting of hope. We can look around at the way things are and like so many on this day, feel the hopelessness of our culture. Yet we are called to be the light.

If someone looked at your light, up close and personal, would it be enough to light their path? We have a great deal fewer heroes than ever before. We have lies that surface from the most unexpected places. We are in dire need of light. It is getting darker out there.

We can't answer all the reasons why the dark has come often and the light seems dim at times. We can only know that living a life that expresses our leaning into the light will open more roads for courage and faith to take a stand. Love and light have always overcome the darkness, even though time feels like it's running out. The questions will not go away, but you won't feel the need to have them all.

Joy to the world, the Lord has come.

"May the God of hope fill you with joy and peace in believing so that by the power of the Holy Spirit, you may abound in hope." (Romans 15:13)

DECEMBER 26

"It will do you a world of good to do a little good in your world."

THE CLERK AT the counter was not smiling. She just wanted to do her job. Or maybe she wasn't feeling well. I don't know. I just decided I wanted to take the gauntlet when the man left. She began to price my strawberries. She asked if I found what I needed. (I think they get points for that.) I said all but yellow bananas, but I was willing to go green for a few days. And we talked about potassium and her knee surgery.

I said, *"You have the perfect hairdo for this crazy windy day."* She smiled and we talked about hairdos. *"That is the best orange juice,"* I whispered. She took note. We talked about getting good food and the prices of some and she was laughing. She even told me not to blow away as I headed for the door.

It was just a matter of minutes. She needed a distraction, a good word, a friend experience. It didn't cost me anything. It wasn't that hard to do. It made me feel good.

I don't always take these challenges. But when I do, I feel both of us letting go of the *"Oh me"* and *"Oh my"* of our own lives. I'm pretty sure she would rather I handed her keys to a fine Mercedes, but that wasn't what I had to give. I gave what I had. Don't be stingy. It will do you a world of good to do good in the world.

Just do it.

"Do not forget to do good and to share with others." (Hebrews 13:16)

"When you get alone with God, don't forget to listen."

E LIJAH HAD A bad day. That song could have been written about him. He had been through the wringer, as my Grandma would say. Bet you've been there too. He told God all about it, finally ending up along the lines of:

I am the only real believer left (we love our self- righteousness).

Look at what l did (we love our credit).

There is nobody I can trust (we love our alienation).

Don't know why I do what I do (we love our need for affirmation).

I feel like no one cares (we love our feelings).

There are people who hate me (we love our fears).

Does that sound familiar? God eventually reminded poor ole Elijah that in His economy, nobody gets to fail and leave it at that. Whatever you do, you cannot live a failure. He reminded him that there were at least 7,000 people he had influenced who were following truth and living in love. He reminds us all that whatever you do for God is never done in vain. No word spoken, no truth shared, no sacrifice made was in vain.

You might not feel or see or know the impact you left, but you don't need to know. Trust God that He used you to be a blessing, to encourage or strengthen. Keep on keeping on.

"After the earthquake, a fire, but the Lord was not in the fire; and after the fire, a still small voice." (1 Kings 19:12)

"Keep dreaming."

WE HAVE A dream. It is not real before us, for others to see. Nevertheless, it is, to us, real. There is a valley where the dream seems too far away, too impossible and we begin to give up. But the Dream Giver is simply taking us to a place to refine our dream.

By the time it is real, we will likely be on to another dream. So, here, in the making of the dream you have today, is the thing to be most treasured. As sure as God is God, and you are you, the accomplishment of your dream will flourish if you hold to it, pay its price, and cherish all it gives you, not just the success of it. Much dissatisfaction has come because we have given up before we were there, or we tried to be settled with less, or we had misread the work before us.

Hold on to your dreams. They shape your life.

"Where there is no vision, the people perish." (Proverbs 29:18)

"A critical spirit reveals death inside."

THE NUMBER ONE consistent root of all divorces is not money, affairs, children or drugs. It is criticism. Small or big, a critical relationship is the strongest indicator of a marriage headed for trouble. It's often the beginning of all the other issues to come. Don't get me wrong. You have the right and sometimes, even the responsibility, to confront your mate. But if you have fallen into the habit of constantly correcting, your habit could cost you the love you want.

Marriage should never be a place where you are afraid to speak; but it should also be a place of thinking before you speak. One of the most valuable things I have found, after being in a long term marriage, is that there are an awful lot of things you just don't need to worry about after all. Who cares if you have to take two seconds and put down the toilet seat? So what if you have to wait till she gets ready.

Watch out if you can't go a day without criticism. If you think it's just the way marriage is, you are sadly mistaken. You should be having fun and constantly complimenting each other with ease and delight. If you can't feel free to do that, then you really do have a problem. A critical home creates insecure, depressed people. Is that what anybody really wants? Let the Joy in.

"But if you bite and devour one another, take care that you are not consumed by one another." (Galatians 5:15)

DECEMBER 30

"It lakes a tremendous amount of time for your internal discipline to ascend to your external. Some of us expect to clear the numberless ascensions in about two minutes." – Oswald Chambers

OSWALD HAS A way of putting it right into our dirty boots, doesn't he? He doesn't praise the next best thing. He contends that the little things matter quite a bit. He says we like to keep our old stuff and our new stuff together too much. We are a race of common threads, often wanting the prize, but tired of the run.

From what I recall, if you want to become a doctor, you are looking at four years of college after high school, and then four *more* years of medical school after that. Then add to that several more years of Internship which means no sleep for a while. Then maybe you get to say you are a Doctor. You can't figure on skipping a year or dropping out of Anatomy Class until you feel better. Nope, it's do or don't do. Who would want you if you didn't do all the requirements anyway?

I get a lot of clients, who tell me right out of the bag, that they are going to help people because of what they have been through. All l can say is you can have that Doctor Dream the first day of school, but as Grandma says, *"The proof is in the pudding."* You have to earn that right to help others. You can give but give yourself time to grow. There's a lot of Joy in growing.

"But grow in the grace and knowledge of our
Lord and Savior Jesus Christ."
(2 Peter 3:18)

DECEMBER 31

"If you see yesterday, let it get through today."

T HERE IS A *"Rachel"* at the movies. She is clapping and squealing while her mother shushes her a hundred times. I smile. It doesn't damper her spirits to be out and seeing *"The Lorax."*

Profoundly retarded children have a way of dancing in the dark. She wiggles in her big, bulky wheelchair. The lights have dimmed and we are fine. She is no rowdier than the other one hundred children in the room. I hope it has relieved her Mama.

I remember the many times of trying to keep our Rachel quiet, especially in church and at the movies. One Sunday she got so loud Dan pushed her wheelchair into a tiny room in the vestibule. Imagine my surprise to come out and find my husband and daughter in the closet!

People look at you, when you have a wheelchair. Some avoid you. In either case, you know you don't quite fit anywhere. The movie soon ended. As I stepped back, I slipped over to Rachel. I told her Mama thank you for bringing her, that I so enjoyed her talking. Her Mama looked at me with a look that I so understood. "It was wonderful," I said. "I have a little girl like her in heaven and I miss her every day. Having the sweetness so close blessed my heart so much. Thank you."

I had to hurry off because the tears had begun...and the Grands were wondering about me. I hope I made her day. She certainly made mine. It's a Joy to see the unseen.

Happy New Year!

"I am forgetting what is behind and straining toward what is ahead."
(Philippians 3:13-14)

9 781796 023770